Oxford Poetry by Richard Eedes and George Peele

I0603125

Dana F. Sutton

Routledge
Taylor & Francis Group

First published in 1995 by Garland Publishing, Inc.

This edition first published in 2018 by Routledge
2 Park Square, Milton Park, Abingdon, Oxon, OX14 4RN
and by Routledge
52 Vanderbilt Avenue, New York, NY 10017, USA

Routledge is an imprint of the Taylor & Francis Group, an informa business

Publisher's Note
The publisher has gone to great lengths to ensure the quality of this reprint but
points out that some imperfections in the original copies may be apparent.

Disclaimer
The publisher has made every effort to trace copyright holders and welcomes
correspondence from those they have been unable to contact.
A Library of Congress record exists under ISBN:

ISBN 13: 978-0-367-18908-2 (hbk)
ISBN 13: 978-0-367-18909-9 (pbk)
ISBN 13: 978-0-429-19914-1 (ebk)

Routledge Revivals

Oxford Poetry by Richard Eedes and George Peele

THE RENAISSANCE IMAGINATION

IMPORTANT LITERARY AND THEATRICAL TEXTS
FROM THE LATE MIDDLE AGES
THROUGH THE SEVENTEENTH CENTURY

edited by

STEPHEN ORGEL
STANFORD UNIVERSITY

A GARLAND SERIES

OXFORD POETRY BY RICHARD EEDES AND GEORGE PEELE

DANA F. SUTTON

GARLAND PUBLISHING, Inc.
NEW YORK & LONDON / 1995

Library of Congress Cataloging-in-Publication Data

Sutton, Dana Ferrin.
    Oxford poetry by Richard Eedes and George Peele / Dana F.
Sutton.
        p.   cm. — (The Renaissance imagination)
    Includes bibliographical references (p.).
    ISBN 0-8153-2161-9 (alk. paper)
    1. Latin poetry, Medieval and modern—England—Oxford—
History and criticism.   2. Latin poetry, Medieval and modern—England—Oxford—Translations into English.   3. Oxford
(England)—Intellectual life—16th century.   4. Eedes, Richard,
1555–1604. Iter boreale.   5. Peele, George, 1556–1596—Authorship.   6. Pareus.   I. Eedes, Richard, 1555–1604. Iter boreale. English and Latin.   II. Pareus. English and Latin.   III. Title.   IV. Series: Renaissance imagination (Unnumbered)
PA8045.E5S88   1995
871'.0408—dc20   95-21074
                                                            CIP

Printed on acid-free, 250-year-life paper
Manufactured in the United States of America

Contents

PREFACE: THE SCHOOL OF WILLIAM GAGER

illiam A. Ringler has described the bleak condition of literature at Oxford when Sir Philip Sidney was up in the late 1560's and early 1570's.[1] By the early 1580's Oxford was the home for a number of highly talented writers, including outstanding poets and dramatists.[2] Doubtless there were a number of reasons for this remarkable change within a span of little more than a decade, but one individual seems to deserve more credit than anyone else for this transformed literary scene, the University's premier poet and dramatist, William Gager (1555 - 1622), whose example went far toward raising the tone of Oxford literature; his influence on a number of his contemporaries is visible. Then too, as will be described in the Introduction to the second item included in his volume, Gager seems to have been instrumental in the foundation of the University press, which offered a nationally visible forum where Oxford writers could display their work.

[1] William A. Ringer Jr., *The Poems of Sir Philip Sidney* (Oxford, 1962) xix f.

[2] Since Oxford was a Latin-speaking and reading institution more often than not these men wrote in Latin; cf. my remarks on the bilingualism of educated England in the General Introduction to Volume I of William Gager's *Complete Works* (New York, 1994), a general survey of the literature produced for this bilingual society has been provided by J. W. Binns, *Intellectual Culture in Elizabethan and Jacobean England: The Latin Writing of the Age* (Leeds, 1990).

Gager belonged to an intellectual and literary circle focused on his own college, Christ Church, at a time when it was presided over by the eloquent and charismatic Dean Tobie Mathew, who provided a hospitable environment in which these writers could cultivate their talent. Other Christ Church members of this circle were the poet-playwrights Richard Eedes and George Peele, and the legal scholar Alberico Gentili, whose brother Scipio was himself a Latin poet of formidable stature. Members who belonged to other colleges included the poet-playwright Matthew Gwinne (the future co-editor of Sidney's *New Arcadia*), and the poet Richard Latewar, both members of St. John's, and the philosopher John Case, a prolific writer.[1] It is a pleasant thought to imagine members of this circle sitting at a table in The Bear, presided over by its landlord Matthew Harrison, a gentleman we are about to meet.

The present volume contains two comparatively lengthy Latin hexameter poems that emanated from this circle. One is by Richard Eedes; the other is anonymous, although for the purposes of this book I provisionally accept Tucker Brooke's attribution to George Peele. Both poems are lively and interesting, and so they serve as excellent illustrations of the vitality of Oxonian literature of the time. At first sight they may seem to have little to do with each other, other than the fact that both were produced by friends of Gager's in the 1580's. But in fact their similarities go considerably deeper: both are works of national significance rather than the merely parochial coterie verse one might expect, dealing with contemporary historical events; both document the growing sense of national self-consciousness and patriotism characteristic of the period. The first one is a satiric travelogue that, for the region of England that it covers, invites comparison with Camden's *Britannia*, and it in-

---

[1] The existence and membership of such literary circles as this one can be worked out from the way they provided liminary verses for each others' books. By this test, another outstanding Christ Church writer of the period, Richard Hakluyt, was not a member of Gager's circle.

spired an entire genre of satiric travel literature. The other began a tradition of Anglo-Latin historical epic, and managed to exert influence, directly or indirectly, on a remarkable number of writers, including John Milton. Both poems deserve to be made accessible to the modern reading public, and both richly reward close study.

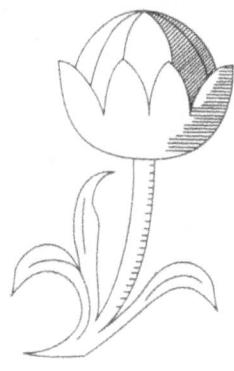

Richard Eedes,

Iter Boreale

with William Gager's *Musa Australis*

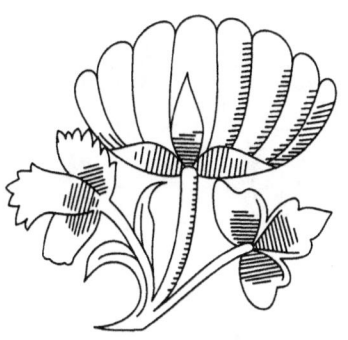

1583

Introduction

niversity wit" is a designation usually reserved for those University men who went down to London and functioned in a literary milieu distinctly anticipatory of Grub Street. Thus used, this term tends to gloss over the fact that there was also plenty of keen and inventive wit, in both the Elizabethan and modern senses of the word, exhibited by others who chose not to leave the Universities and went on to academic careers, or who entered the learned professions. Such men also wrote clever and ingenious stuff for amusement. A fine specimen of academic wit is the lengthy satire *Iter Boreale*[1] by Richard Eedes or Edes (1555 - 1604),[2] a student of Christ Church, Oxford. The circumstances of its composition were described by Sir John Harington in his memoir of Dr. Tobie Mathew, Archbishop of York:[3]

---

[1] The proper title of this poem is discussed the initial Commentary note.

[2] So the *D. N. B.* biography (by Gordon Goodwin), on unstated grounds. Eedes was likelier born in 1552, the birthdate of his exact contemporary at Westminster and Oxford, Martin Heton. William Gager, who matriculated from Christ Church three years after Eedes and Heton, was born in 1555.

[3] *A Briefe View of the State of the Church of England as it Stood in Q. Elizabeths and King James his Reigne, to the Yeere 1608*, edited by John Harington under the title *Nugae Antiquae* (London, 1779, repr. Hildesheim, 1968) I.228f., copied by Anthony à Wood, *Athenae*

Among some speciall men that enjoyed, and joyed most in his friendship and company in *Oxford*, and in remembrance of it since they they were sundred, was Doctor *Eedes*, late Dean of *Worcester*, one whose company I loved as well as he loved his *Thoby Matthew*. He for their farewell, upon his remove to *Durham*, intending first to go with him from *Oxford*, but one dayes Journey, was so betrayed by the sweetness of his Company, and their old friendship, that he not onely brought him to *Durham*, but for a pleasant penance wrote their whole Journey in Latine verse, which Poem he himselfe gave to me, and told me so many pretty Apothegmes of theirs in their younger yeeres, as might make a Booke almost by it selfe.

A product of the of the Westminster School, Eedes matriculated from Christ Church in 1571.[1] He enjoyed a distinguished academic career, being elected Junior Proctor of the University for 1583, and appointed Canon of the fourth stall of Christ Church in 1586. In the same year he was made

---

Oxonienses, Fasti Oxonienses, and *Life of Anthony à Wood* (ed. Philip Bliss, in four volumes, London, 1813 - 22, reprinted Hildesheim, 1969) II.749. [Because of the frequency with which these works will be cited, they will henceforth be abbreviated *A. O.* and *F. O.*] Wood added that Eedes "wrote their whole journey in Latin verse, entit. *Iter boreale*, several copies of which did afterwards fly abroad." He was able to quote the first line of the poem because he owned a copy, one of the mss. on which this edition is based.

[1] No study has ever been devoted to Eedes. The principal source of biographical information is Wood's notes (*ib.* 749 - 50), which provide the basis for the life in the *D. N. B.* Available notices and discussions of his literary work include Frederick S. Boas, *University Drama in the Tudor Age* (Oxford, 1914, repr. New York, 1966), 163 - 5; Leicester Bradner, *Musae Anglicanae: A History of Anglo-Latin Poetry 1500 - 1925* (New York, 1940, reprinted New York, 1965) 66; and David H. Horne, *The Life and Minor Works of George Peele* (New Haven, 1952) 169 - 73. See also Binns, *Intellectual Culture* index s.v.

4

Chaplain to Queen Elizabeth,[1] and created Doctor of Divinity in 1589. He died in 1604, perhaps a victim of the plague then ravaging England. Eedes was a playwright as well as an author of occasional verse. On the strength of his lost play *Caesar Interfectus* the discerning Francis Meres included him in his list of "our best for tragedy" in *Palladis Tamia* (1598); the work seems to have been staged on the same occasion as the first performance of Gager's *Meleager*, in 1582. Only the epilogue of the play survives, which is regrettable, because such a relatively early example it would have been of some interest for the development of the Elizabethan history play, and has even been suggested to have been a source for Shakespeare's *Julius Caesar*.[2] Other than the *Iter Boreale* Eedes' only surviving Latin poetry consists

[1] Evidently an honorific appointment, as he remained at Oxford. Likewise in the dedicatory epistle to Leicester, Chancellor of the University, prefacing the *Exequiae Illustrissimi Equitis D. Philippi Sidnaei, Gratissimae Memoriae ac Nomini Impensae* that he edited in 1587, William Gager refers to Dr. William James, Tobie Mathew's successor as Dean of Christ Church, as Leicester's chaplain. Maybe the individuals honored with such designations were to function in this capacity when Elizabeth and Leicester visited the University. Was this, then, a specialized form of patronage relationship? Eedes continued as Chaplain to James I, though he was Dean of Worcester, and was selected as a Bible translator by James, but his contribution to the *K. J. V.* was precluded by his death soon thereafter.

[2] John Semple Smart, *Shakespeare Truth and Tradition* (London, 1928) 179 - 82 and C. F. Tucker Brooke, "The Life and Times of William Gager (1555 - 1622)," *Proceedings of the American Philosophical Society* 95 (1951) 415 (though this idea is denied by Boas, *loc. cit.*). The epilogue, which reveals nothing important about the play's contents, is preserved by the Bodleian ms. Top. Oxon. e. 5, fol. 359; Boas reproduced it. In his biography (*A. O.* 749) Wood writes "His younger years he spent in poetical fancies and composing of plays (mostly tragedies)." *Caesar Interfectus* is the only play he is known to have written, unless he helped write William Gager's *Dido* produced in June 1583, which shows signs of multiple authorship (cf. Gager's *Complete Works*, New York, 1994, I.246 - 9), although Gager's collaborator may have been George Peele.

of gratulatory verses prefacing various contemporary publications, chiefly by other members of his Oxford circle, and contributions to University commemorative anthologies.[1] Some English work also exists. A prose dialogue on love printed in the 1593 anthology *The Phoenix Nest* (pp. 24 - 9) is attributed to Eedes in one manuscript, but to others by different sources.[2]

Even in an age when University students and faculty were often distinctly younger than their modern counterparts, Tobie Mathew's career was alarmingly precocious.[3] Born in Herefordshire in 1546 and educated at Wells, he came up to Oxford in 1559 at the age of thirteen. A B. A. by seventeen and ordained by twenty, he was unanimously elected Uni-

---

[1] For example, for Alberico Gentili's *Lectionum et Epistolarum quae ad Ius Civile Pertinent, Liber 1* (1583), William Gager's *Ulysses Redux* (1592) and *Meleager* (1593), and John Case's *Speculum Quaestionum Moralium* (1596).

[2] Inner Temple ms. Petyt 538.43, fols. 299f. According to this manuscript the dialogue was spoken before the Queen at Woodstock, evidently in 1592. Both *The Phoenix Nest* and other sources state that it was spoken before the Queen at the house of Sir Henry Lee. For a discussion of authorship—several candidates have been proposed—see the annotated edition of *The Phoenix Nest* by Hyder Edward Rollins (Cambridge, Mass., 1931) 134ff.; E. K. Chambers, *Sir Henry Lee* (Oxford, 1936) 276f.; and Horne, *loc. cit.* It may be the case that one or two anonymous poems in this collection are also by Eedes (see Gager's *Complete Works*, III.xviii). Some vernacular poetry preserved by the Bodleian ms. Rawlinson Poet. 148 has been published in Edward Doughtie, *Liber Lilliati* (Newark, N. J., 1985). Cf. also Bodleian ms. Rawlinson Poet. 172 fol. 6ᵛ and British Library ms. Harleian 6910 fol. 151ᵛ ("Luigi Groto his New Philosophie Englished by Doct. Eedes"). In the seventeenth century two volumes of Eedes' sermons were printed: bibliographical information on these is provided under Eedes' name in the list of Works Consulted at the end of this volume. [Eedes is not to be confused with his Presbyterian namesake, who also published sermons later in the century and died in 1686.]

[3] For his life cf. Wood, *A. O.* II.869 - 77 and the *D. N. B.* entry (by William Holden Hutton) with references cited. There is also a contemporary biographical sketch by Sir John Harington, *op. cit.* I.224 - 35.

versity Orator in 1569 and chosen as one of the eight Canons of Christ Church a year later. He defeated Dr. William James, his eventual successor, in an election for the Deanship of Christ Church in 1576.[1] Mathew seems to have owed his success to his great amiability as well as to his charismatic abilities in the pulpit. Now he was about to take another step up the ecclesiastical ladder, as Dean of Durham Cathedral. Later he would succeed to the bishopric of Durham, and was later translated to the archbishopric of York, not dying until 1628.

A distinctive feature of Christ Church life during the 1580's, was a fashion for passionate friendships, or perhaps more accurately homosexual pairings that were at least supposed to remain platonic. There is plenty of evidence for this fad in William Gager's occasional poetry. In a commonplace book of poems unprinted in his lifetime,[2] Gager documents several such pairings, such as that of Sir Thomas Clinton, grandson of the Earl of Lincoln, and Sir Walter Devereux, younger brother of Essex, and records the ups and downs of his own similar friendship with another Christ Church student, Richard Brainche, evidently a kinsman. On the showing of Wood's account, it would appear that Mathew and Eedes paired off in this way.[3] This friendship supplied the motive for a spur-of-the-moment decision to accompany Mathew to Durham. Mathew's party consisted of two fellow academics, Eedes and Anthony Blencowe,

---

[1] Christ Church, or more accurately The Cathedral College of Christ, is simultaneously an academic college and the seat of the diocese of Oxford. Thus, instead of the normal organization of an Oxbridge college, it has the administrative structure characteristic of a cathedral. It is governed by a Dean, Sub-dean, and a chapter of Canons, and its other members are termed students.

[2] British Library Additional ms. 22583.

[3] One of Gager's poems, CXVI, suggests that at one point he too had such a relationship with Eedes; if so, it must have been of brief duration, as it leaves no further mark on Gager's private poetry although he wrote copiously about his pashes.

Provost of Oriel College, who came along for the companionship. As a sort of traveling factotum and general provider of food and good cheer, a local innkeeper named Matthew Harrison made up the fourth member of the party. Mathew must have been grateful for all the support and comfort his comrades could offer. For he was headed for a tense and tricky situation.[1]

The previous Dean of Durham, Thomas Wilson, had died in mid-June 1581.[2] Choosing a successor and putting him in place proved to be a protracted affair. The story of Mathew's installation is told by Strype.[3] After an attempt on the part of the Cathedral chapter to procure the post for one of the Canons had come to naught, Lord Burleigh nominated Mathew for the post in 1582.[4] Royal assent could not be

---

[1] Blenkowe was trained in the law, and Mathew may have felt the need for a legal advisor and also, perhaps, for somebody who could help make sense out of the Durham finances. Then too, Blenkowe haled from Cumberland and Mathew may have wanted the support of a friend who was himself a northerner.

[2] Wood, *A. O.* II.174.

[3] John Strype, *Annals of the Reformation and Establishment of Religion and Various Other Occurrences in the Church of England during Queen Elizabeth's Happy Reign* (Oxford, 1824, reprinted New York, n.d.) III.i.257 - 9. Strype quoted source documents in modernized orthography.

[4] This nomination rapidly became common knowledge. There is preserved in the library of the College of Arms a letter dated May 3, 1582, from Dr. Robert Lougher, a lay official of York diocese, to the family of the Earl of Shrewsbury announcing Mathew's selection. Mathew had lobbied shamelessly for the post. Cf. his quite discreditable letter to Sir Christopher Hatton, the Lord Chancellor, on September 7, 1581, reproduced by Sir Harris Nicholas, *Memoirs of the Life and Times of Sir Christopher Hatton, K. G.* (London, 1847) 191f., largely devoted to the disparagement of his rival, the Durham Canon Ralph Bellamy. Mathew's main talking-points were that Bellamy's medical background and general obscurity rendered him unfit for the Deanship (he sneeringly asserts that Bellamy would make an ideal Dean if the job involved dispensing quack nostrums such as *aurum potabile*). Other specimens of Mathew's aggressive letter-writing campaign reproduced by Nicholas

procured until the following year, so he did not go up to Durham until the summer of 1583, when he was formally installed on August 31.[1] Due to the incompetence if not actual venality of Bishop Richard Barnes, diocesan finances were in a shambles, and the interregnum (to use Eedes' word at 261) between Deans had not helped matters. Strype quotes a couple of highly illuminating letters from an impatient Mathew (who seems to have enjoyed writing about himself in the third person) to Burleigh written during the interval between his nomination and his installation. The first was written in May 1582. in which he urged Burleigh to press his appointment with the Queen:

> That by his good word, which it pleased his lordship to afford him unto her highness towards the deanery of Durham, to his great furtherance, and greater credit, he was encouraged to move her highness again for her resolution and his despatch. And that he was nothing so importune with his honour, as many good men of that church and country were earnest with him to do what in him lay for expedition...For that he was credibly informed that many things there went to wrack. The houses decayed; the game spoiled; the woods wasted; the grounds unlet...

---

are a letter to Hatton of Feb. 12, 1582 (pp. 232f.), and one to Ann, Countess of Warwick of July 22, 1582 (pp. 255f.). The subject of a further undated letter to Hatton is unclear (pp. 355f.). Interestingly, in canvassing for the position Mathew did not level charges of diocesan corruption.

[1] So *A. O.* II.870, supported by such other authorities as P. Mussett, P., *Lists of Deans and Major Canons of Durham 1541 - 1900* (Durham, 1974). Robert Surtees, *The History and Antiquities of the Country Palatine of Durham* (London, 1816 - 40, repr. Ardsley, Wakefield, Yorkshire, 1972) I.lxxxv note d, erred in giving the date as September 3. [Unless noted to the contrary, all dates cited are old style.]

Not getting anywhere, he wrote even more explicitly on August 25, 1582, promising:

> That he would be his good lord, as he had hitherto been, in the despatch of the deanery: and that especially as unless the dean that next should be might be inducted, and keep his residence there by the space of one and twenty days together, before Michaelmas next, the whole crop, as well of hay as corn, as all other fruits, belonging to the tithes and glebe land, (which was valued two parts of three in that living), must by a local statue of that church accrue to the prebendaries resident this year past: so as the next dean should for the year to come have no manner of provision wherewith to keep house; and so be the less able to do good in preaching or government: where, they said, many regarded hospitality very much; who being lost at the first, would hardly be won a good while after.

He requested Burleigh:

> To remember his lordship withal in what decay and dilapidations the dean's mansion houses were fallen; what spoil and waste, as well of woods as of other commodities belonging to their dignity, had been, and would be, during the vacation; and in how great need the divided church did stand of some indifferent governor: how incommodious the season of the year would hereafter be to remove so far from these parts, &c. Consideration whereof he most humbly referred unto his lordship's great wisdom and favourable furtherance.

Mathew's ominous words "in how great need the divided church did stand of some indifferent governor" hint at mismanagement and the need for a strong and impartial administrative hand. This remark is illuminated by another passage in Strype:[1]

This bishop had a brother John, who was his chancellor, a bad man, addicted to covetousness and uncleanness. He was to be bribed by money to pass over crimes presented and complained of. Which reflected upon the biship himself, and gave him an ill name every where. And when these things were brought to the bishop, he would say, Others were in the fault; but it never came to his knowledge. Gilpin, a reverend and pious preacher in those parts, in a sermon preached before him, told him plainly, that whatsoever he did himself, or suffered through his connivency to be done by others, was wholly his own. The bishop took this well, and, taking him by the hand, said, Father Gilpin, I acknowledge you are fitter to be bishop of Durham, than I to be parson of Houghton; which was Gilpin's parsonage.

Clearly, the diocese was beset by corruption and maladministration. Biographers and ecclesiastical historians tend to fix the blame on grasping brother John rather than on Bishop Barnes himself, who was only guilty of inability to rectify the situation.[2] Eedes provides evidence that the

[1] *Ib.* III.i 680f.—the parish rector in question was Bernard Gilpin of Houghton-le-Spring. The anecdote about Gilpin denouncing Barnes is told more fully by Surtees, *op. cit.* II.168f. (extracted from Carleton's biography cited in the next note). Gilpin plays no part in our story because he had died in March 1583. There is a certain unfortunate symbolic value in the fact that, after Gilpin's death, Bishop Barnes appointed his own son to the vacant parish in the next year (cf. the Commentary note on 483ff.).

[2] Besides the authorities just quoted cf., for example, Thomas Fuller, *The History of the Worthies of England* (ed. P. Austin Nutall, London, 1840, repr. New York, 1965) II.197, a biographical sketch based on

Cathedral chapter was also guilty, at least in the matter of the Deanery estates and income. Eedes took a vigorous dislike to Barnes, in part because the Bishop had Puritan leanings, and so our poet, who detested Puritans, offers a withering portrait. But though he represents Barnes as eccentric, oafish, and cheeseparing, and describes plenty of equivocal behavior on his part, he does not accuse him of peculation. It may be noteworthy that he fixes blame for the despoliation of the Dean's country estate on the Canons collectively, not on Barnes. Then too, collegiate and diocesan wealth consisted chiefly of landholdings, and in reading both academic and ecclesiastical histories of the period, one rapidly becomes aware that squabbles involving real or imagined abuse of rents and leases were endemic; charges of incompetence or maladversion were easily made and readily heard. William Gager, for example, at least imagined that some sort of scandal, probably of this type, was occurring at Christ Church during Mathew's time as Dean.[1] And manufacturing a crisis atmosphere so one can come forward as the man of the hour is a time-honored ploy for incoming administrators.

Bishop George Carleton's *The life of Bernard Gilpin, a man most holy and renowned among th' northerne English*, printed by William Jones at London, 1629, and Alexander Grosart's *D. N. B.* life.

[1] In his notebook poetry Gager writes rather obscurely of some Christ Church fiscal scandal involving courtiers, expressing his irritation at Mathew for being unable to suppress it (after Mathew left the scandal continued unabated and Gager went on fuming). See particularly poem CXXI, an item entitled *Wulsaei Umbra*. At a guess, some members of the Christ Church chapter were renting out college lands to courtiers at knocked-down rates in exchange for absentee ecclesiastical livings, a common academic scam. Presumably the courtiers in question were too highly placed to be defeated. To give another example involving a member of Eedes' circle of Christ Church friends, Martin Heton's later rule over the see of Ely (commencing in 1601) was seriously tainted by similar issues. Cf. James Bentham, *History and Antiquity of the Cathedral Church of Ely* (Cambridge, 1771) 195 - 7.

One thing, in any event, is beyond dispute. Eedes accepted Mathew's assessment of the situation at face value—and so came up to Durham with a strong predisposition to dislike whatever he found. This attitude colors everything he writes and generates the rather savage satire that marks the Durham part of the poem.

Understandably, as far as his dealings with ecclesiastics went, Mathew's visit went off disastrously and supplied Eedes with plenty of material for splenetic comedy. Bad blood existed on both sides. Barnes seems to have snubbed him when they first met, at least by Eedes' standard of how Mathew deserved to be treated, and avoided him as much as possible thereafter. It may be significant, for example, that in Eedes' admittedly sketchy description of Mathew's installation ceremony his presence goes unmentioned: did he boycott the event? Barnes had a well-developed talent for making himself scarce, which Eedes attributes to a desire to avoid the expenses involved in entertaining visitors. One might see in his equivocal behavior the furtiveness of guilt, or perhaps strong resentment if he knew Mathew had been complaining to the government about the quality of his stewardship. Or we could be more charitable and attribute Barnes' absences to an otherworldy character (Grosart's assessment) or to simple shyness, though Eedes describes the man as gross, fleshy, and anything but ethereal. In the same way, Eedes provides a strong hint that the welcome extended Mathew by the Canons of the Cathedral chapter was equally chill. The newcomers' Oxonian superciliousness (with which *Iter Boreale* is saturated, inadvertently supplying another level of humor) doubtless did its part to worsen the situation. This was the rather daunting situation which Mathew encountered, with the support of Eedes, Blenkowe, and Harrison. He was obliged to stay longer than planned in order to the lay the foundation of his future administration, and took a first step towards righting matters by prolonging his stay so that Sir Francis Walsingham, Elizabeth's great

Secretary of State, could force Barnes and his Canons to cough up the rent monies accruing to the Deanship, which they had been diverting for the past two years. Equally forward-looking was the time invested in social entertaining, forging of ties with prominent local families, and cultivation of such Durhamite clergy as were willing to be won over (Henry Ewbanke being a case in point). All this activity seems to have been sensibly subsumed by Mathew under the general heading of foundation-laying.

Mathew simultaneously encountered a second difficulty. Matters between England and Scotland appeared to be near the breaking-point. J. B. Black has sketched the result of the failed diplomatic mission of Walsingham, who met James VI of Scotland in early September:[1]

> Meanwhile Elizabeth was anxiously watching Scotland, where another revolution had taken place in July 1583, leading to the overthrow of the Ruthven clique and the return of Arran to power. In September, hearing of a renewal of French machinations in the northern kingdom, she sent Walsingham with a splendid embassy to remonstrate with James, and to see what he could do to restore English influence. The veteran diplomatist was no lover of the Scots, whom he regarded as a mercenary nation to be won only by hard cash—a method of persuasion he knew Elizabeth would never sanction. From the first, therefore, he fought a losing battle. He had nothing to offer—no gifts of money,

---

[1] J. B. Black, *The Reign of Elizabeth, 1558 - 1603* (Oxford, 1936). A more detailed account is furnished by Conyers Read, *Mr. Secretary Walsingham* (Oxford, 1925) II.204 - 24, though Read does not mention Walsingham's stopover at Durham on the way back from Scotland. Source documents emanating from Walsingham's embassy may be read in Volume VI of William K. Boyd (ed.), *Calendar of the State Papers Relating to Scotland and Mary Queen of Scots* (Edinburgh, 1910).

no promises with regard to the succession: the anti-English party was in a strong position; and the king, though friendly, was in no mood to listen to expostulation on his 'crooked ways.' It is hardly surprising that Walsingham's report was a bitter one. He pronounced James 'an ingrate and such a one as if his power may agree to his will, will be found ready to make as unthankful a requital as ever any did that was so greatly beholding unto a prince, as he hath been unto your Majesty.' Nay, he concluded that the only way to deal with him was to have him 'bridled and forced, whether he will or no.'

The situation was serious and might lead to war, as Eedes indicates at 474f. Various measures had to be taken. A commission was established to inquire into the repair of the borderland defenses,[1] and the convocation of the Council of the North described by Eedes was for the purpose of meeting with these commissioners as well as with Walsingham. Durham occupied a critically sensitive position in the border country. The County Palatine of Durham, governed by a Prince-Bishop with considerable secular powers, had an important role to play in defensive preparations. During his Deanship Mathew held a kind of watching brief for the Queen's principal advisors vis-a-vis Scotland, and also was active in curbing recusants.[2] Eedes describes a meeting of the Council at which Walsingham was present on his way back from Scotland. Mathew extended his visit and played a part in the resulting confabulations. It is likely that at their meeting Walsingham recruited him as a political observer and instructed him how the government wanted the diocese to be managed. Nothing could be clearer than that Bishop

---

[1] Cf. the charge issued to this commission on August 18, at Mary Anne Everett Greene (ed.), *Calendar of State Papers (Domestic)* (London, 1872, repr. Nendeln, 1967) XII.92 - 4.

[2] So the *D. N. B.* biography; some of his political reports are extant.

Barnes was unsuited for such responsibilities; it is possible that the real reason he went into hiding was not to avoid the costs of hosting such a large number of guests or because he had been looting his diocese, but because he wanted to dodge any involvement in this matter. In view of his general gormlessness, the government must have eagerly fixed on Mathew as the right man to put some spine into Durham diocese.[1]

This delay turned out to be a lucky break for Eedes. For all his grumbling about the protracted stay at Durham—though he confesses that the place came to grow on him—he had the opportunity to be introduced to Walsingham and favorably impress him. It would be excessive to claim that this meeting laid the foundation for his future academic and ecclesiastical success: having been elected a University Proctor, he was already a marked man.[2] But students of preferment (and there must have been many in his Christ Church audience) would have appreciated that this meeting did not exactly harm his chances.

A third source of anxiety for our traveling companions as they headed for the North country was more generalized: not entirely without reason, southerners tended to regard the North as uncivilized, uncouth, and dangerous. In several respects the North was a violence-prone place. If war with Scotland (supported, perhaps, by France or Spain) were to break out, it would bear the brunt of invasion. Memories of the northern rebellion of 1569 led by the Earls of Northumbria and Westmoreland, and of its bloody suppression, were fresh, and indeed some of the individuals we shall meet in *Iter Boreale*, notably the Earl of Huntington, were involved

[1] But one must admit that the fact that Mathew assumed the Deanship under crisis conditions makes the leisure with which he moved up from Oxford difficult to understand.

[2] The next vacancy in the Christ Church chapter of Canons was reserved for Martin Heton, who soon became Sub-dean; Eedes got the following one.

in putting it down. The Council of the North may have governed the region, but so far it had failed to impose anything like true law and order on the region. Eedes provides evidence for this when he records that fear of a robber currently plying his trade in the vicinity under the name Jock the Scot, deterred Blenkowe and himself from amusing themselves by a side-trip to Newcastle.

Southerners were also prejudiced against the North because it was perceived as culturally backward. This attitude colors a complaining letter from Bishop Barnes, a Lancashireman, to Burleigh written soon after his appointment to Durham:[1]

> I assure your good Lordship, [the people of York-shire] are far more plyable to all good order, than those stubborn, churlish people, of the country of Durham, and their neighbours in Richmondshire, who shew but, as the proverb is, *Jack of Napes charity* in their hearts. The customes, the lives of these people, as their country is, are truly salvage [*sic*]; but truly such hast to amend (though it be fore some) as is zelous, and yet non extremity shewed to any, otherwise than be threatening, which hath wrought *panicum timorem* in their minds, and in the Clergy a good readiness to apply their travells[2] to their calling, only that *Augie Stabulum*, the Church of Durham, exceedes; whose stinke is grievous in the nose of God and man, and which to purge far passeth Hercules' labours. The malicious of this country are mervailously exasperated against me; and whereas at home, they dare, neither by words nor deeds, deal undutifully against me, yet abroad, &c. they deface me by all slanders, false reports,

---

[1] (February 11, 1576). Quoted by Surtees, *op. cit.* I.lxxxi.
[2] I. e., their travails, I suppose. (I cannot identify the Latin quote at the end of this passage.)

and shameless lyes; though the same were never so inartificial or incredible, *according to the Northern guise*, which is never to be ashamed, however they bely and deface him whom they hate, yea though it be before the honorablest. *Pessimum hoc genus hominum ex aliqua invidia laudem sibi quaerens.*

In his *Musa Australis* (reproduced as an appendix here) Gager is obviously indulging in a good deal of clowning, but in his humorous way he gives voice to all these prejudices about the North. He portrays Durham as a gelid and sunless region somewhere up around Ultima Thule (although in another poem in his series on Mathew's departure he adds that it is infested by tigers), populated by marauding bandits and mean-minded yokels who wouldn't know a decent preacher when they heard one, but who would resent his presence if they did. But for all the comic exaggeration, his concern for Mathew's welfare may well have been genuine.

If such attitudes about the North helped shape Eedes' reportage, *Iter Boreale* is informed by various other views and prejudices. Two of these, obviously, are a dislike for Puritanism, evidenced by the disdain with which he describes his encounter with extreme Low Church practice at Northampton, and a standard Oxonian sense of general superiority. Another concerns the nature of Christian preaching. Here, Gager is a valuable witness. In *Musa Australis* he says a lot about the prestige that accrues to an excellent and learned preacher. In an oration in praise of eloquence, delivered at Christ Church in early 1585,[1] he lays it on the line even more explicitly:

> *quid porro tam gloriosum quam cum auditum sit*
> *hominem eloquentem esse dicturum, loca in sub-*

---

[1] Printed in Vol. IV of Gager's *Complete Works*. Compare the similar ambition of the hapless Dr. Emmanuel Barnes in this poem.

*selliis occupari, compleri forum, gratiosum unum-
quemque esse in dando et cedendo loco, coronam
multiplicem omnes erectos videre? cum vero surgit
is qui dicturus sit significari a corona silentium,
deinde crebras assensiones, multas admirationes,
risum cum velit, cum velit fletum esse? hic enim
unus est in quo homines exhorrescunt, quem stupe-
facti dicentem intuentur, in quo clamores illos non
potest melius plaususque etiam tollant.*

["And what more glorious than for every seat to be
occupied when it has been heard that an eloquent
man is about to speak; for the forum to be filled, everyone graceful in giving and yielding place; to see
everybody bolt upright in a packed throng; when
the speaker rises to his feet, to have the crowd cry
silence; for there to be much applause, much approval; for there to be laughter or weeping, as he
wants? He is the sole man in whose presence all
men tremble, whom they gaze at with amazement
as he speaks, for whom they shout 'couldn't be
better' and raise their applause."]

Unless Gager is stating a very idiosyncratic philosophy—but
he had the habit of appointing himself spokesman for orthodox views—it would seem as though Anglican preaching
was valued largely as an occasion for rhetorical display.
Like one of those Greek rhetoric professors of the Second
Sophistic, the successful preacher, eloquent and learned,
was lionized.

So Eedes was accompanying a sort of touring superstar.[1]
This consideration renders understandable a number of

---

[1] This word is not inappropriate: Harington, *op. cit.* I.228 wrote of his
Christ Church supporters "[his] name grew so popular and plausible, that
they thought it a derogation to their love, to adde any title of Doctor or
Deane to it," almost like Fabian or Prince.

things: it explains why Mathew was repeatedly invited to preach along the way, and why so many people were eager to offer him hospitality. It also explains why Eedes mordantly reviews the generally deplorable professional competence of the Durham clergy with virtually exclusive reference to their forensic abilities. In some passages it is almost as if he is describing a contest, smugly reporting that his Oxford paladin always comes out on top.

The rest of the story can be told briefly. Mathew and his party lingered in Durham for a full month after the installation, then returned to Oxford. This protracted stay was purchased at the cost of good traveling weather, and their return journey was repeatedly disrupted by storms and floods. Mathew remained in Oxford through the winter, not demitting the Christ Church Deanship until early 1584.[1] Even then, giving a good imitation of a yo-yo, he came down to Oxford yet again and preached a farewell sermon to Comitia on July 12, leaving nary a dry eye among his auditory.[2]

At its beginning Eedes states that he composed the *Iter Boreale* on the road as a diversion. Whether such was or was not his original intention, it may be the case that the poem was put to a specific use.[3] Gager wrote a sequel entitled *Musa Australis*,[4] dated November 11, 1583. The only

---

[1] Gager's commonplace book of unprinted poetry contains several items about Mathew's departure from Oxford. One of them, written to Mathew when he was laid low by a fever (poem CXLIX), suggests that bad health may have been a reason why it took Mathew so long to remove to Durham, though one must also allow for winter weather and bad roads.

[2] This phrase comes from a biographical notice appended to the Bodleian Rawlinson ms., found also at Wood, *A. O.* II. 877.

[3] But it was written to be read rather than recited: a number of allusions would be virtually incomprehensible to a hearer without access to Eedes' marginal annotations.

[4] Poem CXXXVIII. Gager wrote a number of other items having to do with Mathew's departure from Oxford (CXXXVIII - CXL, CXLIX, CL). The *Aegloga ad Matthaeum* (CL) was a major farewell poem un-

other dated poems in Gager's commonplace book collection of unprinted work were written for a recitation at a Christ Church Michaelmas dinner on September 26 of the same year,[1] and so it would seem that the *Musa Australis* was written to be read at a testimonial dinner for Mathew. *Iter Boreale* may have been recited on this same occasion. At the very least, Gager's poem shows that Eedes' poem had circulated through Christ Church to the point that he could presume familiarity with it on the part of his hearers.

From what has been said so far, it might seem that *Iter Boreale* is a recherché collegiate work, of interest only to specialist historians. But it acquires national significance as a specimen of travel literature, for within the scope of the regions traversed by Eedes the quality and detail of his observations are in no wise inferior to those of those two great Tudor travel writers, John Leland and William Camden. In the appendix to Johann Bucheler's *Phrasium Poeticarum Thesaurus* printed at London in 1624 is a taxonomy of Renaissance poetic genres,[2] one of which is the Hodoeporicon, or journey-describing poem, a class to which *Iter Boreale* belongs. The classical model for such poetry is Horace, *Sermo* I.v, the account of a journey to Brundisium as a member of Maecenas' retinue. While Eedes does not assiduously imitate this work,[3] the general dramatic situation of a poet accompanying a Great Man on a journey is obviously similar and he provides much the same sorts of notes: about other members of the company, sights seen along the way,

---

printed in his lifetime, from which he later borrowed much material for the second of the two eclogues on the death of Sir Philip Sidney printed in the 1587 Oxford memorial anthology (XXXIV).

[1] CXXXIV - CXXXV.

[2] Discussed by Binns, *op. cit.* 62ff.

[3] The closest imitation is in the last two lines of the poem, *sic coepit, sic clausit iter locus unus et idem, / quique dies conclusit iter, mihi carmina clausit*, which may be compared with Horace's conclusion, *Brundi-sium longae finis chartae viaeque est.*

traveler's hardships, exceptionally good or bad food and lodging, and so forth. In writing this he was no doubt catering to his audience's curiosity about their national geography. The evident originality of this idea is noteworthy. It would be three years before William Camden first published his *Britannia*, a later edition of which moved Thomas Campion to write (*Epigram* I.lxix, printed in 1619):

> *lectorem utque pium decet, hoc tibi reddo merenti,*
> *per te quod patriam tam bene nosco meam.*

["As befits a pious reader, I give you this deserved thanks, for it is your doing that I am familiar with my native land."]

Far-flung regions such as Wales, the North country, and Scotland were still remote, exotic, and rather forbidding locales. Information about them must have been eagerly accepted, all the more so when it was colorful and sometimes blood-curdling. Likewise, Mathew's Christ Church contemporaries would have been glad to have their curiosity satisfied about the place their Dean was going and matters of high politics. Those who were, or were in training to become, churchman would take a professional interest in the ecclesiastical information he provides. But the *Iter Boreale* is no mere travelogue of the Horace variety. Eedes was a divine singularly deficient in Christian charity. From the standpoint of his spiritual welfare this may be deplorable, but the reader can only be grateful, for he has given us a memorable example of muscular and interestingly malicious Renaissance satire. It is as if Juvenal rather than Horace had taken the trip to Brundisium.

It is worth comparing Eedes' observations with those of others who traveled, at least in part, the same roads he did, and what they wrote occasionally illuminate his remarks. John Leland made his journey around England in the 1530's or '40's. Although he made his observations a generation before Eedes, he visited many of the same places and saw many of the same sights, and it is often interesting to compare their notes.[1] Then too, though in his *Britannia* William Camden was more often concerned with gathering antiquarian information than in reporting his own observations and impressions, at various points his testimony is useful. In his expanded 1607 edition Camden, who had by then read the *Iter Boreale*, incorporated one of Eedes' remarks, which permitted a later traveler, Daniel Defoe, to make a shrewd comment on his observations about the great bridge over the Wharfe at Tadcaster (cf. 71f. with the Commentary note *ad loc.*).[2] Finally, on the theory that much of the English road net did not substantially change between the sixteenth and eighteenth century, I have traced our companions' route on the county maps provided in an early atlas of Britain, *The Royal English Atlas*, printed in 1760 by Emmanuel Bowen and Thomas Kitchen.[3] In this collection, on all of the relevant maps save those for the three Yorkshire Ridings road distances are noted in English statute miles. I reproduce these distances in appropriate Commentary notes.

A pair of lines on the Tadcaster bridge is not the only mark Eedes made on later literature. A later Dean of Christ Church, Richard Corbett (1582 - 1635, Dean 1620 - 28), wrote a lengthy and satirical travelogue also entitled *Iter Bo-*

---

[1] I have read Leland's *Itinerary* in the edition of Lucy Toulmin Smith (Oxford, 1907 - 10, repr. Carbondale, Ill, 1964). A glance at Map I, included at the end of Vol. I, shows that he visited virtually all of the places mentioned by Eedes. Especially in Yorkshire and Durham they often traveled over the same roads.

[2] I have consulted both Camden's original 1586 edition and the expanded one of 1607; for the reader's convenience, since the latter has been selected for modern reproduction (Hildesheim, 1970) page references for the 1607 version are cited. All of Camden's words quoted here also stand in the 1586 edition.

[3] Reprinted Newton Abbot, Devonshire, 1970.

reale, that begins:[1]

> *Foure Clerkes of Oxford, Doctours two, and two*
> *That would be Docters, having lesse to do*
> *With Augustine then with Galen in vacation,*[2]
> *Chang'd studyes, and turn'd bookes to recreation:*
> *And on the tenth of August, Northward bent*
> *A iourney not so soon conceiv'd as spent.*

Both the work's title and its content strongly suggest that Corbett knew Eedes' poem and learnt from it. Corbett, Leonard Hutten, the Sub-Dean of Christ Church,[3] two other unidentified academics, and Hutten's servant Thomas, a somewhat Harrison-like figure, took a summer trip into the Midlands slightly before Corbett assumed the Deanship. He fills his poem with observations of the people and places encountered along the way, some mordantly satirical, all identified by sidenotes precisely in the manner of those found in the manuscripts of Eedes' work. Like Eedes, Corbett was a churchman—he went on to become Bishop of Oxford and latterly of Norwich—and so both observers tend to focus on ecclesiastical matters, often reviewing them with a critical professional eye. The only element in his observations that finds no counterpart in Eedes is a tendency to include historical and antiquarian notes as well as personal observations; doubtless these are inserted after the example of

---

[1] The poem can be read in J. A. W. Bennett and H. R. Trevor-Roper (edd.), *The Poems of Richard Corbett* (Oxford, 1955) 31 - 49.

[2] Corbett's editors thought this line may be corrupt. The gentlest emendation would be to change *then* to *and.*

[3] Hutten provided a living link with Eedes' generation of Christ Church *literati*: William Gager had written a new prologue and epilogue for a performance of his *Bellum Grammaticale* in connection with the Queen's 1592 Oxford visit; on the same occasion Hutten, Gager, and Matthew Gwinne, another member of Gager's literary circle, were members of the entertainment committee.

Camden.[1]

His poem proved enormously successful—it exists in a number of manuscripts as well as printed versions—and spawned a series of Oxonian imitations throughout the seventeenth century written in both English and Latin. Corbett's editors cite Richard James' *Iter Lancastriense* (1636), Thomas Master's *Iter Boreale* (1637, published 1675), Thomas Bispham's *Iter Australe* (1658); Jeremiah Well's *Iter Orientale* (1667); George Wither's lost *Iter Boreale*, and even Davenant's *Journey into Worcester* (1673). Hence, via Corbett, Eedes fathered an entire genre of topographical poetry, a special manifestation of rising national self-consciousness.

Anthony à Wood wrote of the *Iter Boreale* circulating freely in manuscript, and in this form it was read by Harington, Camden, and Corbett. It is preserved in four known copies, the remnants of what must have been a considerably richer tradition:

> **B** British Library Additional ms. 30352. Eleven numbered pages written in a scrawling hand; much necessary punctuation is omitted. The poem is entitled *Musae Boreales sive Iter Boreale*. On the title page are written two names, "John Bur

---

[1] Like Eedes, Corbett wrote *Iter Boreale* purely for the amusement of his Christ Church audience: the poem has as a concluding colophon a couple of lines from Horace, *Sermones* I.iv, *non recito cuiquam nisi amicis, idque coactus, / non ubivis, coramve quibuslibet.*

[2] *Ib.* 118f.; they also mention John Earle's manuscript poem *Satyra Itineraria* and further items cited by R. A. Aubin in his *Topographical Poetry in Eighteenth Century England* (New York, 1936).

rows of Harford" and "John Erdwell (?) of Sydmouthe." Therefore this ms. appears to have been owned successively by two members of Magdalene College, John Borroughs (B. A. 1594) and John Erdall (B. A. 1601).

C Corpus Christi College (Oxford) ms. 309 (pp. 85ff.). Included in a commonplace book of vernacular and Latin poetry (including, *inter alia*, an early biographical sketch of Shakespeare and some unedited material by William Alabaster of Cambridge) compiled by William Fulham, a Fellow of Corpus Christi (expelled 1648, restored 1660). For a history of this manuscript cf. E. K. Chambers, *William Shakespeare* (Oxford, 1930) II.255f. [In the copy supplied me by the firm acting as commercial agent for Corpus Christi, pp. 86^v - 87^r, containing lines 81 - 142, are omitted. Since the significant readings of **C** are also contained in the closely related ms. **W** this is not troublesome.]

R Bodleian Library ms. Rawlinson B 223 (once owned by the antiquarian Dr. Richard Rawlinson), a short manuscript containing sixteen numbered pages It is written in a tolerably good secretary hand, with a few corrections by a later reader. Provided as appendices on unnumbered pages. are short biographical sketches of Eedes and Mathew, written in the original hand (the one for Mathew also appears in Anthony à Wood's biography). Since Eedes' death is recorded, the manuscript cannot have been written prior to 1604. At a later time someone else has entered further biographical notes drawn from Wood's *Athenae Oxonienses* (first printed in 1692) and a reconstruction of the itinerary, with some calculations of mileage, almost all wrong.

W Bodleian Library ms. Wood 8853 (the antiquarian Anthony à Wood's personal copy). Eleven numbered pages written in a handsome italic hand, possibly a presentation copy. No evidence for dating.

In inspecting the *apparatus criticus* at the foot of each page of text, the reader will immediately see that **B** and **W** have strong affinities with each other, over against **R**. They frequently, though not invariably, share the same readings where **R** has something else (though often an equally acceptable lection), and **R** has a pronounced tendency to drop lines retained by **BW**. One of Eedes' rhetorical mannerisms is to repeat words or phrases in successive lines, and this led **R**'s copyist, or at least that of some manuscript in **R**'s background, either to skip lines or to telescope them by wrongly splicing together the first part part of one line with the latter part of the next. So **BW** and **R** represent different sectors of the textual tradition. In this context, it may be relevant that **R** was not executed for over twenty years after the composition of our poem.

B and **W** each contain readings, errors, and omissions not found in the other.[1] This principle is illustrated, for example, by omitted, telescoped, or otherwise mangled lines. **B** botches 308f., leaves out 406, telescopes 576f. into a single line, and garbles the passage at 617ff. **W** for its part shares with **R** the single telescoped line that substitutes for 421f., and omits 526. Observations of this sort exclude the possibility that either manuscript is an apograph of the other. Leaving out of consideration the evidence of sidenotes, it would almost be possible to think that both **B** and **W** are copies of the same manuscript; but **W**'s telescoped line at 421, a feature shared with **R,** suggests that their relationship is somewhat more complex.[2] The closeness of **BW** is especially illustrated by the shared misplacement of 617ff.

The position of **C** in the history of the text poses a more complicated problem inasmuch as it has a hybrid ancestry. According to the marginal notations of its copyist, William Fulman, the first 309 lines are copied from one manuscript with corrections written both marginally and in the text itself

---

[1] For the purpose of this discussion I do not take into account the fact that the sidenotes in these manuscripts are often quite different, which is possibly liable to a special explanation, given below.

[2] This process of omitting or telescoping lines may have been gradual rather than a phenomenon introduced at one time.

ex ms. Sheldon. The exemplar must have been a copy of inferior quality, for a large number of corrections needed to be introduced. That manuscript evidently broke off at 310, unless for some reason Fulman lost access to it when he reached this point, for a marginal note at that point reads *ex hinc Ms. Sheld. sol.* From now on the number of foolish copying errors and subsequent corrections decreases markedly.

The place of this bad manuscript in the tradition is difficult to ascertain (save that it had no obvious affinities with **R**). More important is that of the lost Sheldonian manuscript against which it was collated and corrected, and which supplied the text from 310 onward. It is clear that this latter copy was closely related to **BW**, and that it had a special affinity to **W**. In the portion of the poem beginning at 310 there are 30 readings common to **BCW** and 34 common to **CW**, including a number of uniquely shared sidenotes and the placement of 617ff. after 622. This may be contrasted with only 7 readings uniquely shared with **B**. On the other hand, the only signficant resemblance of **C** to **R** is the omission of 475. It looks permissible to think that **W** and the Sheldonian manuscript standing behind **C** (call it **S**) were copied from the same manuscript (call it **Y**, with **Z** used to represent **C**'s second source), and that **B** and **X** were in turn descended from a common ancestor. The relationship of **R** is obviously remoter. The general scheme can be represented by a diagram in which Ω represents what Eedes actually wrote:

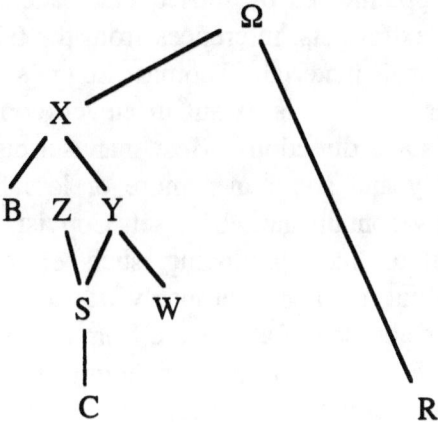

Remarkably few errors have infiltrated the tradition in its entirety: the only mistakes shared by all four extant copies not involving proper names are at 292, 541 and 656 (to which may possibly be added 53). Save for simple mistakes that could occur independently, readings shared by **R** and one or more of the **BCW** family are likely to be correct.

Frequent confusions abound in manuscript renderings of proper nouns. I have written the correct proper name in the Latin text under the theory that unfamiliar names easily confused copyists (sometimes Eedes himself may have been confused by northern pronunciation of the names of people to whom he was introduced).

A distinctive feature of these manuscripts is their more or less copious marginal annotation. Doubtless most of these are the responsibility of the author himself. This is strongly suggested because a number of them supply information that serves to clarify the text or even, in some cases, to render it intelligible. A couple (**B**'s sidenotes against 193 and 469) are written in the first person. Others, notably **B**'s annotations on 159 and 338, unambiguously represent readers' observations. One suspects that there was a core of the author's own annotations which was freely paraphrased, modified, and supplemented by subsequent readers and copyists who added extra facts, inferences from the text itself, and interpretational material. Thomas Legge's trilogy *Richardus Tertius* of 1579[1] is extant in eleven copies, which contain many stage directions. Most manuscripts include these selectively and sometimes more or less freely paraphrased, and few contain the whole set. Copyists felt no need to be scrupulous in reproducing such extra-textual material. Something similar is probably true in the present case, so that the absence of a sidenote from one or more manuscripts is no necessary reason for doubting the accuracy of the information it contains. Factual problems posed by several of them will be dealt with in appropriate Commentary notes.

I should like to take this opportunity to express my gratitude to C. B. L. Barr, Sub-Librarian of the York Minster Library and a specialist on Tobie Mathew; Peter Cane, Fellow Librarian of Corpus Christi College, Oxford; and Mrs. M. Kirwan, Librarian of Oriel College, Oxford, for useful assistance, information, and advice. And I owe a special word of thanks to my U. C. L. A. colleague, Professor M. W. Haslam, an acute critic and a Yorkshireman, for a number of suggested improvements.

[1] Cf. Legge's *Complete Plays* (ed. D. F. Sutton, Bern - New York, 1993), Vol. I.

[2] This is why it is dangerous to rely overmuch on the evidence of sidenotes in ascertaining the history of the text: the considerable differences between **B, C** and **W** in this respect do not call into question the conclusion that these manuscripts are closely related.

Iter Boreale

quid mihi cum Musis? quid cum Borealibus oris?
quo feror incerto, certo pro tempore, cursu,
non animo solum sed corpore? mens mihi gestit
scribere nescio quid, quod (si vere loquar) ipse
nescio quo pacto feci, sed scribere gestit,   5
scribere (si dici possit) qui carmina dictat,
et per iter fundit, nec certa, nec ordine certo,
quod nullo fieri pacto mihi posse putabam.
nam cum Decanum, Oxonia comitabar euntem,
officio, sed amore magis, rediturus eodem   10
quo via caepta die, o sum longius ire coactus,
quam vel ego statui, vel ferre negotia possent.
nam vel amore viri, quo non charior alter,
vel comitante viri, quo non festivior alter,   13A
vel Domini Blencow, quo non fallacior alter,
vanis promissis, ficto sermone trahebar   15
ultra propositam tam longo in itinere metam,
nulla recusandi mihi facta licentia, posthaec

---

9. *Dr. Matthewes, Deane of Durham* **BCRW**   14. *Dr. Blincow*   (*Blinco* **B**, *Blenco* **W**) *Provost of Oriel Colledge*
BCRW, *who promised to returne the next day at the*
†*rothel*† add. **B**

---

titulus. *MUSÆ BOREALES SIVE ITER BOREALE, 1584* (sic) **B**, *ITER
BOREALE* **CRW**   1. v. laudavit A. à Wood, *Ath. Oxon.* vit. nostri auc-
toris, e ms. **W**   2. *feror* **C** ante corr.   3. *certe* **C**   4 sq. om. **R**   9. *Oxonia* **C** ante corr.   11. *o* om. **B** et **C** ante corr.   13 - 13A. sic **W** (cum *qui*
pro *quo* in 13A), unum v. *nam vel amore viri, quo non festivior alter* cet.
(*num* **R**, *nam* corr. in *num* **C**, *charior alter* **C** ante corr.)   14. *Blinco* **B**,
Blincow corr. in *Blencow* **C**, *Blincow* **R** passim, *Blenco* **W**   17. *potentia*
pro *licentia* **B** | *posthac* **C** | *nulla recusandi mihi posthac copia facta* **W**
(sic **C** marg.)

A Northern Journey

What have I to do with the Muses? What with northern climes? Where am I being borne on this uncertain course, for a certain time, not only in my imagination but bodily? My mind craves to write I know not what, about that which I did (truth to tell) I know not how; but my mind craves to write, to write down the poem it dictated (if such can be said) and poured forth over the course of the journey: an unsure poem, written in no sure order, a thing I never imagined could befall me. For when I escorted our Dean as he was departing Oxford, as a duty but even more out of affection, I was minded to return home on the selfsame day I went out. Oh, I was forced to go further than I had planned or than my affairs could have carried me! For when I was lured into this long journey, venturing beyond my proposed limit, whether by affection for the fellow (no man more beloved), or by his company (no man more delightful), or by the empty promises and lying talk of Dominus Blenkowe (no man more deceitful), I had no further chance to refuse or make my excuses, or to say my good-byes, obtain permission

nulla excusandi, nec dicta forte salute,
nec facta venia, positis nec in ordine rebus,
a non ingratis discessi ingratus amicis. 20
hinc volui, ut potui, Musa lenire loquaci
taedia longa viae, nullo discrimine, quicquid
in buccam venit, fudi, quasi fundere sat sit,
tempore pro tali, tales extempore versus,
et longum longo describere carmine cursum. 25
prima defessos accepit nocte Northampton,
quae vult pura quidem (quamvis impura) videri
sed tota in verbis, nam moribus hic ut ubique
vivitur impuris: si nomen forte requiris
templi, respondent, Nicolai, sive Ioannis, 30
Mariae, aut Thomae, non audent dicere, Sancti.
unum quod veteri fuerat cognomine dictum
Allhallowes timide, vel non omnino loquuntur.
non impura modo vox illa, sed impia vulgo est,
proque die Sabaoth scelus est ibi dicere Sunday. 35
hic ad Decanum multi venere rogatum
ut velit ille loqui; loquitur non praedicat illic,
qui populum instituit; qui dicit "praedicat" errat.
proxima se nobis offert Leicestria, magna,

---

26. *Northampton* **BCRW**   31. *Maries, Johns* **C**   35.
Sabbath not Sunday **C**   37. *Speak not Preach* **C**   39.
Leicester **BCRW**

---

20. *gratus amicis* **C** ante corr.   21. *hic* **R** (sic **C** ante corr.)   23. *si
fundere* **C** ante corr.   24. *ex tempore* **BW**   26. *Norhampton* **C** ante corr.
27. *urbs impura quidem (quamvis vult pura videri)* **R**   28. *et* corr. in *ut*
C   29. *requiras* **BCW**   30. *Nicholae* **R**   32. *fuerat veteri* **C** ante corr.
34. om. *est* **BCW**   35. *Sabathi* **R** I *Sonday* **B**   38. *dicit* corr. in *dixit* **C**

to travel, or set my affairs in order; and so I, being a bad friend, took leave of my good friends. Hereupon I conceived the desire, insofar as I could, of relieving the tedium of a long journey by means of my chattering Muse, and I poured forth whatever came into my mouth, as if at such a time it was sufficient just to produce such extemporaneous verses and describe our lengthy travels in a lengthy poem.

On the first night Northampton received us weary folk, which wants to be deemed pure, no matter how impure it may be. Its piety exists only in name, for here as everywhere else men live according to unclean habits. If perchance you ask the name of a church, they answer Nicholas', John's, Mary's, or Thomas', but don't dare add the word Saint. There is one called by the ancient name of Allhallows, which they mention timidly if at all. Their manner of speaking is not only incorrect, but also blasphemous, and there it is a crime to call the Sabbath Sunday. Here many approached the Dean, asking him to *speak*. There anyone who gives moral instruction to the people *speaks* but does not *preach*, and he who calls this *preaching* is mistaken.

On the following night Leicester presented itself to us, a

sed dispersa tamen; seges est ubi multa fuisse   40
temporibus priscis veterum monumenta videmus.
hinc male dispositam, positamque in rupe Notingam
venimus. hic poteras de vivo cernere saxo
excisas aedes, poteras hic cernere diros
tanquam ex inferno spirantes undique fumos.   45
non magis horrendum, credo, dat Avernus odorem.
nos veluti canis ad Nilum bibimus fugimusque,
   atque adeo Mansfield contendimus. haud habet illa
quod quis miretur, nisi sit mirabile, plusquam
  sexcentos illic, idque una nocte morari,   50
quos a portendo dicunt, quia nil nisi portant.
prima in Eboraci comitatu nos Rotherama
accipit, haec solis caruit lusoribus, illic
quovis excellunt simul hospes et hospita lusu.
   Wakefeild in viridi, viridi, virida, viridino   55
hospita ab hospitio mihi saepe vocabitur, illic
accipimur dapibus lautis et piscibus, illic   56A
implemur veteris Bacchi, pinguisque ferinae,
atque in quo multis uno sint omnia potu

---

42. *Nottingham* **C**, *Notingham* **BW**, *Nothingham* **R**   48.
Mansfeild **BR** *Mawnsfielde in Sherewoode* **CW**   50. *600.*
Carriers **W**, *600 Carriers horses inned there one night* **R**
carrier<s> **B**   51. *Packhorses* **CW**   55. *Wakefield in a*
green **B** *Wakefield* **R** *Wakefeilde on(e) the Greene* **CW**

---

42. *Nothingham* **BC**   43 et 44. *poteras* corr. in *poteris* **C**   48. *Mandfeild*
R, *Mawnsfeilde* **W**, **C** corr.   52. *proxima* pro *prima* **R**, **C** ante corr. |
Rotherana **R**   53. *excipit, huc* **R**   55 et 60. *viridam* **C** (corr. u. v.)
56A. *solum habent* **BR** (vid. comm. not.)   57. *dulcis ...veterisque* **BCW**
sed cf. Verg., *Aen.* I.215   58. *sunt* **BCW**

large town but a scattered one. There were fields where we see that in olden times there had been many monuments of the ancients. Thence we came to Nottingham, badly laid out and built on a cliff. Here you could see homes hewn out of the living rock, you could also see evil fumes rising up as if from the Inferno. I do not imagine Avernus emits a more horrible stench. We had a drink, like the dog from the Nile, and made our escape, pressing onward to Mansfield. There is nothing notable there, unless it is worthy of note that more than six hundred carrier horses inned there one night (so-called because they do naught but carry baggage). On the following night Rotherham was the first town in Yorkshire to receive us; it only wanted its gamblers, though its landlord and landlady are adroit at all manner of gaming. I shall often speak of the verdant hospitality of greeny Wakefield all on a green, because of its inn where we were received with dainties and fish, where "we had our fill of vintage wine and fat game,"[1] and a drink so strong that one

[1] Quoting a line of the *Aeneid.*

tam forti, ut vere dicatur Martius esse.
non procul a Wakefeild, viridi, virida, viridino,   60
(nam sic cantus habet) iacet Aberfordia, villa
parva (sed in parvis satis est habuisse volentes).
hic habitat proprio viduata Philemone Baucis,
sola quidem, neque sola tamen, comitata duabus
filiolis venit, pulchras dicam anne modestas,   65
nescio; mixta rosis te lillia cernere credas.
mites Autumni fructus, poma et pyra promunt
et Bacchum Cereris, non Bacchum e vitibus ortum,
pocula magna, putes divinum opus Alcimedontis,
dumque unam pellunt, facta est sitis altera maior.   70
sed Domino Antonio referenda est gratia nostro,
pro quo, tam laeto facta est ea gratia vultu.
nil Tadcaster habet Musis et carmine dignum,
praeter magnifice structum sine flumine pontem.
proxima quae sequitur, domus Archipraesulis Ebor,   75
Thorp sibi nomen habet, tam re quam nomine sedem.

---

59. *March beere* **BCW**   61. *Aberford* **BCR**   63. *a tenant of
small colledge* **B** *Tenant to Oriell Colledge* **W**   68. *Strong
beere* **C**,   *ale and not wine* **R**   71. *Dr. Blencow* **C**   73.
Tadcaster **BCRW**   75. *Bishops Thorp* **BRW**, *Bishop
Thorpe* **C**

---

61. *namque ita cantus* **BC**   65. *pulchris...modestis* **BW, C** post. corr. |
post. hunc v. habet **C** *hae sedare sitim nobis nostraeque* (corr. in
nostrisque) *volentes* **C**   67. *ponunt* **R**   70. *expellunt* **R**   71. *Anthonio*
W, *Blincono* **R**   72. *tecto* pro *vultu* **B**   73 sq. laudavit Camdenus, inde
Defoe: vid. Comm. not.   73. *Todcaster* **C** ante corr. | *habes* laudavit
Defoe per errorem | *vel* pro *et* Camdenus | *Apolline* corr. in *carmine*
altera manu (fort. ex Camdeno) **R**   76. *Thorpe* **CW**

cup is enough for many a man, and one may rightly call it the drink of Mars.

Not far from greeny Wakefield all on a green (for so it says in the song) lies Aberford, a humble village, but it suffices a man to have dwelt content among humble things. Here dwells a Baucis, widowed of her Philemon, living alone but in fact not alone, for she approached us with her two daughters, and I know not whether I should call them more comely than bashful; you would think them lilies mingled with roses. They set before us the ripe fruits of Autumn, apples, pears, and that Bacchus who born of the grain, not the vine, in great huge mugs (you'd think them Alcmedon's divine handicraft); "while they slaked one thirst, another grew greater."[1] Thanks be to Dominus Anthony,[2] to whom our gratitude is expressed with a wide grin.

Tadcaster has nothing worthy of the Muses and my song, save for a grand bridge *sans* river. The next house to come up belonged to the Archbishop of York, having the name of

---

[1] An adaptation of a line from Vergil's *Aeneid.*
[2] Blenkowe.

praesulis esse putes, lauto est ita splendida vultu.
hic est ad tempus data causa quietis, in ipsis
hic fundamentum posuit Decanus arenis
tutius et melius, quam si confideret illis   80
rupibus horrendis, quae sunt Aquilonis in oris.
namque ut sunt durae, firmas vix credo futuras.
  est in Eboraco, quod laudes, quodque requiras.
urbs bene magna quidem, sed non bene structa, nec
                                                   aedes
sunt satis ornatae, nec publica structa viarum;   85
quamquam intra Petri non paucas septa videmus
claras et claris instructas usibus aedes.
sed quae Canonicum minime referantur ad usum,
nam pro Canonicis multi sine canone degunt.
  septima lux oritur, cum nos in septa ferarum   90
et nemorum saltus educit Episcopus Ebor
venatum, solus Decanus defuit, ille
sive invitus iit, sive invitatus Eborum.
nos primo excepit saltus, qui nomine Rider
dicitur. hic cursum sine cursu fecimus, ante   95
quam sequimur, cecidisse feram vox certa sonabat.
linquimus, inde nuces (quibus ante vacavimus) omnes
consequimur, quo nos clamor vocat; ecce iacentem
cernimus, et proprio faedatum sanguine damam.
hinc alium petimus saltum Thorp nomine dictum,   100

---

79. *Sandes* **B**, *Sandys, Archb. of York* **C**   83. *Yorke* **BCRW**
90. *hunting with the Archbishop* **B** *Edwin Sandys* **R**   94.
Rider park **BW** *saltus. 1. Rider* **R**   100. *Thorpe* **B** 2. *Thorp*
R [...]*pe parke* **W**

---

80. *consideret* **R**   83. *laudem...requiram* **BW**   86. *saeptu* **R**   88.
referuntur **R**   94. *Rider* **BR**, *Ryder* **W**   95. *ferimus* **R**   96. *recidisse* **R**

40

Thorp, being his estate in fact as well as in name. You'd think it belonged to a Bishop, such was its elegant façade. Here we had cause to rest for a while, and here our Dean built his foundation on *sand* more safely and soundly than if he had placed his trust in those rugged crags of the North. For though these be *durable*, I doubt they will *endure*.

York has everything you could find praiseworthy, everything you could want. It is a large city, indeed, but not a well built one, and its buildings and streets are not especially fine. Nevertheless once within Petergate we saw no few edifices that were handsome and made for distinguished purposes. But this does not apply to those assigned to the Canons for their use, for instead of the Canons many men live unruly in the Minster Close.

On the dawning of the seventh day, when the Bishop of York led us out to hunt in his forests, only the Dean was absent, either because he was unwilling or because he was invited to tarry in York. First we were received by a park called Rider, a course we traveled with no coursing; for before we could take up the chase the cry went up that the quarry had fallen. We took our leave and went a-nutting (previously we had gone without nuts) when a hallooing summoned us and we saw a deer lying, dyed with its own blood. Next we sought out a second park, named Thorp, a

41

longum iter, et frustra factum, nam fallimus illinc
spemque diemque simul, rara est aut ulla voluptas,
non puto tam damis, quam dumis esse refertum.
restabat saltus, qui Rest, tam nomine quam re
dicitur: hic requies datur, et non parva voluptas.   105
non hic, ut reliquis in saltibus, una videtur,
aut fortasse duae, concurrunt agmine facto,
hinc atque inde ferae, et maiores undique cervi.
nos canibus missis cursu praevertimus unam,
quae bene magna fuit, quam dixit se dare velle   110
Decano praesul si non ingratus abesset.
nec potuit licet ingrati tam immemor esse
Praesul Decani. vidit cervicibus altis
maiorem, servumque iubet sibi tendat ut arcum,
et sermone prius Decano dedicat illam   115
quam videt esse suam, nam frustra est missa sagitta:
solvimus inde canes, cursu superaverat omnes
illa canes; fugere canes fessi, aut quasi nollent
Decano absenti praedam donarier ullam:
sola illi fortuna favet, quam nec valet arcus,   120
nec superare canes, luto defixa iacebat.
sic fera natura infoelix, quia territa vivit
non expectato perit infoelicior ense.
sic et Decano absenti, et minus inde merenti,
dama datur casu, pro cervo maxima magno.   125

---

104. *Rest by Lawood* **B** *3. Rest* **R**

---

101. *num* **B**   103. *non vult* **B**, *nec puto* **R**   106. *nam hic* **W**   109. *superavimus* pro *praevertimus* **R** (fort. desumptum de v. 117)   110. *qui...magnuis erat, quem* **R**   111 - 113. *Decano praesul, vidit cervcibus altis* habet   ceteris verbis omissis   111. *abisset* **W**   115. *sermone prius sermone dedicat* **B**   *illum* **R**   116. *suum* **R**   121. *dama fixa* pro *defixa* **B**   122. *vixit* **R**   124. *minimo* pro *absenti, et* **BW**

long journey and a pointless one, for there we were cheated of our hopes, and of a good portion of the day, and there is little or no pleasure in that pleasure park, for I do not think it is so stocked with beasts as with brambles. There remained a park called Rest (its nature answered to its name), where we found repose and no mean pleasure. Here one did not see one or perhaps two deer, as at the others, for they gathered in herds from all sides, with great stags. We loosed the hounds and ran down a doe, who was of a right good size. The Bishop averred that he would have granted her to the Dean if the ingrate were not absent, and yet he did could not fail to be mindful of the Dean, ingrate though he might be. Seeing another to be taller than the others with her high neck, he bade a servant string his bow. With his words he dedicated this animal to the Dean before he had made her his own, for he shot his arrow in vain. Thereupon we set loose our dogs, but she outran them all and the dogs retreated in exhaustion, or as if they wished no prey at all to be given the Dean for being absent. Only good luck (not to be undone by arrows or dogs) favored our Dean, and our quarry lay stabbed in the mud. Thus a beast is unlucky by nature, for it lives its life in fear but is cut down by an unexpected sword. And so a deer was granted to the Dean, absent and thus less deserving, a large doe in lieu of a great stag.

iamque dies extremus adest, cum nos aliunde
cogit iter, lautaque iubet discedere mensa.
aspice, conveniunt ex omni parte ministri,
ut nostro dicat Decano quisque salutem.
nempe Archipraesul prius invitarat ut illic   130
illius adventum celebrent Aquillonis in oras.
egerat et pariter cum Decano ante, ut ab illo
possit haberi ad tam numerosum concio clerum.
hic vidi, vidisse iuvat, meminisse iuvabit,
praesulis ad mensam plus quinquaginta ministros,   135
quorum quisque Dei mysteria pandere posset.
    hinc nos invitat proprias Bourcherus ad aedes,
nomine vir magnus, sed maior amore, suumque
haeredem mittit, qui nos per fluminis alti
deducat ripas, et dulcia pascua prati.   140
ad mare quisquis iter quaerit, sibi quaerit et amnem
pro duce, nos vero iucundus dirigit amnis
ad largum hospitii fontem, et sine fine benignum.
singula quid referam? structa est, instructaque laute
ipsa domus, labor est quid quaeras dicere. sunt
                                                                          hic   145
omnia, quaeque essent satis, etsi multa deessent.
quid quod et hic pictis iuvat impallescere hortis?
hic viget, a stomacho sumpto qui nomine gaudet,
lusus et ursinus, iugulum qui scinde vocatur;

---

135. *50 ministri* **R**   137. *Mr. Bouser* **B** *Bouserus* **R** *Sir*
Ralphe Bowrcher **W**   148. *Maw* **CR**

---

128. *assidue veniunt* pro *aspcice, conveniunt* **B**   130. *ut* om. **W**   131.
oris **R**   133. *numerosam* **W**   135. *in mensa* **BW**   137. *hic* **BR** |
Bouserus **R**, *Bowserus* **BW**   146. *omnia quae* **C** ante corr.   147. *chartis*
BCW   149. *lusus maro, Loadam* **C** ante corr.

Now day was done, when our journey beckoned us
elsewhere and we were obliged to abandon the Archbishop's
groaning board. Lo, ministers flocked from all sides to greet
our Dean, as the Archbishop had previously invited them so
as to celebrate his arrival in the north country. And he had
already arranged with the Dean that he should deliver an
address to this numerous congregation of clerics. Here I saw
(and it was wholesome to see, "and will be wholesome to
recall,")[1] fifty ministers at the Bishop's table, each one qual-
ified to celebrate the Eucharist.

At this point Bourchier invited us to his manor, a man of
great name but greater affection, who sent his firstborn son
to lead us along the deep river's banks and the sweet
meadowlands. Each of us makes his way towards the sea,
seeking to use the river instead of a guide, and the pleasant
stream led us to a generous fountain of hospitality, friendly
beyond measure. Why relate every detail? The house itself
was sumptuously built and furnished. It would be hard work
to recount each thing of you might ask. Everything needful
is there, though much be lacking. What is the point in
making yourself haggard here working a parti-colored
garden?[2] Here grows that herb which rejoices in a name
taken from the stomach, the garlic called (like the card

---

[1] Quoting a tag from Vergil's *Aeneid.*
[2] Quoting in modified form a tag from a satire by Persius.

omne tulit punctum, qui miscuit utile dulci. 150
  non ego te, Topcliffe, dignarer carmine nostro,
ni bene dilutum vinum, et bona pruna dedisses,
quanquam nota tuo satis es de nomine Musis,
quarum rima fuit sedes in culmine rupis.
iamque mihi vere Boreales cernere partes 155
sum visus, nil terra prior distabat ab Austro;
sola Northallerton gelido mihi nata sub Arcto
creditur, in lectos ita duros cogit et arctos.
hic vidi, vidi? imo tuli mala, quae mihi fama
garrula fortassis, sed vera loquetur in Austro. 160
nam primo ingressu, pleno est data copia cornu
ut cives, armenta boum cum cornibus altis
implevere forum, veluti dictura salutem.
proxima respondent primis, nam quae domus una
visa parata viris, bobus hanc stabulum esse putares; 165
panis equinus erat, vel equino pondere maior,
carbonem redolet potus. coquus omnia praestat
caetera, quae proprium tulerat Decanus in usum.
perdices, quas attulimus sub nomine pulli,
Harrison horrisonus stertens male devorat omnes. 170

---

149. *Loadam, alias Cut throate* **C** *Lodam* **R** *Loadem alias Cut throat, a play at Cardes* **W** 151. *Topcliffe* **BCR** (*Topliffe* **R**) 157. *Northallerton* **BCRW** (*Northalerton* **R**) 162. *I thinke he means a market of beasts* **B** 170. *Harrison that sung the base* **R**

---

151. *Toplif* **R** 153. *satis es* **C** ante corr. 154. *quarum prima* **C** 157. *Northarlton* **R** | *solum* **R** | *gelida* **CRW** | *nota* **C** ante corr. 158. *artus* **C** ante corr. | *in lectis ibi duros cogimus artus* **R** 159. *male* **C** ante corr. 165. *boum* **C** ante corr. | *hanc* om. **W** 169. *quae* corr. in *quem* **C** 170. *Harrison Harissonus* **C** ante corr.

game) cut-throat. "He who mixes the useful with the pleasant destroys the whole point."[1]

Topcliff, I would not dignify you with mention in my song, had you not given us well-watered wine and fine plums, although you are well known by name to the Muses, who dwell in a nook on your pinnacle. And now I truly seemed to be seeing northern territory, for no previous terrain looked any different than the southland. Only Northallerton struck me as having been born under the freezing Great Bear, it compelled us to take to hard and narrow beds. Here I saw—saw? rather I experienced in the flesh what chattering but truthful Rumor will tell down South. For at our first entry a cornucopia of townsmen, cattle, and high-horned oxen thronged the market-place, as if come to greet us. The next development mirrored the first, for you'd think the single house seemingly built for human use was a cow-barn. The bread was suitable for horses, nay, heavier than horse-bread, and the drink tasted of charcoal. The rest of the stuff the cook served up consisted of things the Dean had brought along for our personal consumption. But rumbling, harsh-sounding Harrison naughtily ate up all the partridges

---

[1] Quoting Horace's *Ars Poetica*: cf. the Commentary note.

inde imus cubitum. mens hic mihi gestit iambos
fundere, et in lectos magis execrabile carmen.
quis cladem illius noctis, quis damna loquendo
non vocet ardentes Furiarum in carmina taedas?
durus erat lectus, quid dico durus? in imo   175
mollius ossa cubant, credo, non pauca sepulcro.
non ullus labor est lectos ibi sternere, nulli
cedunt, nec referunt vestigia corporis usquam.
quanquam illo contentus eram nisi (quod magis urit)
naribus afflasset tetrum pulvinar odorem.   180
hic ego quam volui, quod fingitur Endimioni,
mortiferum induci somnum, ne forte quietem
dirus odor raperet mihi cunque quiete salutem!
sed somnum prohibent pulices mihi, quique videntur
his magis audaces (ita stant ad vulnera) vermes.   185
in multam noctem vigilamus, surgimus ante
solem, nox tamen est longe longissima visa;
optavi talem soli illa nocte quietem,
ut citius surgens lustraret lampade terras.
sed quid plura? dies malui tres carcere claudi,   190
quam tali in lecto noctem dormire vel unam.
  de nos inde via cogebat Episcopus ille

---

171. *a hard bed* **B**   192. *tmesis* **R** I *The bishop* [...] *by the
seaside out of the way caused us to go out of oure way* **B**

---

172. *scribere* pro *fundere* **R**   173. *noctis?* **R**   177. *ullis* **C** ante corr. I *ibi
lectos* **C**   178. *unquam* **R**   180. *efflasset* **R**   183. *caperet* **C** ante corr. I
salutem? **C**   184. *quaeque* **BW**   186. *vigilavi* **C** ante corr.   189.
lustrarit **R** I *lumine* pro *lampade* **C**   190. *mallem* **R**

we had brought (we had told him they were chickens). And so to bed. At this point my mind yearns to pour forth iambics, a lampoon against that accursed bed. "Who in describing the catastrophe of that night,"[1] its injuries, would not invite the Furies' burning torches into his poem? My bed was hard—why do I say hard? I believe plenty of bones rest more comfortably in the depths of the tomb. Making the beds there is no chore, for they receive no imprint of your body. But I would have been content, save that I was more anguished by the foul stench of the mattress assaulting my nostrils. At this point how I would have enjoyed that death-like sleep Endymion is supposed to have experienced, as I wished, if this wretched stink had not deprived me of sleep and health! But the fleas forbade sleep, and also the vermin, which seemed even more insolent as they collected at the fleabites. We lay awake most of the night, and rose before sunrise, but still that night seemed the longest in my life. I was hoping the sun was having as bad a night of it as I was, so it would more quickly rise and bathe the land with its light. Need I say more? I'd have rather be locked in jail for three days than sleep a single night in that bed.

Next the Bishop possessing the title of Durham requested

---

[1] Quoting a half-line from the *Aeneid.*

49

devius ire suam, cui dat Dunelmia nomen
nempe in secretam terrae discesserat oram,
quae nec iter multis, nec multis causa videndi.   195
noverat (et certe est sapiens) iam tempus adesse,
in quo consilium propria ius dicat in urbe
atque ideo praeses comes Huntingdonius adsit,
cui dedit imperium princeps Aquilonis in oris.
quid? quod et in Scotiam faciens hoc tempore
                                        longum   200
Walsinghamus iter, fuerat venturus ad illum,
non facerent quaestum, facerent haec omnia sumptum.
nos sequimur quamvis fugientem ad littora, littus
praestat ei sedem, quae trunci dicitur antrum.
lautius accepit quam sperabamus, et ipse   205
obvenit, et multis procedunt undique servi.
filius imprimis mage Doctor, quam bene doctus.
miramur molem, miramur corporis artus,
inflatumque nimis vultum; Decanus et ipse
cum simul ambo sedent, referunt pullum
                                    et petasonem.   210
nec solum in nato praeposterus ordo tenetur
ante sit ut Doctor quam doctos, fecit id ipsum

---

204. *Stockden* **BR** (*Stocden* **R**), *Stockden a house of the Byshops of Durham* **CW**

---

193. *devius, ille suum* (cum *ille* corr. in *ire*) **C**   194. *namque* pro *nempe* **C** ante corr. I *secesserat* **CW**   195. *qua* **W**   196. *ut certe* **R**   197. *concilium* **W**, **C** post corr.   198. *adeo* **W**   199. *oras* **B**   201. *fecerat* pro *fuerat* **C** ante corr. I *rediturus* **R**   202. *faceret* **BCRW** I *sumptu* **R** 204. *praestat eis aedes* **C** ante corr.   205. *excepit* **R** I *at ipse* **BRW**   206. *obvius* pro *obvenit* **C** I *praecedunt* **C** ante corr.   207. *in primis* **W**   209. *et ille* **CR**   211. *non solum* **R**   212. *doctus* **BW** I *ferit* **R**

us to swerve from our route and track him down, for he had gone off to his secluded retreat, a place to which few men travel or have cause to visit. Since he was a canny fellow, he was aware that the time was now at hand when the Council of the North was to sit in his city. Hence the Earl of Huntingdon was present, whom our sovereign had made President of the North. Why? Because at that time Walsingham had made a long journey to Scotland, and was coming to him, so he feared lest all this would mean not profit but expense. We tracked him down, even though he had retreated to the coast. For the coast supplied him with an estate which took its name from a den in a tree-stock.[1] He received us more lavishly than we had expected, coming out to meet us himself and preceded by many servants, and particularly by his son the Doctor—what a learned man! We were astounded at his size, his huge frame, his haughty expression. When he and the Dean had taken their seats, they produced chicken and ham. A preposterous order of precedence was observed not only in regard to the son, that the Doctor should sit above the learned: it also applied to his

---

[1] Stockden.

in natis; natas quas credas iam modo natas,
vidimus uxores, iurares esse puellas,
ni patris ad dextram, primaque in sede sederent.   215
nil vulgare facit, nil non mirabile; Gallam
duxit in uxorem gallinam, noluit Anglam:
sed quid miramur facta haec emblemate digna?
ille quidem totus fuit emblematicus. omnis
pars domus inventis illius splendet, eadem   220
picturas fingit, qua scribit Pallade versus.
unam qua valde delectabatur, et in qua
ipse sibi nimium placuit, quam Pallade dextra
se finxisse putat, proponi iussit in aula;
parturiunt montes, nascetur ridiculus sus.   225
fingit nempe sui cacanti insidere Papam,
foedatosque illis, qui caudam forte trahebant,
vili (quo melius nil pictum) stercore vultus.
spectatum admissi risum teneatis, amici?
a porco mage quam de porco ficta videtur   230
fabula, nam quid habet Musis et Apollone dignum?
multa essent dicenda mihi, sed plura tacenda,
illius in nugis inopem me copia fecit.
    hac veluti scaena recreati, prorsus ab illo
ridendo mage quam risum faciente comoedo   235

---

221. *one of his verses in the picture with thee was
†ambited† shee* **B**

---

213. *natas quam* **C** ante corr.   218. *emblematicus, eadem* cum v. 219
om. **R**   220. vid. comm. not.   222. *delectebamur* **C** ante corr.   223. *et
prodit ridiculus mus* corr. in *sed prodit ridiculus sus* **C**   227. *faedatisque*
C ante corr.   231. *vel Apollone* **W**   234. *ad tempus* pro *prorsus* **B**

children. For we observed that girls who appeared to be newborn were actually wives, though you'd swear they were children if they had not sat at the right hand of the father, in the seat of honor. The Bishop did nothing in the ordinary way, nothing that was not surprising. He had taken a French pullet to wife, for he wanted nothing to do with an English-woman. But why be surprised at these things, worthy of an emblem? The man was emblematic through and through. Every part of his house shone with his inventions, and he painted pictures by the same creative impulse that inspired his versification. There was one painting in which he took particular delight, over which he was especially pleased with himself, that he fancied he had executed with Minerva's guidance, and he had ordered that this be displayed in his hall. "The mountain labor, and give birth to a ridiculous— pig!"[1] For he had painted the Pope astride a shitting swine, and men befouled by tail-dragging demons, their faces smeared with dung (naught painted better). "Friends, having been let in to see this sight, can you restrain your laughter?"[2] This scene seems to have been devised *by* a hog rather than *about* one, for what does it contain worthy of Apollo and the Muses? Though there may be much for me to say, there is more about which I must remain silent, and, when it comes to his follies, "the abundance renders me helpless."[3]

Refreshed by this stage-play, so to speak, this comedy more laughable than laughter-provoking, we hastened on

---

[1] A comically distorted quotation of a line from Horace's *Ars Poetica.*
[2] Another line from the *Ars Poetica.*
[3] Quoting a half-line from Ovid's *Metamorphoses.*

maturamus iter, vix passus mille, relicto
Stockden, occurrunt ex omni parte coloni
qui dominum terrae Decanum habuere, salutant
quoque modo possunt, gratum advenisse loquuntur,
hinc alii atque alii veniunt ex urbe frequentes.   240
imprimis Praebendarii, qui lege tenentur
Canonicum obsequium Decano offerre creato.
expectata diu tandem Dunelmia prodit,
clara quoad templum Cathedrale in monte locatum.
namque urbem quotusquisque est qui vidit in urbe.   245
longa nimis, neque lata satis, sunt strata, forumque
scindunt, non secus ac mathematica linea centrum,
nec nisi de summo poteras decernere templo.
circa urbem fluvius sinuoso flectitur arcu,
in se qui rediens tantum non efficit isthmum.   250
   Decani domus ascensu quasi regia primo
magna est ad speciem, sed multo maior ad usum.
omnibus officiis magis ampla sit, an magis apta,
difficile est dictu; molles habet illa recessus,
quam vellem reditus aequales aedibus essent.   255
intrat tota cohors, illa se iactat in aula
Harrison, et mensam summa cum laude secundam
ornat; maiori cum maiestate sedere
haud credo, possit fundator nobilis Ursae.

---

237. *the deanes tenants* **B**   243. *Durham* **R**   251. *Deanes house* **B**   259. *Mr. Furze Dr. Beare in Oxon.* **R** *Thomas Furse of the Beare in Oxford* **CW**

---

238. *et gratum* **B** 239. *ex parte* **R**   244. **C** *ante corr.* 245. *urbe?* **C** 246. *longe...late* **R**   248. *poteris* **C**   250. *istmum* **B**, *Istrum* **R**   254. *multos* pro *molles* **BC** 259. *vix* **CW** I *posset* **W**

our way and, with Stockden behind us, had scarcely covered a mile when farmers ran up to us from all directions who had the Dean for their landlord, and greeted him in every way they could, saying his arrival was welcome, and afterwards more and more people came thronging out of the city. In particular there appeared the Prebends, obliged by law to pay their Canons' duty to their appointed Dean. At length long-awaited Durham came into sight, a distinguished city at least insofar as the Cathedral is placed on its own hill. For it is a rare man who gets a good view of the city once inside it: the street is long but narrow and cuts through the market-place just as a geometer's lines bisects the center of a circle, but you cannot take this in this save from the Cathedral's steeple. A river makes a sinuous arc around the city and, doubling back on itself, all but creates an isthmus.

The Deanery, which you come across like a palace as you climb the Cathedral hill, is large to the eye but much larger in relation to its purpose. It is difficult to say whether it is more ample or more apt for all its official requirements. It has comfortable rooms (and how I wished the houses in which we would stay during the return trip would be similar!). Our entire company entered, and Harrison hurled himself about the great hall itself, serving as an ornament to a bounteous dinner served *summa cum laude*; I do not believe that the noble landlord of The Bear could have taken his seat with greater dignity.

Bellamy postridie, qui dicitur ante fuisse   260
aemulus imperii (licet aemulus impar Achilli)
instituens populum, legit quasi clericus alte;
spem tamen is nostram longe superaverat omnem,
quae nulla est, poterit facile expectatio vinci.
hinc omnes imus Decani invisere sedem,   265
quae dicta antiquo, sed falso nomine, Dear Park;
nempe interregni spoliarunt tempore, quando
regnum inter sese Decano absente tenebant,
qui Praebendarii minus a praebendo vocantur.
quodque magis miror (quid enim sibi cornua
                     quaerant?)   270
abstulerant damas, quae cornua cunque gerebant;
quamquam terra ferax et robore consita firmo
et viridi prato, et placido spectabilis amne;
quod delectat, habet, quodque et referatur in usum,
non tam iucundus, non tam foecundus in Austro   275
est locus. hic non est quod dicunt copia cornu,
quae tamen esse potest sine cornu copia summa,
in medio posita est, quae paulo distat ab urbe
clara domus, iucunda situ, iucundior usu;
sive etenim placidi delectant murmura fontis,   280

---

260. *Doctor Bellamy* **B** *Bellamy* **R** *Doctor Bellamy a Praebendary of Durham* **CW** 266. *the Deanes house called Deare park* **B** *Derepark belonging to the Deane of Durham* **CW** 279. *The Deanes first sermon* **B**

---

260. *Bellamus* **C** ante corr. 261. *(licet impar congressu Achilli)* **B** 262. *alter* **BCW**: vid. Comm. not. 263. *superaverit* **C** ante corr. 265. *tendunt* pro *imus* **R** 266. *Beerparcke* **B**, *Dereparke* **W** 270. *quierant* **B** 271. *gestabant* **R** 272. *concita* **W** 273. *paulum* **C** 274. *delectet* **B**, fort. recte | *ad usum* **CR** 278. *positum* **B**, *paulum* **W** 280. *etiam* pro *etenim* **W**, **C** post corr.

On the following day Bellamy, who is said to have been a rival for the throne, though a rival "unequal to Achilles,"[1] preached to the congregation, reading aloud in a high clerical voice. Nonetheless, he vastly exceeded our expectations—when there are no expectations, they are easily surpassed. Next we all went to visit the Dean's estate, which is called by the ancient but misleading name of Deer Park, For this had been despoiled during a period of interregnum, when the Prebends (who do not get their title from providing anything!) shared the power amongst themselves in the absence of any Dean. And I find it more remarkable that they had done away with all the antler-bearing deer—what possible use had they for antlers? Still, the land is fertile, good sound soil and verdant meadowland, made handsome by a placid brook. It is endowed with all that pleases, all that is needful, and there is no place so fertile down South. You can't exactly say there's a horn of plenty here, but an abundance of all good things (minus the horn). In the middle of the park stands a fine manor, somewhat removed from the city, pleasing for its location, even more so for its utility. If the babble of a tranquil

---

[1] A tag from Vergil.

seu spectare placet florentis gramina prati,
seu cupias suaves inspiret ut aer odores
seu peragrare iuvat sylvas, seu scandere colles,
natura locus omnia sensibus omnibus offert.
   iamque dies aderat solis, quo tempore primum   285
possedit proprii Decanus pulpita templi.
magna adventantis fuit expectatio, maior
laus hominis (de quo quasi de Carthagine praestat
nulla quidem quam pauca loqui). superaverat omnes
ante alios, iam nunc coepit superare seipsum.   290
ille quidem foelix tam divite sede, sed illi
plusquam foelices tam docti divite vena.
nec minus interea (mage quod pars maxima spectat)
corpora pascit eis, quod vix conceditur uni.
praestat utrumque simul; patet omnibus aula
                              domusque   295
interior, curam levat hac in re bene magnam
Harrison, accipiens cum summo quemque decoro.
   nos procul a patria, vastis Aquilonis in oris
coepit amor post quinque dies non parvus eundi
Oxoniam, Oxoniam longeque diuque relictam.   300
sed nos, sed noster, sed fallacissimus ille
Blencowe (ne gravius quid dicam) fallit, iterque
praetendit verbis quod non intendit habere;
Decanus, non dico rogat, iubet, imperat, orat,

---

302. *Doctor Blenco* **W**

---

281. *campi* pro *prati* **CR**   282. *sive* **B**, *sive cupis* **C** | *suavet* **B** | *ut spiret hortus* corr. in *inspiret ut aer* **C** | *arbor* pro *aer* **R** | *odore* **R**   284. *omnibus omnia sensibus* **R**   292. *plus quam* **B** 294. *iis* **R**, **C** ante corr.   297. *excipiens* **RW** 298. *non* **R**   300. *longe* **R**   302. *Blinco* **BW**, *Blincow* **C** ante corr. | *(ne dicam gravius quid)* **R** | *fallit* corr. in *fallet* **C** 304. *urget* **B**

fountain delights you, or if you take pleasure in gazing at the lawn of a flowery yard, crave for air so as to breathe its sweet fragrances, or wish to amble in the woods or climb hills, by its nature this place purveys everything for all your senses.

Now it was the Sunday on which the Dean was to take charge of his own pulpit in the Cathedral. The expectation of his arrival was great, the praise given the man even greater (about whom, as about Carthage, it is preferable to say nothing than too little). Previously he had surpassed everyone else; now he outdid himself. He was fortunate in having such a divine appointment, but they were even more fortunate to have the blessed talent of such a learned man. And at the same time he also fed them bodily,[1] a thing rarely possible for a single man, especially because the larger part of the congregation was present. He offered them a spiritual and corporeal feast, for the interior of his hall and his house were thrown open to the public, and Harrison took charge and greatly lightened his burden in this matter, receiving each guest with the greatest ceremony.

After five days had passed, being in the vast North country far from our native land, we were overcome by no small desire to return to Oxford, Oxford which we had put far behind us for so long. But our most deceptive friend Blenkowe (to say nothing worse about him) deceived us, and spoke in his conversation about the return journey, which he had no intention of making. And I won't say the Dean asked us—

[1] As well as spiritually.

et tenet invitos, mensem maneamus ut unum,   305
etsi mens esset (quod dicunt) mensis eundi.
se quamvis habeat multos multoque habiturus
quoque die plures videatur, se tamen inter
illos absque suis solum putat esse futurum.
nec tam gratus erat (quamvis gratissimus) illas   310
illius causa quod venissemus in oras,
quam fuit iratus quod in illis linquere terris
ante volebamus quam fundamenta locasset.
nos illi morem gerimus, tempusque diei
longum excercitio nunc hoc nunc fallimus illo.   315
hic vetus Harrisonus iugulum ad nos scinde vocavit,
seque gerit similem sibi semper, namque vocabat
more suo chartas, sine more renunciat omnes.
saepe Novum Castrum voluit Blencowus adire,
saepe recusavi; dominus mihi Iocche timorem   320
fecerat, hunc referunt passim et sine lege vagari,
in lectisque homines somno iugulare sepultos.
praecipue, mihi crede, aliis puer ille placebat
qui stans ad mensam placide cantare solebat
atque Scoto Scoticos Scotice magis edere cantus.   325

---

316. *Loodum* **B** *Harrison called them to Lodam* **CW**   319.
New Castle **BRW**   320. *a Scottish outlaw* **BCRW**   323. *the
boie that song the Scottish song* **B**   326. *Tunstall the Vice
Deane* **BW** *Tunstall Vice-deane of Durh.* **C** *Dunstall* **R**

---

306. *(quam dicunt mensis)* **B**   307. - 9. vv. om **R** (*se tamen illos /
absque suis* **B**)   309. *solum sese* **BCW**   310. *quanquam* **R**   311. *ob
causam* **R**   315. *excercitia* **R**   316. *ad vetus Harrisonus iugulum nos
scinde vocavit* **C** | *ad* om. **B** | *vocabat* **B**, *recusat* **RW**   317. *nempe
recusat* **BW**   319. *Blincous* **BW**, *Blenconus* **C**   320. *Loche* **R**   321. *et*
om. **R**   323. *praecipue mihi, credo aliis* **C**   324. *tentare* pro *cantare* **R**

he ordered, commanded and exhorted us, holding us against our will, that we linger for a month, even though we were minded (as they say) for a travel-month. Although he saw many men and seemed to be seeing more by the day, he imagined that he would be stranded among those folk with none of his own people. Nor was he as grateful (though he was most grateful) that we had come to these climes for his sake, as he was furious that we were willing to leave him behind in those lands before he had laid the foundations of his Deanship. We humored him, and passed our days now in this recreation, now in that. Hereupon ancient Harrison invited us to play a game of cut-throat, behaving in his typical fashion, for he asked for his cards, as was his wont, and made his discards with unwonted abandon. Blenkowe often wished to visit Newcastle, and I often refused. For Master Jock had made me fearful, since they said this outlaw was ranging freely, murdering sleeping men in their beds. In particular (you must trust me) that boy pleased the others who used to sing calmly at our table, performing Scots songs Scottishly in a Scots dialect.

posthaec Dunstallus (Tall Dunsum dicere possis)
praedicat, in tanta tenuem pinguedine sensum
miror, certe habuit (nisi me sententia fallit)
tam tenuem, ut tantum possis non dicere nullum.
vox maior quam vis dicendi, verba profecto   330
pondus habent, sed pondus iners, et ponderis expers;
scilicet audaces facit ignorantia stultos;
textum ex undecimo Matthei sumpserat, illum
nempe locum, quo Christus eos quicunque laborant
seque sui cernunt peccati pondere pressos,   335
convocat ut levet et pondus grave leniet illis.
plumbeus hic asinus, vel si quid durius isto,
(namque favere nimis videar, cum sic loquar) illos
esse laborantes dixit, quicunque labori
dant operam, pariterque hortatur cuique laborem.   340
si natura neget, daret indignatio versum.
cum plumbo gravior, pluma leviora loquatur,
hoc tamen hoc uno est visus satis esse modestus
quod vel avaratiae, vel turpis crimina vitae
cum notat, ad pectus sese ferit; haud putat illum   345
posse movere alios, qui non moveatur et ipse.

---

333. *come to me all ye that labour and I will refresh you* B
338. *I* †*inerve*† (i. e. *interpret?*) *it as hee tooke all of them
that labour of (as?) laborers so hee did not take them that
are heavie loden as porters* B

---

326. *Tunstallus* BCW, fort. recte (sed vid. Comm. not.)   329. *possis
tantum* CW   336. *convocat ut levet et pondus leniet illis* BW, *convocat,
ut levet, grave pondus leniat illis* C, *convocat ad sese, ut grave pondere
levitet ipsis* R   337. *illo* B   338. *videor...loquor* BCW   341. *facit* pro
daret R   342. *pluvia* BRW   343. *hoc tamen hic* BRW, C post corr.
346. *movetur* R   346. *vice Decanum* R

Afterwards Dunstall[1] preached (you could just as well call him Tall Dunce): unless my judgment fails me, he spoke so drearily on such a trifling theme that you could all but proclaim he was saying nothing. His lungs were more powerful than his eloquence; to be sure, his words had weight, but it was dead weight, insubstantial heaviness. Thus ignorance emboldens the stupid. He took his text from the eleventh chapter of *Matthew*, I mean that passage in which Christ summoned to Himself all those who labor and know themselves to be oppressed by the weight of their sins, so that He might relieve them of their burden and lighten their heavy load. This donkey fashioned out of lead, or some substance even denser (and when I speak thus, I seem to be flattering the man), spoke of those who labor as those who work for a living and urged everyone to seek employment. "Even if natural talent is wanting, indignation makes one write satire!"[2] Though heavier than lead, the fellow spoke stuff lighter than a feather, but in this one single respect he appeared to be satisfactorily modest, that as he railed against avarice and the crimes of a base life, he thumped himself on the breast, since he scarcely imagined that anyone could move others who wasn't moved himself. When this

---

[1] Actually he was named Tunstall.
[2] Quoting a line by Juvenal.

hic Vicedecanum cum sese intelligit esse
illius officii non unum perdit iota,
nec sane perdet, Decani nomine salvo,
quod reliquum est, totum me iudice semper habebit.   350
  iamque Lougherus adest et cui dedit ipsa iuventus
nomen—digna quidem cui se daret ipsa iuventus.
tam bene de rebus multis et ab omnibus audit,
non alio multis est Wallia nomine clara,
quam quod eos tulerat, Doctorem nempe
                   Lougherum   355
et Dominam Yongham. multis e millibus unum
haud quenquam invenies, qui non his cedit utrisque,
tam sunt egregiis, et honestis moribus ambo.
nobis Oxoniam nova spes est facta videndi
illorum adventu, sed spes est irrita; semper   360
fit nova causa morae. magis est mora longa molesta
quam via longa fuit, finis spes magna levabat
taedia longa viae, finis spes nulla levabat
taedia longa morae, fit spes minor, et mora maior.

---

351. *D. Louher, Mrs. Yong* **B**, *Dr. Loher [et Dna. Young]* **C**
Dr. Losher **R** *Doctor Loher* **B**   356. *D. Yongham* **R**

---

348. *officio* **R** I *unum non* **C** I *perdat* **BCW**   351. *Loherus* **BC** I *adest,
cui* **C** ante corr. I *iamque Losherus adest, cui se dedit ipsa iuventus* **R**
cum v. 352 om. (sed nomen habet recte expressum **W** v. 590)   353.
audet **C** ante corr.   354. *chara* **B** 355. *tulerit* **BCW** I *Loherum* **BCW**
356. *dominum Yongam* **R** I *de millibus* **R**   357. *haud quaquem* **BW**,
haudquaquam **C**, *quapiam* **R** I *qui nos* **R** I *cedat* **W** I *utrisque* om. **B**
359. *petendi* **B**   360. *tamen* pro *est* **C** I interpunxit post *semper* non post
irrita **CRW** 362 sq. *levabit* **BCRW** 364. *et mora* **BRW** 365. *suadet* **R**
I αμνησιαν vel fort. αμνηστιαν **C** (lacunam habet **R**)

gentleman perceived he was Vice-Dean he did not let go one iota of that dignity, nor (saving the title of Dean) will he ever let it go, and in my opinion will always clutch it in his grasp.

At this point Lougher made his appearance, and she to whom Youth has given its name, who has deserved it that Youth itself has granted this gift. She enjoyed a fine reputation with everybody for so many good points. For no other reason is Wales renowned than that it has produced Dr. Lougher and Mistress Young. Nowhere will you discover a single man out of thousands who does not yield to these two, thus are they distinguished by their excellent and honest morals. At their arrival our hopes of seeing Oxford were rekindled, a hope that was constantly being dashed: for there arose a new cause for lingering. This lengthy delaying was more oppressive than our long journey, for the hope of making an end to traveling lightened our journey, whereas no hope of making an end lightened our delay. Hope lessens as delay lengthens.

suadit ἀμνησίαν simplex Holydaius, in eius   365
simplicitate tamen subtilia multa latebant.
Graecula Romanis miscebat, sacra profanis.
sed tamen est illi cur ignoscamus id unum,
certe erat ad captum quod derivabat ab illis,
quodlibet est Graece praeterquam Graeca loquutus.   370
hunc sequitur cui lingua fluit melle atque butyro
mollius, inter eos velut inter Luna minores
excellens stellas; Borealis Tullius ille,
Naunton, dicendi princeps, princepsque docendi.
huic inimica fuit nimia expectatio, docti   375
nomine famosus, docti vix rettulit umbram.
nempe locos in communes nimis expatiatus
dixit de quovis quod possis dicere textu.
inde vicem caepit Decanus habere secundam,
anseribus miscetur olor, apis Attica fucis,   380
et de more suo tantum supereminet omnes
quantum lenta solent inter viburna cupressi.
sed quid apis mel dulce valet, quid cantus oloris,
cum sese in lucem profert non garrulus anser
ignavumque pecus, verum Iunonius ales   385

---

365. Holidaie praebendarius **B** *Holyday* **R** *Mr Hollyday a praebend of Durham* **CW**   371 *Nanton* **B** *Naunton* **R** *Mr. Nawnton a praebend of Durham* **CW**   379. *the Deane* **B**

---

367. *prophanis* **BCW**   368. interpunxit post *ignoscamus* non post *unum* **B** 370. *quidlibet* **C** 374. *Nanton* **B**, *Nawnton* **CW** I *loquendi* **R** 367. *vix docti* **C** 378. *possit* **B**, *posset* **W** 379. *invicem* **R** 380. *fusis* **R** ante corr. 382. *cupressus* **R** 385. *Iunovius* **R**

Simple Holiday urged forgiveness of the offences we have received, but in his simplicity lay concealed much subtlety. He mixed morsels of Greek in with his Latin, tidbits of sacred learning in with his secular conversation. But we forgave him on this single score, that what he drew from these sources was readily comprehensible; whatever he said was more Greek-like than actually Greek. Next came a man whose tongue flowed smoother than honey and butter, shining among them like the moon among lesser stars. This person, Naunton, was the Tully of the North, the prince of oratory, the prince of preaching. The great anticipation he had created proved his undoing, for he had a reputation for learning, but was scarcely the shadow of an educated man. He went on and on with his rhetorical tropes, saying all you could say about any text of Scripture you care to name.

The Dean spoke second in his turn; a swan come in among the geese, an Attic bee among the drones, and (as was his habit) he surpassed them all, "just as the cypress are wont to overtop the swaying viburnums."[1] But what is the use of bees' honey, what is the value of a swan's song, when no mere chattering goose or lowborn beast thrusts himself into the light: when indeed Robson, a veritable bird of Juno,

---

[1] Quoting a line from one of Vergil's *Eclogues*.

Robsonus ostentans plumas pavonis et alas?
quam vellem misereri hominis! sed vanus in illo
atque ingens animus magnum quid nescio spirat,
tam male tam misere naturam torquet et artem
ut neque naturam videatur nosse nec artem.   390
quicquid alit color est, sed plane decolor; affert
flores, sed flores ornatu et flore carentes.
Mercurium e ligno et duro quasi marmore fingit,
qui studet invita Cicero novus esse Minerva.
hunc Dunelmensis tamen omnis praesulis esse   395
delicias dicunt, et dicunt non male, namque
praeter delicias nihil est quod dicere possis.
Browne minor ad speciem, re maior, lenior illo
fertur, sed fertur multo quoque plenior illo
more fluentis aquae, tacito quae murmure cursum,   400
quando est plena, facit, quando est tenuissima, spumat.
Bunnius Oxoniae qui dulcia mella putatur
e Magdalenae mammis hausisse videtur,
inter Canonicos longe doctissimus omnes.

---

386. *Robson of Cam* (i. e. *Cambridge*) *the bishops chaplen*
BD Cantabrigia **B** *Robson* **R** *A bachelor of divinity in*
Cambridge **CW**   398. *Mr Browne MA Oxon* **B**, *Browne* **R**
A Master of Arte of Oxford **W**   402. *Mr Bunny that was of*
Magdalen colledge Oxford praebend **B** *Bunnie* **R** *Mr Bunny*
a Praebend of Durham **CW**

---

387. *quum* **R**   391. *alit* pro *ait* **R**   393. *ex ligno* **R**   397. *nil* **W** |
possunt **BCW**   398. *lenius* **BCW**   399. *plenius* **BW**   402. *Bunneus* **C** |
delicia mella **R**   403. *e* om. **R**   405. *Decanus* corr. superscr. in *Decani*
R | *Eubanck* **B**, *Ubank* **R**, *Ubanck* **CW**

shows off his peacock feathers and wings? How I wanted to

feel pity for this man! But his vain, colossal ego, full of God

knows what, distorted both nature and art so miserably, so

wretchedly, that he seemed to have learnt nothing of either

nature or art. Whatever he cultivates is his stylistic col-

oration, but a discolored one; he introduces flowery pas-

sages, but florid without beauty or bloom. It is as if he

makes a Mercury out of wood and hard marble, who craves

to be a new Cicero against Minerva's will. But they say he is

the Bishop of Durham's darling and they don't say this

amiss, because there's nothing they could call him except

"darling." Brown is smaller in stature, but larger in accom-

plishment. He swept along more gently than Robson, though

much more substantially, and he speaks in the manner of

flowing water, which follows its course with a quiet murmur

when it is at the full, but tends to foam when shallow. Bun-

ney is held to be Oxford's sweet delight, and he seems to

have been nursed at Magdalene, the most learned among the

inde Capellanus Decani prodiit Eubank   405
nec bene multa quidem, sed nec male cuncta loquutus.
frigidus in calido fuerat, ieiunus in amplo
textu, quam suadet, fervens dilectio frigit.
iamque iterum discessuros nova causa moratur,
fama reversuri Scotorum a rege legati,   410
nollet ut ante suis Decanus ab aedibus irem
quam Walsinghamo, domino mihi iure colendo,
dixissem (fateor quam me debere) salutem.
nulla mora est mihi iusta magis, quam quae datur inde,
nulla molesta minus; caepit Dunelmia tandem   415
ipsa placere mihi, dedit haec occasio causam,
cur de praeterito minor esset tempore cura.
vix ter caelestem cursu confecerat orbem
Phaebus, et Oceani radios immerserat undis,
cum tolluntur equis comes Huntingdonius, atque   420
Decanus noster magna comitante caterva
ut dominum Walsinghamum comitentur in urbem.
hic ut praeriperet reverendus Episcopus omnem

---

405. *Mr Eubanck that prayed for the Deane in his sermon* **B**
Ubank **R** *A follower of the Deane of Durham* **CW**   *His text
above all things have fervent love* **B**   408. *returne of the
Embassador out of Scotland* **B**   418. *his driving into
Durham* **B**

---

406. v. om. **B**   407. *fuit* **BC**   408. *textu quum suadet fervens dilectio
frigit* **B**, *qui suadet Domino delicta fateri* **R**   409. *iam* **W, C** ante corr.
417. *minus...curae* **B** 418. *vix vero* **C**, *vix dum* **RW** (vid. Comm. not.)
419. *immiserat* **R**   421. *Decanus, quo Walsingham comitentur in urbem*
cum v. 422 om. **R**, idem habet **CW** cum *ut* pro *quo*   423. *his ut
praeriperet praepinquis* **B**, *his ut praeriperet nobis* **CW**

70

Canons. Next Ewbanke, Chaplain to the Dean, came forth, who couldn't say much well (but who didn't say everything badly). He waxed chill on a text that required warmth, threadbare on one that demanded amplitude, and the fervent love he urged was frigid.

And now yet another reason delayed us as we were on the point of departing: rumor that the ambassador to Scotland was returning, with the result that the Dean did not wish me to leave his house before I had paid my respects to Walsingham, a Lord I was duty-bound to honor. I had no more legitimate reason for delay than the one then offered, nor one less irksome. And at length Durham had started to please me, and this development gave me an excuse to pay less attention to time's passage. Scarce had Phoebus thrice completed his course through the sky and plunged his rays in Ocean's waves, when the Earl of Huntingdon and the Dean rode out on horseback, accompanied by a large retinue, to escort Lord Walsingham into the city. Hereupon the

gratiam, in Aurora clam se subduxerat, inque
finibus extremis, pluvialibus obvius Austris.   425
a nona ad quartam consedit sordidus horam;
abiectos mores non mutant regis honores.
serior occurrit, sed multo gratior illo
nostra cohors, oleum et operam sic perdidit omnem.
magnus erat numerus noster, sed maior eorum   430
qui sese comites Domini fecere legati.
inter eos primus Comes est Essexius, inde
custodes ambo praefecti finibus illis
qui Scotiam attingunt, dominus Scroope, et ferus ille
Foster, quem dicunt bene custodir seipsum.   435
hinc ambo fratres, et clari insignibus ambo
milites aurati, Russelli vera propago
illius Comitis, cui dat Bedfordia nomen.
accedunt istis, queis purpura fulget et aurum
Mildmaius, doctusque libros tractare Nevillus   440
et generosa satis pubes Aquilonica, Lowther,
Widdrington, Barnston, doctique equitare caballos,
Musgravii, spoliisque Scoti Fenwickus opimis,
flammeus ipse satis natura, sed magis illi
flammam auget, patris ut mortem ulciscatur in illos   445
illo qui puero patrem trucidasse feruntur.

---

423. *Richard Barnes* **R**   431. *Robertus Comes Essex* **R**

---

425. *asteris* corr. in *Ausris* **R**   428. *senior* **R**   429. *atque* pro *et* **R** sed vid. Comm. not.   434. *Scroop* **B**   436. *huic* **B** u. v., **C** ante corr.   438. *praeclari* pro *illius* **R**   439. *cui* pro *queis* **C**   440. *Mildmanus* **B** 441. *Lader* **B**, *Loader* **R**, *Looder* **CW**   442. *Wittington, Daleton* **B**, *Whittington, Barnston* **R**, *Wythrynton, Darston* **CW**   443. *ffanocus opimus* **B**, *Fenwicus opimus* **W**   446. *patrem puero* **CW** | *occidisse* pro *trucidasse* **B**

reverend Bishop, so that he might steal a march in
gaining Walsingham's favor, furtively went eastward
into the farthest borderland, exposed to the rainy South
wind, and waited, covered in mud, from nine in the
morning to four in the afternoon. Honors conferred by
the sovereign do not alter his contemptible habits. So he
was the earlier to meet Walsingham, though our group
was much more welcome in his sight, and thus the
Bishop "wasted his time and oil."[1] Our number was
great, but still was greater that of those who composed
the Lord Ambassador's retinue. Foremost among them
was the Earl of Essex, then the two Wardens of the
border country, Lord Scrope and fierce Foster (whom
they say to be good at guarding himself). There too were
two brothers, both distinguished by the golden Garter,
the true scions of Russell, that Earl to whom Bedford
lends its name. Joined to them were others resplendent
in purple and gold, Mildmay, Neville, distinguished for
his book-learning, that right noble lad of the North,
Lowther, Widdrington, Barnston, the Musgraves, skilled
at horse-riding, Fenwick, rich with Scots spoils, a man
fiery enough by nature, his flame fanned higher by the
hope of exacting revenge on the men who had killed his

---

[1] Quoting a line from Plautus' *Poenulus.*

mitto alios, mittoque horum cuiusque catervam,
nec numerare licet, nec si, numerare referret.
his urbem Walsinghamus simul intrat et implet
non satis est toti Dunelmia tota cohorti.   450
ipse quod iturus Domino promiserat Heathus
illius hospitio, nocte una gaudet, ab urbe
cui bene magna domus vix passus mille iacebat.
  postera lux oritur Matthaeo dicta diemque
occupat in proprio proprio de nomine templo   455
Doctor Matthaeus; cupit hunc audire legatus,
atque adeo hospitium senis Heathi mane reliquit.
Decanus nunquam non creditur optimus esse
et primum placet et postremum perplacet idem.
est semper similisque sui. duri atque rebelles   460
Catholici qui dicuntur quo nescio iure
hunc auditum veniunt ex urbe frequentes.
alternis vicibus dominum accepere legatum
in mensa comes et Decanus, solius autem
utitur hospitio Decani, nosque cubili   465
depellit nostro, pulsi depellimus ipsi
Harrisonum, dominumque domus, domini esse videmur.
ut primum ingreditur Decani tecta legatus,
gratulor adventum longo sermone, quod ille

---

450. *Mr. Heathe's house neare Durham called the keeper* **R**
(l. *called of Kepier*) *Mr. Heath* **W**   454. *7ber 21* **R**   469. *I was apointed to speak before hym* **B**

---

447. *catervas* **R**   448. *referre* **W**   451. *Heatho* **BCW**   454. *Mathao* **B**,
Matthaeus **R**   458. *eius* pro *esse* **BCW**   459. *est primum* **B**   460. *et semper* **R**   461. *ut dicunt, quamvis quo nescio iure* **R**   462. *audituri* **R**
463. *excepere* **R**

father in his boyhood. I pretermit the rest, I omit each man's outriders, as it would be impossible to enumerate them nor, if it were, would there be any point. They all entered along with Walsingham, filling the city, but Durham was not sufficient for such a throng. Because Heath, who himself was leaving town, had promised the hospitality of his house to his Lordship, he enjoyed the pleasure of a night's stay in that man's grand manor, scarce one mile distant.

The following day that dawned was called that of St. Matthew, and Dr. Mathew was busied about his own name-day in his own Cathedral. The Ambassador conceived a desire to hear him, and so left old man Heath's hospitable house in the morning. The Dean was always held to be the best, at first giving pleasure, in the end giving complete delight. He is always the same: they say that even the savage and rebellious so-called Catholics emerged from the city to hear him in droves, though I do not know by what right. The Earl and the Dean took turns entertaining the Lord Ambassador, although he only took advantage of the Dean's hospitality. He chucked us out of our beds, and we, being thus turfed out, did the same to Harrison and the Major Domo, so we seemed to be masters of the house. As soon as the Ambassador entered the Dean's house I delivered a lengthy

quo solet, accepit, vultu laeto atque benigno,   470
et bene multa licet mihi se fecisse sciebat,
se maiora tamen multo debere fatetur,
quodque erat officii pro signo ducit amoris.
totos quinque dies illa consistit in urbe,
vel quia defessus, vel (quia mage credo)   475
Decani domus aula minor pro tempore visa.
nuntius hinc atque inde venit velocior Euro
quoque die, nova semper habens, quaecumque geruntur
vel Scotici regis, vel in aula principis Anglae.
arcana imperii mitto, neque nota cuique   480
nec noscenda viro. Scotia est quasi fabula vulgo
quod fieret nostris inimica et inhospita tellus.
  tempore Decano facturo verba secundo,
pulpita praeripuit patris decus, o decus, inquam
Emmanuell Doctor bullatus, transque marinus,   485
scilicet ignotum nolebat Episcopus esse,
se non Doctorem, Doctorem gignere posse:
sed neque natus erat Doctor puer ille, creatum
Basiliae dicunt, et dicunt iure creatum,
non solet ex nihilo genuina creatio dici.   490
nec tamen est veritus quicquam cordatus asellus
Davidis tractare lyram, tractare prophetas,
metaphorasque loqui, quas non intellegit ipse,

---

485. *Barnes B. of Durham* **C** *Dr Barnes* **R**

---

475. v. om. **CR**   478. *quaeque dies* **R** | *habent* **R**, *habemus* **W**   479.
Scotii **R** | *Angli* **B**   480. *multa* pro *mitto* **R**   481. *mihi* pro *viro* **B** | *quae*
pro *quasi* **R** | *vulgi* **CW**   482. *fuerit* **BCW** | *nostri* **C**   483. *facturus* **W**
484. *pecus o decus* **CW** | *ah* **B**   485. *Immanuel* **BCW**   486. *noscebat* **B**
490. *nam* pro *non* **BCW**   491. *movere* corr. in *morari* **R**

welcoming sermon, and he accepted it, as was his wont, with a happy and kindly expression, and though he was aware he had favored me, he acknowledged that he was much more indebted to me because he interpreted my duty towards him as a sign of affection. He tarried in the city for five days, either because he was exhausted or (as I prefer to think) since the Dean's house seemed a small palace for the occasion. Daily messengers flew hither and thither, swifter than the east wind, always bringing news, telling everything done in the court of the Scottish king or of our English sovereign, secrets of state, scarce known or fit to be divulged to any common fellow. A rumor, as it were, is circulating that Scotland has become hostile to us, an enemy land.

At a time propitious for preaching in the Dean's presence, that ornament (yes, I say that ornament) of his father, Dr. Emanuel with a nice sealed diploma from over the sea, took over the pulpit, for evidently the Bishop did not wish it to be unknown that, though no true Doctor himself, he could procreate one. But this man was not born a Doctor as a boy: they say he took a doctorate at Basle, and he took *his* one quite legitimately. True creation cannot be said to proceed *ex nihilo*. This wise donkey did not shrink from trying a tune on David's lyre, handling the Prophets, spouting metaphors

et quasi de caelo cherubinus hosanna sonare.
spectante modo verum cedente perito,   495
et tamen obtinuit (quo sensu dicere parco)
quod voluit, possit, nimirum ut dicier "hic est."
ulterius non ulla potest nos causa morari,
cogimur innumeris de causis cedere tandem,
Decanus licet invitus permittat abire,   500
et nummos, quasi nos pretio conduxerat, offert,
nos minus abiecti nummos contemnimus eius
et dedignamur quod nobis offerat illos:
Walsinghamus iter facturus quas neque debet
Decano grates, Decani nomine solvit,   505
promittitque suum Blencowque mihique favorem.
Decanum tanto tantum debere profecto
gaudeo. vix credas qua cura, quoque labore
illius causam cum Praesule, Canonicisque
egerit, atque adeo totam susceperat in se,   510
ut solvant illi vacuo pro tempore fructus,
quos vi, nempe suo Boreali iure, tenebant.
quis non Harrisoni vultus miretur et ora?
quo gemitu Dollae, quo risu dicere Furzo
caeperit, et reliquis qua maiestate salutem!   515

---

499. *reditus versus Hutton* **R** (vid. Comm. not.)   514. *Furze & Doll his wife the hostesse of the Beare in Oxon* **R** *A mayd of the beare in Oxford* **CW**

---

493. *intellegat* **W**   494. *Cherubim Eloimque sonare* **B** | *cherubino Osanna* **C**   495. *spreto ante* pro *spectante* **R**, *spreta ante* **CW** | *credente* **B**, *sedente* **R**   497. *ut* om. **R** | indicia loquentis supplevi   499. *discedere* **CW**   500. *permittit* **BCW**   501 *quos* corr. in *quasi* **B**   502. *minas* **R** | *omnes* pro *eius* **R**   504. *facturis* **BCW**   505. (init.) *Decanus* **BCW**   506. *Blincoque* **BCW**   507. *tantum tanto* **CW**   509. *Decani* pro *illius* **R**   510. *totum* **CR** | *susceperit* **BCW**

which he himself scarce understood, bawling like one of the Cherubim singing hosanna in the sky, with our expert not only a member of the congregation but also deferring to his talent. He nonetheless obtained his object, for, understandably, he became somebody of whom it could be said "this is the man!" (I forbear to say in what sense).

No further argument could compel us to remain, yet for countless reasons we were obliged to yield, albeit the Dean unwillingly permitted us to go and proffered some coins, as if we were in his employ; we, not so degraded, disdained his money and scorned to accept his offer. Walsingham, on the point of departure, extended unnecessary thanks to the Dean by paying off his debts, and promised his favor to Blenkowe and myself; and indeed I rejoice that our Dean is indebted to such a great man. You would scarce credit the great care and industry with which he dealt with the Bishop and Canons, taking the whole matter upon himself, so that they would turn over to Mathew the rents accrued during the time the Deanship had lain vacant, which they retained by the violence which passes for law in the North. Who would not be astonished at Harrison's expression? With what groaning he addressed Doll, with what laughter he addressed Furze, and with what dignity he bade farewell to the rest! He

stabat ut οἰκονομός magnusque magister in aula.
tandem (quod fieri vix posse putavimus) imus,
iamque recedentes domus optima Praesulis, Auckland,
accipit, huc sese cum forte receperat ille
ut dominum acciperet (quem fugerat ante) legatum.   520
nos gratos dixit, n on fecit, scilicet eius
nec multus, nec suavis erat mensae cibus illi.
nam tenui miror tantum pinguescere victu,
sed magis ille bibit quam vescitur, immediate.
e cella in cellam post prandia ducit, et haurit   525
spumantem pateram, pleno et se proluit auro.
non cedit patri (quia Doctor), filius. esse
Doctorem vere germanum se probat, atque
maiorem. antiquis cyathum propinat amicis.
inde Northallerton cane peius et angue perosi   530
dirigimus cursum, qua nos Richmondia ducit
qui locus est Londinum illis Borealibus oris.
divitis et mundi nomen sibi vendicat, at qui
dives mons debet, non dives mundus haberi.
nam nec ab ornatu mundus, nec dives ab usu,   535
nil magnum praeter fraenum et calcaria vendit.
si procul aspicias vetus esse videtur Ulissis
Ithaca celsa loco, et pendentibus aspera saxis.

---

525. *Dr Barnes* **R**   529. *erat utrique e Coll. Magd. Ox. A.
M. 1581*   530. *Northalerton* **R**   539. *Ubank* **R**

---

514. *Dallae...Furso* **BCW**   516. *ut* om. **R** l *oeconomus* **C**   518. *ultima*
pro *optima* **B** l *Aukeland* **BW**, *Ubank* (sic) **R**   519. *excipit* **R**   520.
exciperet **R**   522. *multos* **R** ante corr. l *erat mensa cibus; illum* **C**   523.
non **R** l *pinguedine* **R**   525. *a cella* **R**, *cella* corr. in *sella* **C** l *haustus* **B**,
hausit **CW**   529. *cialtrum* **B**, *Yakum* corr. in *Yahum* **R** u. v. ex
phototypo l   *proponat* **C** ante corr.   530. *Northarlton* **R**   531.
Richmundia **W**   533. *sibi nomen* **BCW** l *atqui* **BCW**   536. *fraena* **C**

stood there, acting the Major-Domo, acting the master of the hall.

Finally, though we could scarce believe it possible, we departed. And just as we were leaving Auckland, the Bishop's finest manor received us, since he had chanced to return there to entertain the Lord Ambassador, whom he had previously been dodging. He set a table that was neither pleasant nor bountiful. He said that we were welcome, but did not make us such, for his table was not set well or lavishly: I am amazed that he had grown so fat on such thin fare. But he drank more than he ate, uninterruptedly. After the meal he led us from room to room gulping from his foaming tankard, wetting his whistle from a full golden cup. Being a Doctor himself, his son did not yield to his father, showing himself a right germane Doctor and greater than his sire, as he toasted his old cronies with an even larger bumper.

From there, since we hated Northallerton "worse than dog or snake," we directed our journey by the Richmond road, a place which is "the London of the North country." Although its name proclaims it is rich and mundane, it ought to be called Richmont rather than Richmond. For it is neither mundane in its elegance, nor rich in commerce, and has nothing to sell beyond mortar and lime. If you look at it from afar, it appears to be Ulysses' ancient Ithaca, lofty in its site and craggy with its overhanging rocks. Here

hic dedit Eubankus lautam pro tempore caenam
illius in patriam ut gratos venisse doceret.   540
faceret hoc ipsum primo quoque mane, sed ante
nos fugimus, memoresque viae, memoresque diei.
cumque diem medium fecisset clepsydra nostra,
(nam solem dormisse puto radiosque per omnem
abscondisse diem) subito divertimus omnes   545
ad villam Musis datam de nomine Topclyffe,
quam vix dignabar proficiscens carmine nostro.
gratior ille locus, quem nos pluvialibus Austris
acti expectamus; datur anser, alauda, ferina,
caetera praetexto quae sunt vulgaria mensa   550
instructa est melius quam fert Aquilonia tellus.
callidus Harrisonus prius hoc invenerat, atque
hunc dominum domino similem praedixerat Ursae;
sensum eius in tali causa sine teste probabo.
    postquam larga quies facta est, mensaeque
                                          remotae,   555
nullaque iam poterat caeli spes esse sereni.
rebus in extremis medios penetravimus imbres,
et veluti immersi madidis in fluctibus Ousae
amnis Eboracum multa sed nocte venimus.
deterior semper sequitur fortuna cadentes: 560
obtigit hospitium gratum minus imbribus ipsis,
namque cubile datur, sed nullis usibus aptum,

---

539. *Ubank* **R**   553. *Mr. Furze* **R**   560. *Mrs Yongham* **R**

---

539. *Eubanckus* **B**, *Ubankus* **R**, *Ubanckus* **CW**   541. *fecerat* **BCRW**
546. *notam* pro *datam* **C**   548. *quem* corr. in *quum* **R**, *quam* **CW**   549.
laeti pro *acti* **R**   550. *(caetera...vulgaria)* **B**, *praeterea* pro *praetexto*
CW   558. *velut* **C**   559. *sed multa* **B**   560. *semper sequitur* **R**

Ewbanke gave us a meal elegant enough for the occasion, so as to demonstrate that we were welcome to his homeland. He would have done the same thing the next morning, but we made our escape beforehand, mindful of our journey, mindful of the day. And when our clock showed that it was noon (for I think that the sun had gone to sleep and had hidden its beams the whole day) we suddenly swerved aside to the hamlet called Topcliff by the Muses, which I had scarce condescended to include in my poem during the outward trip. But the place was more welcome to us now as we, done in, waited out a rainy aouth wind there. Goose, lark, and game, and the other adornments of the prevalent fare there, were offered us, all better than what the South has to offer. Clever Harrison had already sniffed this out, proclaiming our landlord the equal of the master of The Bear. I accept his opinion in such a case with no witnesses being summoned.

After we had rested a long while and the table had been cleared, there could be no more hope of fair weather. Reduced to extremity, we braved the dense rain and, as wet as if we had been ducked in the currents of the Ouse, we arrived at York, but late at night. Ever greater misfortune always hounds those in trouble, and our inn turned out to be even more unwelcome than the rain, for we were given a room, but one unfit for human use, and (what we craved the

83

quod summe cupimus, non est locus ullus ad ignem;
ad stabulum mittuntur equi, quod longius absit:
non domus hospitibus minus hospita cernitur
                       unquam.   565
  dura verecundum nescit fortuna pudorem;
cogimur ad dominam Yongham deducere tandem
nos, et equos, cui magna domus, cui copia maior.
illa invitarat prius, et promiserat illi
nomine, Decanus, nostro, sed nos pudor inde   570
detinuit, seri quod venissemus in urbem.
ut videt ingressos, laetatur adesse, doletque
fortunam, miserata viam, miserata labores,
seque adeo nostrae fortunae plura fatetur
quam nobis debere, tulit quos casus ad illam: 575
hinc nos laeta domum deduxit in interiorem
magnifice extructam textilibus atque tapetis
omnigenis, ignemque parat, caenamque parari
iussit, et (officiis plusquam vulgaribus usu)
ostendit quodcunque potest; supra omnia vultus   580
accedunt hilares, nec mens pauperque voluntas.
inde per eximium spatium, variisque decorum
picturis, ad magnificum clarumque cubile
ducit, ubi damus nos membraque lassa quieti.
quid referam ornatum insignem tectique locique?   585

---

583. *Galerie* **B**

---

565. *hospitii* **B**, fort. recte, *hospita* **C** } *usquam* **C** post corr.   567.
Yongam **BC**   569. *ministrat* pro *invitarat* **C**   570. *inde* om. **R**   571. *sero*
C   573. *vias* **R** I *laborem* **B**   574. *sed* pro *seque* **W**, **C** ante corr. I   576
sq. singulum versum *huic* (u. v.) *nos laeta domus textilibus atque tapetis*
habet **B** I *dederit, inque interiorem* **R**   577. *instructam* **CW**   579. *e* pro
et **B**   581. *iners* pro *mens* **C**   584. *ibique* **R** *demus* **W** I *laesa* **R** I *quieto*
W   585. *illustrem* pro *insignem* **R** I *lectique* **BCW**

most) there was no fireplace. Our horses were sent off to a stable which ought to have been farther away. I have never seen a guesthouse less hospitable to its guests.

Hard luck knows no shame: we were at length obliged to foist ourselves and our horses onto Mistress Young, owner of a large house and a larger storehouse. She had previously invited us, and the Dean had promised in all our names that we would come; but our sense of bashfullness had restrained us, since we had entered the city so late. When she saw us coming in, she rejoiced at our presence, and clucked over our misfortune, commiserating with us about our travels and travails; she averred that she was even more indebted to our fortune than to ourselves, for it had brought us hardships but also brought us to her. Hence she gladly opened her home to us, admitting us into its interior, magnificantly decked out with all manner of textiles and tapesties, had a fire laid, and bade a meal be made ready. And with uncommon kindness she pointed out everything she could for our use. Atop of everything else, her face beamed and she was unstinting in disposition and good will. Afterwords she led us down a long gallery, past the splendor of various paintings, to a magnificent, noble room, and there we gave ourselves and our tortured limbs over to slumber. Why should I describe the splendor and brilliance of that edifice and its setting?

apta domus dominae, domus illam illustrat et ornat,
illa domum. sunt digna animis quae maxima magnis.
nos velut obliti nostri, somnoque sepulti
in multum dormisse diem non sensimus, ipse
donec adest Doctor Lougherus, et excitat, urgens   590
ut tollamur equis, et ad Archipraesulis aedes
tendamus, prius expectarat saepius, atque
nunc rediise sciens, deduci ad prandia iussit;
 surgimus, egredimur, celeresque volamus ad illum;
cui sedes passus bis mille ab urbe iacebat.   595
ille sui similis, Decani nomine partim,
partim etiam nostro (quis enim magis unus utrisque
favit academicis?) reditu laetatur, et una
accipit in mensa, solito de more benigne,
multa super Boream, super Austrum multa requirens. 600
hinc labor alter erat discedere tempore nostro;
tres urget remanere dies, non possumus unum.
rursus Eboracum non pauca negotia Blencowe
me quoque non levia ad Yongham promissa vocabant.
postquam nulla potest nos causa morarier, ille   605
nos, nostrosque Deo liberos commendat, et urget
nummos invito mihi, quamlibet ipse recusem.
vix ad Eboraci perventum est moenia, quando

---

591. *Arch. Sands* **R**   594. *Mr. Hutton the Deane of Yorke*
(vid. Comm. not. ad 609) **R**

---

586. *visa* corr. in *velque* pro *apta* **B**   588. *veluti* **C**   589. *multam* **C** I
ipsos **BCW**   590. *Louherus* **B**, *Losher, excitat, excitat, urgens* **R**   591.
tollemur **R** I *Archiepiscopales* **R**   592. *atqui* **BW**   594. *celeres* **CW**
595. *vix mille* **R** I *iacebat ab urbe* **BC**   596. v. om. **B**   598. *academiis* **C**
ante corr.   599. *benigno* **R**   601. *hinc* vel *huic* **B**, *hic*.**R** I *erit* **R** ante
corr.   603. *Blinco* **BCW**   604. *Yongam* **BCW**   606. *libros* **C**

The house suited its mistress: the house ennobled her and she ennobled the house. Great possessions befit great souls.

Plunged in sleep, as if forgetful of ourselves, we slumbered well into the day unawares, until Dr. Lougher himself arrived and tried to awaken us, bidding us mount our horses and make our way to the Archbishop's palace. He had already been on the lookout for us and now, learning we had returned, bade us be escorted to dinner. We arose, went out, and quickly flew to him, whose manor lay scarce a mile from the city. Always the same good fellow, he rejoiced at our return, partly on account of the Dean, partly on ours (what single man was more favorable to both us academicians?), and graciously extended us the hospitality of his table in his usual way, asking many questions about the North, many about the South. Here it was yet another chore to get away on schedule. He urged us to tarry for three days, but we could not for even one. Our not inconsiderable affairs and also our weighty promises to Mistress Young recalled Blenkowe and myself to York. The Archbishop commended us and our progeny to God and pressed some coins on me, no matter how much I refused, reluctant as I was. We has scarcely arrived at York's walls, when Dr.

nos doctor Parsons, nos et Decanus Ebori
invitant. prius at possiderat hospita Yongham,   610
illa dedit lautam coenam, dedit hospita cantus
in mensa, famulos hunc ipsum servat ad usum.
hanc multos ambire procos, ambireque frustra
non miror, fortuna animo respondet, eumque
quam iuvenis debet, iuveni bene servat amorem.   615
sola manet iuvenis, quae non nisi sola maneret.
hinc urbe egressi, quam saepe precamur ut illi,
quae semper iuvenis, renovetur ut saepe iuventus
more aquilae, ut veniat nunquam vel sera senectus.
Doctori Parsons dicturi mane salutem   620
uxorique simul, quoniam aequa lege tenemur,
namque vel invitis ientacula lauta parantur
    quae Tadcaster erat sine flumine, pulvere plena,
nunc habet immensum fluvium, et pro pulvere lutum.
quales ante dedit, dedit Aberfordia tales   625
iam fructus, mora noster minor, sed gratia maior.
mittitur ignotis qui nos deducat ab oris.
longe aberat Wakefeild, ideo divertimus illinc

---

609. *Doct. Hutton* **R**   623. *Tadcaster* **BR**   625. *Alberford*
B *Aberfordia* **R**

---

609. *Person* **B**, *Perseus* **C**, *Persens* **W**   610. *primum* pro *prius at* **R** I
Younga **B**, *Yonga* **C**, *Yonge* **W**   611. *coenam cantusque suaves* **BCW**
612. *in usum* **R**   615. *quem* **BC** I *dedit* pro *debet* **C**   616. *quod* pro *quae*
C   617sqq. *hinc urbem egressi quam semper precamur ut illi / quae
semper iuvenis renovetur saepe iuventus / atque illi ut veniat nunquam
vel sera senectus* **B** (scripti post v. 622), *hinc urbe egressi, quam saepe
precamur ut illi / more aquilae ut veniat nunquam vel sera senectus ,*
versos supradatos habent **CW**, sed post v. 622 scriptos 620. *Pierso<n>*
CW   621. *non* pro *quoniam* **CW**   628. *illac* **CW**

Parsons and the Dean of York issued us an invitation, but our hostess Mistress Young took precedence and gave us an elegant banquet; our hostess entertained us with song while we were at table, for she retained servants for this very purpose. I am not surprised that she has many suitors, but that they have wooed her in vain, for her fortune corresponds to her disposition and, as a Young ought, she preserves her affection for youth. She alone remains young, though no one should stay young but she. Hence when we had departed the city we prayed that for her, since she is a Young, her youth be ever renewed, Phoenix-wise, so that old age would visit her late or never. This we did in the morning, as we were going to pay our respects to Dr. Parsons and his wife, for we were equally beholden to both, for they had prepared a breakfast for us, even though we were protesting.

Tadcaster, previously riverless and dusty, now had an immense river, and mud in place of the dust. Aberford offered us the same produce as before; our stay was shorter, but our gratitude was greater. A fellow was sent to guide out of this unfamiliar region. Wakefield was far distant, so we

qua iacet oppidulum, quod fracto a ponte vocatur
Pomfret, nil habuit praeter laudabile castrum.   630
quae Rotherama prius caruit lusoribus, illis
iam scatet, hospitio prohibens qui ludere nescit.
nos (licet indigne tulimus prohiberier) illinc,
in melius tamen et magis amplum forte redimus
hospitium, quandoque iuvat quod obesse videtur.   635
semper habet Mansfeild qui portent, semper in ipsis
non intermittunt festis solisque diebus.
mitto Nottingham, quam si laudare putarem,
quam vereor, ne laus eius sorderet ut ipsa.
iamque ultra Trentam apparet Lecestria, quando   640
Blencowus noster caepit minus esse superbus,
atque Aquilonares animos dimittere novit,
in nostra patria posse et nos esse superbos.
tandem sed sero multisque ambagibusque usi
Butleri attigimus dictum de moenibus Aston.   645
huc cursus fuit, hic suscepti meta laboris;
hic datur accipitri perdicibus accipiendis
una dies, datur una dies leporisque sequendo;

---

628. *Pomfret* **B** *Pontefract* **R**   631. *Rotheram* **BR**   636.
Notingham **BR**   640. *Lester* **B** *Leycester* **R**   645. *Ashton in
the wall* **B** *Aston on the Walls in the Countie of
Northampton* **R**

---

629. *opidulum* **W** I *facto* **B**   630. *nilque* **R**   631. *Rotherana* **R**   632.
prohibent **R**   633. *volumus* pro *tulimus* **B**   634. *venimus* pro *redimus*
CW 635. *abesse* **R**   638 sq. scripti ante 636 sq. **R**   636. *Mawnsfeild*
C   638. *Nottinghamiam* **B** I *studerem* pro *putarem* **CW** 640. *Trentum*
B I *patuit* pro *apparet* **W**   641. *Blincous* **B**, *Blinconus* **C** 642. *dimittere*
corr. in *demittere* **C**   645. *dictam* **C**   646. *haec suscepti* **C**   647.
perdices accipiendi **R**   648. *lepori* **C**

swerved aside to a village named after a broken bridge,
Pomfret, which had nothing beyond a praiseworthy castle.
Rotherham had previously lacked gamesters, but now it
swarmed with them, and anybody ignorant of gambling was
barred from the inn. Although irked at being excluded, we
chanced on a bigger and better hospice: sometimes a
seeming difficulty works out to one's advantage. Mansfield
always has people transporting goods, and they do not inter-
rupt their work even on festivals and holidays. I say naught
of Nottingham, for if I were minded to praise her, I fear that
Praise herself would become as shabby as she is. And now
Leicester appeared on the far side of the Trent, when
Blenkowe began to drop his arrogance and learned to
abandon his Northern pride; he also learned that we too
could wax haughty on our home ground.

At length, but only after taking many roundabouts, we
arrived at Butler's estate at Aston, named after walls. This
was our goal, the object of our journey; we had earmarked a
day here for hawking for partridge, and another forr

una dies, datur una dies leporisque sequendo;
dira voluptatem tempestas abstulit omnem
cogit et in medio cursum intermittere cursu.   650
Blencowe ne semper non falleret, atque suprema
aequa essent primis, hic deserit atque recusat
Oxoniam mecum, mihi quod promiserat, ire.
ut primum Oxoniae turres et moenia vidi,
culta bonis studiis, doctis cultissima Musis,   655
nescio quo pacto, citius quam posse putarem
defecisse mihi vires in carmine sensi.
rustica Musa silet, gelido quae nata sub Arcto,
atque inter Musas metuens ne forte politas
quae rudis obstreperet nimium, velut inter
                            olores   660
anserulus; tanquam in Boream expirata refugit.
respicio, revocoque simul, procul avolat illa
ex oculis, velut umbra fugit, et non respicit unquam.
quam volui per eam nostro misisse salutem
Decano, misisse aliis quam debeo multis!   665
sed nec opinati mihi dixerat illa salutem.
sic coepit, sic clausit iter locus unus et idem.
quique dies conclusit iter, mihi carmina clausit.

---

628. *Pomfret* **B** *Pontefract* **R**   631. *Rotheram* **BR**   636.
Notingham **BR**   640. *Lester* **B** *Leycester* **R**   645. *Ashton in the wall* **B** *Aston on the Walls in the Countie of Northampton* **R**

---

648. *lepori* **C**   651. *Blinco* **BCW** I *utque* **C**   656. *putaram* **BCRW**
661. *refrigit* **R**   663. *icta* pro *umbra* **B**, *ita* corr. in *icta* **C**, *ita* **W** I
usquam **CW**   664. *voluit* **B** ante corr.   667. *omnis* pro *unus* **B**   668.
quaeque **BW** I *claudit* **BW**

rabbiting. But a terrible storm destroyed all our pleasure, and compelled us to break off our hunt in in mid-chase. Blenkowe, so as to be unfailingly deceptive and finish in the manner in which he had started, deserted us here and refused to travel on to Oxford with me, as promised.

When I first caught sight of Oxford's walls and spires, Oxford, splendid for its excellent studies, most splendid for its learned Muses, in some way I failed to understand, quicker than I could imagine, I perceived my poetic powers failing. My rustic Muse, born under the freezing northern sky, feared lest she make a rude noise amongst the polite Muses, like a gosling amongst swans. As if wafted northwards, she made her escape. I looked over my shoulder, calling her back, but she flew away out of view, fleeing like a shadow, and never looked backwards. How I wanted to use her to bid farewell to the Dean and to the many others I should! But it was she who unexpectedly bade farewell to me. Thus one and the same place began and ended my journey, and the same day that brought it to its conclusion also ended my song.

Commentary

Title The three Oxford mss. call this poem *Iter Boreale*,[1] the title by which it was known to its imitator Richard Corbett, while the British Library ms. has the double title *Musae Boreales sive Iter Boreale*. It is possible that it circulated under yet a third, for when William Camden quoted lines 71f. in the 1607 edition of his *Britannia* (p. 569) he wrote in a sidenote *Itinerarium T. Edes*. But the word *itinerarium* is more likely a genre-specifying word than a title, and the fact that he got the author's name wrong possibly diminishes his credibility as a witness. *Musae Boreales* commands no confidence, since our poem contains only one Muse, and **R**'s evidentiary value is likewise tainted because it dates the poem to the wrong year. But it is not out of the question that Eedes called his work *Musa Borealis*, for two reasons. At the end of the poem (649ff.) he writes of the sudden flight of his *rustica Musa gelido nata sub Arcto*. Then too, the name of William Gager's sequel, *Musa Australis*, suggests that he knew the poem under this title. But the evidence favoring *Iter Boreale* obviously preponderates.

10f. **B**'s sidenote is corrupt, or at least the final word is illegible on my microfilm. Perhaps the original plan was to go as far as Banbury, spend the night, and then return (cf. the Commentary note on 26f.).

13a Here (as opposed to its one after 17, which seems indefensibly weak) **W**'s extra line makes rhetorical sense and finds a measure of support in **C**'s original reading *charior* at

---

[1] Since Anthony à Wood read the poem in the ms. designated **W** here, his citation of the work by this title has no independent evidentiary value. In his description of how it came to be written, upon which Wood's account is based, Sir John Harington mentioned no title.

13.

14 Anthony Blenkowe or Blenkow, Provost of Oriel College (1546 - 1618). What little is known about him is summarized by G. C. Richards and C. L. Shadwell, *The Provosts and Fellows of Oriel* (Oxford, 1922). He came from Little Blencowe, Cumberland; entered Oxford as a Dudley exhibitioner in 1560; admitted to the B. A. in 1563, and incepted M. A. in 1566; elected Senior Proctor of the University for both 1571 and 1572; elected Provost of Oriel College in 1574, a position he held for the rest of his life; received the D. C. L. in 1586. Little of a circumstantial nature seems known about the man beyond a eulogy written by his successor William Lewis:

> *26 Jan. anno d^{ni} 1617* [i. e., 1618 new style] *convocatis sociis in sacellum per Decanum consilium inivit moestissima societas de modo et forma quibus duceretur funus desideratissimi Praepositi qui 15to die eiusdem mensis naturae cessit, non sine ingenti luctu et veris lacrymis Collegii, quod per tot annos foelici et moderatissimo regimine caput charissimum beaverat. funus sine pompa (quam cum adhuc in vivis esset deprecatus est) per laudes et memoriam virtutum celebre fore rati, statuerunt eum festinantius et sine strepitu honestae tantum, qui meruerat honorificam, tradere sepulturae, Gulielmus Lewis Decanus.*

Blenkowe bequeathed Oriel £1300 for the repair of its fabric as well as 67 books for its Library. There is a 1601 portrait in the Provost's Lodge, listed, but not described or reproduced, by Mrs. Reginald Lane Poole, *Catalogue of Portraits in the Possession of the University, Colleges, City and Country of Oxford* (Oxford, 1927) II.80.

Any university man admitted to the B. A. was entitled to

call himself *Dominus*, alone or in combination with other academic titles. This is a problematic word to render, and in the end I decided not to translate it all: *Dominus* is the Latin translation of "Sir" when writing of a nobleman or knight, but in the case of an academic "Sir" conveys entirely the wrong impression. One cannot translate it "Master," because that English word must be reserved for *Magister* (someone who had incepted for the M. A.); "Dom" would make the individual seem monkish, "Don" sounds Spanish, and "Dan" too Chaucerian. But in the case of non-academics "Sir" or even "Lord" are of course the proper translations.

16 The second syllable of *itinere* is improperly scanned long.

19 Eedes departed too abruptly to apply for a leave of absence (the institution of the Long Vacation lay far in the future). But in his case requesting travel permission would have only been a formality: how much hot water could he get into, accompanying the heads of two Colleges and having been elected one of the two University Proctors for 1583 in the previous April (Wood, *F. O.* 223)?

22f. Eedes was evidently thinking of Martial, *Epigrams* XII.xxiv.4f:

> *hic mecum licet, hic, Iuvate, quidquid*
> *in buccam tibi venerit, loquaris.*

26 Leland wrote (*Itinerary* I.7), "The toune of Northampton stondith on the north side of the Avon ryver, on the brow of a meane hille, and risith stille from the south to the north. Al the old building of the toune was of stone, the new is of tymbre."

Mathew's party had gone north to Banbury on a road following the west bank of the Cherwell (reckoned as 16.4

English statute miles by the *Royal English Atlas*), then turned northeast through Northamptonshire (a road stated to be 21.5 mi. by the *Atlas*).

27ff. Northampton was a Puritan town. Since 1572 its churches had been regulated by a covenant entitled *The Orders and Dealings in the Church of Northampton* (1572), described by W. H. Freer, *The English Church in the Reigns of Elizabeth and James I (1558 - 1625)* (London, 1905, repr. New. York, n.d.) 168f. These injunctions prescribed very Low Church practices, and that Calvin's catechism was to be used in lieu of that of the *Book of Common Prayer*. By Eede's testimony, at least some extremists rejected the idea of Saints and refused to call the Sabbath by a pagan name. The tone of his initial remarks shows that he regarded Puritanism with distaste, an attitude which colors his subsequent evaluation of the crudely outspoken anti-Papist Bishop Barnes and his Basle-educated son.

31 "S. Thomas Hospitale is with oute the toune, and joinith hard to the West Gate" (Leland, *Itinerary* I.9). Eedes also refers to St. Mary's (by the Castle) and either the Chapel of St. John the Baptist, Kingsthorpe (attached to St. Peter's church), or to the Hospital of St. John's. The survey of Northampton churches in William Page (ed.), *The Victoria History of the Country of Northamptonshire* (London, 1970) II.40ff. mentions no religious establishment consecrated to St. Nicholas.

33 "Paroche chirches in Northampton withyn the waulles be 7. whereof the chirch of Al Halowes is principale, stonding yn the harte of the toune, and is large and welle buildid" (*ib.* I.7.). This church is more commonly known as All Saints'.

37f. *The Orders and Dealings* described in the Commentary note on 27ff. gave instructions on how preaching was to be done. It would seem that Mathew adhered to these injunctions, to the extent that Eedes thought that he had given a talk but had been unable to deliver a genuine sermon.

39 They went north to Harburough in Leicestershire and then onward to Leicester, a total distance of approx. 24 mi. according to the *Atlas*. **R** puts the distance at 16 miles. **R**'s mileage calculations are almost always short (only accurate for the Tadcaster - York leg of the journey); perhaps some obsolete long mile was employed.

41 Possibly Eedes had in mind Vergil, *Aeneid* VIII.356, *reliquias veterumque vides monimenta virorum.* This line may refer to the monastery ruins mentioned by Camden, *Britannia* p. 388, *alteram urbis partem inter laetissima prata, quae Soarus irrigat, monasterium fuit.*

42 Our companions had traveled to Nottingham via Mobray, a total of 25.5 mi. according to the *Atlas*, though **R**'s appended itinerary makes the distance 19 mi. Nottingham's castle is built on a rather dramatic sandstone bluff honeycombed with caves, Castle Rock, overlooking the River Trent. The stench of which Eedes complains presumably emanated from the marshland down by the river. 1583 appears to have been a dry summer (cf. the Commentary note on 73f.), which may have amplified the problem.

Nottingham made a more favorable impression on Camden (*Britannia* p. 412): *urbs est loci ingenio amoena, hinc ad flumina spatiosa procumbunt prata; illinc faciles consurgunt colles; omnibus etiam quae ad vitam pertinent copiosa.* Camden added *sic enim Saxones dixerunt a subterraneis speluncis, et meatibus quae in receptacula, et habitationem excavavit antiquitas sub praeruptis illis saxis in Australi parte qua Linum fluviolum despectat.* These caves were inhabited, perhaps by squatters, when Eedes saw them.

44 Cf., perhaps, Vergil, *Aeneid* I.167, *vivoque sedilia saxo* (imitated by Ovid, *Metamorphoses* V.317).

47 Pliny the Elder (*Natural History* VIII.cxlix) wrote of Egyptian dogs *certum est iuxta Nilum amnem currentes lambere, ne crocodilorum aviditati occasionem praebeant.*

48ff. Leland (IV.15) wrote "Maunsfeld a market town longing to the King in Notinghamshire (it is yn Shirwode)...miles from Rotherham in the hy way to Nottingham." It is on the river Mann or Maun. **R** reckons it as 12 miles beyond Nottingham (13.6 according to the *Atlas*).

52 "Rotheram is a meately large market towne, and hath a large and fair collegiate chirch" (Leland, *Itinerary* IV.14). According to the *Atlas* it is 23.4 miles beyond Mansfield.

53 I am not sure of my translation here: *solis* may be a corruption common to all four mss.

55 Wakefield is in the West Riding of Yorkshire, on the river Calder. Camden (p. 565) praised this market town: *Wakefeldiam alluit Calderus re pannaria, sua magnitudine, aedificiorum elegantia, foro frequenti, et ponte inclytam.* **R**'s itinerary places it 13 miles beyond Rotheram. The *Atlas* gives no mileage, but by applying its scale one sees that it is more like 20 English statute miles.

Eedes is alluding to the ballad "The Jolly Pinder of Wakefield," for which cf. Francis James Child, *The English and Scottish Popular Ballads* (Boston - New York, 1888 - 90) III.129ff., where it is registered as no. 124. It begins:

> *In Wakefield there lives a jolly pinder,*
> *In Wakefield, all on a green.*

In introducing this ballad, Child noted that a printed version was entered in the Stationers Register in 1557-58. There is probably a special point in Eedes' allusion: at the conclusion of the ballad the pinder offers a banquet for Robin Hood and his merry men, just as Mathew's company is treated to a feast now.

57 This line = Vergil, *Aeneid* I.215 with *implentur* altered to *implemur.*

58f. As **BC**'s marginal note indicates, they are offered a special brew called March beer. Evidently this was powerful stuff. Lithgow in his *Travels* of 1632 (III.16, quoted by the *O. E. D.*) writes of "strong March-Ale, surpassing fine Aqua-vitae."

61f. Aberford is a village in the West Riding about 14 miles northeast of Wakefield and 4 miles southwest of Tadcaster, well known in Eedes' day for the manufacture of pins: Camden (p. 567) wrote *qui nunc viculus est situs ad viam illam militarem, et aciculis conficiendis, quibus primas mulieres deferunt, celebris.*

63 Ovid tells the story of Philemon and Baucis in Book VIII of the *Metamorphoses.* They stayed with this woman because Blencowe was the Provost of the college from which she held her lease.

66 Cf. Vergil, *Aeneid* XII.67f.:

> *si quis ebur, aut mixta rubent ubi lilia multa*
> *alba rosa, talis virgo dabat ore colores.*

This image influenced Ovid, *Amores* II.v.37, *quale rosae fulgent inter sua lilia mixtae*, and also Statius, *Silvae*

I.ii.22f., *tu modo fronte rosas, violis modo lilia mixta /
excipis.*

This representation of feminine beauty was often imitated
by the Elizabethans, both in English and in Latin, because it
corresponded to their own, especially as enhanced by lead
and vermilion. Cf., for example, Thomas Watson's Ἑκατομπαθία (1582), Passion vii.9, *On either cheeke a Rose
and Lillie lies.*

67 The outward trip was made in August, by which time
Yorkshire apples are ripe.

69 Cf. Vergil, *Eclogue* iii.36f.:

*pocula ponam
fagina, caelatum divini opus Alcimedontis.*

70 This imitation of Ovid, *Metamorphoses* III.415,
dumque sitim sedare cupit, sitis altera crevit, hints that the
more ale they drank, the more attractive the widow's
daughters came to look (the Ovidian line describes Narcis-
sus becoming enamored of himself whilst drinking from his
pool). Or is this a sly allusion to the inevitable consequence
of enthusiastic beer consumption?

73f. Cf. Leland, *Itinerary* I.43, "The bridge at Tadcaster
over Warfe hath 8 faire arches of stone. Sum say there that it
was laste made of parte of the ruines of the old castelle of
Tadcaster." This town is built at the confluence of the
Wharfe and the Ouse, and it was the former of these that ran
dry, or at least stood so low that the bridge struck Eedes as
absurdly oversized. On the return journey, when he saw this
same river swollen by floods, he was disabused of his
impression (622f.).

This bridge was also mentioned by Camden, *Britannia* p.
569, who added in the 1607 edition *et sane mihi neutiquam*

admiratione indignum videtur, quod Wherf tot aquis ad-
auctus aestivo tempore tam tenuis sub hoc defluat, ut
quidam adulta iam aestate cum huc venisset lepide cecinerit.

nil Tadcaster habet Musis vel carmine dignum,
praeter magnifice structum sine flumine pontem.

A sidenote credits these lines to *Itinerarium T. Edes.*

Daniel Defoe had the same experience with another bridge
over the Wharfe (*A Tour Thro' the Whole Island of Great
Britain*, London, 1727, repr. London, n.d., II.618):

The River *Wharfe* seemed very small, and the Water
low, at *Harwood* Bridge, so that I was surprised to
see so fine a Bridge over it, and was thinking of the
great Bridge at *Madrid* over the *Mansanares*, of
which a *Frenchman* of Quality looking upon it, said
to the *Spaniards* that were about him, *That the King
of* Spain *ought either buy them some Water, or they
should sell their Bridge.* But I was afterwards
satisfied that was not the Case here; for coming another time this Way after a heavy Rain, I was con-
vinced the Bridge was not at all too big, or too long,
the Water filling up to the very Crown of the Arches,
and some of the Arches not to be seen at all.

When he comes to his description of the bridge at Tadcaster
(*ib.* 635) he added:

Mr. *Cambden* gives us a little Distich of a learned
Passenger upon this River, and the old Bridge, at
Tadcaster; I suppose he pass'd it in a dry Summer,
as the *Frenchman* did the Bridge at *Madrid*, which I
mentioned before.

nil Tadcaster habes[1] muris vel carmine dignum,
praeter magnifice structum sine flumine pontem.

But I can assure the Reader of this Account, that
altho' I pass'd this Place in the middle of Summer,
we found Water enough in the River, so that there
was no passing it without a Boat.

73 Tadcaster is nine miles from York, and here our companions picked up the great London-to-Berwick highway
that would lead them northward to Durham (although, as we
shall see, on both their outward and homeward journeys
they were required by Bishop Barnes to swerve from the direct route). According to **R**'s itinerary, accurate for once,
one passes through Bishopthorp on the way from Tadcaster
to York, about two miles south of the city. Here the Arch-
bishops of York had owned a manor and hunting park since
the thirteenth century. This imposing moated edifice backs
onto the Ouse. Cf. Peter F. Ryder, *Medieval Buildings of
Yorkshire* (Ashbourne, Derbyshire, 1982) 110. Leland, *Itinerary* IV.12, wrote "In the midde way I saw hard on the
right hond a veri fair large maner of the bisshops of Yorke
caullid Bishops Thorpe."

76 "Thorp" is an Anglo-Saxon word meaning "hamlet,
village, estate"; as can be seen from the *O. E. D.* examples,
it had not quite gone out of usage in Eedes' period.

77 The rather complex thought of these lines is based on
Matthew 7:6 - 7, *And every one that heareth these sayings of
mine, and doeth them not, shall be likened unto a foolish
man, which built his house upon the sand: And the rain descended, and the floods came, and the winds blew, and beat
upon that house; and it fell: and great was the fall of it.* The

---

[1] Defoe's error for *habet.*

point of the pun is that the Archbishop is named Sandys, and Eedes grimly predicts that Bishopthorp will prove safer and securer for Mathew than Durham Cathedral, although the latter is set on a rocky hill (cf. 244), and simultaneously that Sandys is more trustworthy than Barnes. There may well be a pun intended in *durae* at line 82. Later in the trip Mathew speaks of laying the foundation of his administration (313— since it is repeated, we may probably assume this was his actual phrase). It is easy to imagine that the reason for his protracted stay at York, lasting at last a week (90) was such foundation-laying. It would prove useful for him to cement relations with the most powerful Anglican prelate in the North and with the York clergy. Possibly his absence from the hunt laid on by the Archbishop (92f.) involved some discreet form of politicking.

88f. Cf. P. M. Tilmot (ed.), *A History of Yorkshire: The City of York* (printed at London for the Oxford University Press, 1961) 341f., "The Old Residence, a house standing at the southeast corner of the minster, was probably built in the early eighteenth century to house canons during their period of residence. Nothing is known of any previous communal residence."

89 Eedes was a habitual punster, and some of his Latin and bilingual puns and word-plays are untranslatable. In this case he plays on two meanings of *canon*, "Canon" and "rule."

88 Hunting was a favorite sport of the upper classes and was also a popular university recreation (cf. James McConica "The Collegiate Society" at James McConica (ed.) *The Collegiate University*, (Volume III of *The History of the University of Oxford*, Oxford, 1986) 151. Therefore a number of items of academic literature have passages calculated to appeal to devotees of the sport, such as the lengthy de-

description of a boar hunt in William Gager's *Meleager* of 1582 (793 - 880).

91 Archbishop Edwin Sandys (1516? - 1588); there is a biography in the *D. N. B.* His second son, Sir Edwin, was currently a member of Corpus Christi College, and may have been an acquaintance of our Oxonians.[1] Gager wrote an epitaph for young Edwin's aunt Cicely in 1584 (poem CLII). Mathew was well advised to cultivate Sandys, as Durham diocese lay within the province of the Archbishop of York. Sandys, already an admirer of Mathew, and a supporter of him for the present position, was a natural ally since as long ago as 1577 he had created one of his typical imbroglios by complaining about excessive Puritanism at Durham. Cf. John Strype *Annals of the Reformation* II.ii 107. We may note that, despite Sandys' knack of becoming involved in squabbles with all and sundry, Mathew managed to remain on his good side. In his will, dated Aug. 1, 1587, Sandys offered Mathew first pick of "all my books of learning, save as are in English."

94 The park of Ryther, frequently spelled Rider in contemporary documents, adjoins the archiepiscopal palace at Cawood, about three miles downriver from Bishopthorp. Cf. Edmund Boggs, *Old Kingdom Emet: York and the Ainsty District* (London, 1902) 245 - 51.

104 Rest Park was a moated archiepiscopal manor near Sherburn: cf. William Page (ed.), *The Victoria History of the Counties of England: Yorkshire* (London, 1974) II.46f. *Restabat* of course involves a bilingual pun.

---

[1] Two of Sandys' sons were involved with the colonization of Virgina: Sir Edwin was treasurer of the Virginia Company, and his younger brother George wrote part of his translation of Ovid's *Metamorphoses* while sailing to Jamestown.

105 Evidently an echo of the Vergilian *Culex* 89, *illi dulcis adest requies et pura voluptas.*

113 Cf. Vergil, *Aeneid* II.219, *superant capite et cervicibus altis.*

114 *Arcum tendo* designates the act of drawing a bow (Horace, *Odes* II.x.20, Ovid, *Metamorphoses* II.604, Persius, *Satire* iii.60, Statius, *Achilleis* II.134, etc.). The Latin would sustain the idea that he had his man fit an arrow to his bow and hand it to him ready to shoot; it may not be impossible that an elderly prelate would require such help, but it seems likelier that he asked for his bow to be strung prior to taking his first shot.

117 Eedes was remembering Lucan, *Bellum Civile* I.183, *iam gelidas Caesar cursu superaverat Alpes.*

134 Cf. Vergil, *Aeneid* I.203, *forsan et haec olim meminisse iuvabit.*

137 Mathew's host was Sir Ralph Bourchier of Benningborough, a town on the Ouse about twelve miles southeast of York as the crow flies, in the Ouse and Derwent wapontake of the East Riding of Yorkshire. He was a grandfather of the regicide Sir John Bourchier, whose biography is in the *D. N. B.* For the family pedigree cf. Joseph Foster, *The Visitation of Yorkshire made in the Years 1584/5 by Robert Glover, Somerset Herald* (London, 1875) 62f.

144 *Singula quid referam?* is from Ovid, *Amores* I.v.23.

147 The relevance of this tag taken from Persius, *Satire* v.62, *impallescere chartis* ("to go pale over your books") preserved in **BCW** is far from self-evident. **R**'s *hortis* is far superior: what is the point in growing pale laboring over flower gardens (rather than herb gardens)? This idea sets up the contrast drawn between the *utile* and the *dulce* at 150.

148 The sidenote shows Eedes is describing maw, a dialect variant of mallow (cultivated for its medicinal virtues).

149 Loadem was a popular card game of the time (cf. the *O. E. D.* entry), but I find no evidence for it being called cutthroat. Nor in his compendious treatise *The Herball or Generall Historie of Plants* (London, 1633, repr. New York, 1973) does John Gerard list either loadem or cut-throat as a popular name for any member of the garlic family.

150 Eedes quotes Horace, *Ars Poetica* 343. Horace wrote this line to admonish playwrights not to mix elements of tragedy and comedy in the same play. The evident idea here is that we are supposed to think of the inadvisability of mixing useful herbs and decorative flowers in the same garden. (At Williamsburg I recently learned that colonial gardeners alternated rows of flowers with rows of herbs or vegetables. Possibly Yorkshiremen anticipated this practice and earned Eedes' disapproval.)

This line would have been fresh in the ears of Eedes and his Christ Church audience, for in June of this same year William Gager had produced his tragedy *Dido* on the occasion of a state visit, and in the Prologue had paraphrased this line in the form *tulit omne punctum tristia admiscens iocis.*

151 Our travelers took the north road out of York, paralleling the Ouse, for approximately 21 miles, and came to Topcliff. The Topcliff School occupies the site of a former chantrey: cf. William Page (ed.), *The Victoria History of the Counties of England: Yorkshire* (London, 1974) I.46f. Hence the playful allusion to the Muses. Leland (*Itinerary* I.66) describes Topcliff as "an uplandisch toune."

155 They continued about twelve miles further on the same road to Northallerton. It is, as a Chamber of Commerce brochure would say, a gateway to the northern moor country.

157f. Note the *Arcto...arctos* pun.

161 Cf. Horace, *Epistulae* I.xii.29, *Italiae pleno defudit copia cornu* (cf. also his *Carmen Saeculare* 60).

162f. The author of **B**'s sidenote was right: Northallerton was famous for its cattle market.

167ff. There may be a hostile implication to this passage. Leland (*loc. cit.*) records that "At the west side of Northalverton a litle from the chirch is the Bisshop of Dyrham's palace, strong of building and welle motid" (Camden gives the history of this manor at *Britannia*, p. 575). The modern reader wonders why our four travelers were obliged to stay at a ghastly inn rather than at the episcopal manor. They may have asked themselves the same question. This would appear to be the first of a number of slights to which Mathew was subjected by Bishop Barnes and the Durham chapter.

Fama is called *garrula* at Seneca, *Hercules Furens* 193.

169 The partridges were perhaps acquired in the manner indicated by line 647.

170 Matthew Harrison, with the help of his wife Doll (cf. 514), was proprietor of an Oxford inn, The Bear. He kept a tame bear, Furze, as a mascot. Eedes reports that he was an animal of considerable dignity. The Bear was located on Alfred Street, between Christ Church and the High, and so was the Christ Church "local."[1] See further the Commentary note on 258f.

Within his own sphere, Harrison was no less destined for a distinguished future than Eedes and Mathew.[2] He was one of the two Oxford Bailiffs in 1588 and Mayor of the city in 1611, by which time he could describe himself as a mercer; in recording his burial on 20 March, 1630, the parish register of St. Aldgate's calls him an alderman.[3] He married Helena Levins, his Doll, at St. Aldgate in 1581. After her death in 1590 he married Mary Plumpton at St. Martin's. When Eedes calls him *vetus* at 307 he is only indulging in humor.

Harrison, talented at sniffing out provender and whipping up meals, seems to have been brought along as a kind of Major-Domo (Mathew's 1582 letters quoted in the Introduction show he was anxious about the quality of the establishment he would find there and aware of the necessity of entertaining the locals). One gathers that the travelers amused themselves on the road by singing, and one of Harrison's responsibilities was to supply the bass, which he did badly, sounding more as if he were snoring than singing. He was a devotee of the card game cut-throat, though he did not play it well (316ff.). Evidently he went along on the trip as a vacation from Doll, for he seems to groan at the prospect of returning to her, though he did miss Furze (513ff.). His

---

[1] The original inn was pulled down in 1801 and the present public house of that name occupies an ostler's house attached to the main building (Christopher and Edward Hibbert, *The Encyclopaedia of Oxford*, London, 1988, 35f.). Possibly the horses ridden by our travelers came from Harrison's stable.

[2] Cf. Anthony à Wood, *Survey of the Antiquities of the City of Oxford Composed in 1661 - 6* (ed. the Rev. Andrew Clark, Oxford, 1899) vol. III, index s.v.

[3] Interestingly, Harrison's career nearly duplicates the wish expressed by the freedman Crobolus in Edward Forsett's academic comedy *Pedantius* (1581, printed 1631), pp. 9f., who aspires to become an innkeeper and thence to work his way up in society, eventually arriving at the exalted station of a municipal magistrate.

presence imparts an interestingly democratic tone to the expedition, but we note that when Mathew had too many guests to put up it was Harrison who lost his bed (466f.).

William Gager's tragedy *Dido*, produced a few weeks previously in June 1583, was filled with spectacular (and quite expensive) stage effects. In one scene a procession of hunters crosses the stage with a pack of hounds, and then later recrosses it when returning from the hunt (stage direction after 610). Although the stage directions, and Raphael Holinshed's description of the performance, do not mention this detail, one cannot help observing that it would have hugely pleased the audience to have the hunters return with Furze in tow.

Eedes may have got the adjective *horrisonus*, which he employed for the sake of the play on Harrison's name, from Edward Forsett's comedy *Pedantius* (p. 142) where it is applied to artillery. For Eedes' possible familiarity with this play see the Commentary note on 479.

173f. Cf. Vergil, *Aeneid* II.361f., *quis cladem illius noctis, quis funera fando / explicet(?)*.

176 Cf. the Ovidian formula *molliter ossa cubent* at *Amores* I.viii.108, *Heroides* vii. 162, and *Tristia* III.iii.76.

180 My student Margaret Smith pointed out that *taetrum...odorem* is used of the smell of the plague by Lucretius VI.1156, and of the stench of the Harpies at Vergil, *Aeneid* III.228.

181 For Endymion's eternal sleep cf. Robert Graves, *The Greek Myths* (New York, 1955) § 64.

189 For *lustraret lampade terras* cf. Vergil, *Aeneid* IV.6 and VII.148.

192 Eedes now introduces the villain of the piece, Dr. Richard Barnes (1532 - 87). Cf. Alexander Grosart's sympathetic biography in the *D. N. B.* as well as Wood, *A. O.* II.826f.

As stated in **R**'s sidenote, *de nos inde* involves the tmesis of *deinde*.

197 Save for the Duchy of Lancaster, all of England north of the Trent (Yorkshire, Durham, Northumberland, Cumberland, and Westmoreland) was governed by the Council of the North, which had sweeping administrative and judicial authority. It was composed of leading northern noblemen and ecclesiastical notables, though much of its routine work was carried out by full-time professionals. Cf. R. R. Reid, *The King's Council in the North* (London - New York, 1921).

198 Henry Hastings, third Earl of Huntington (1535 - 95), the Lord-President of the Council of the North. He also bore ultimate responsibility for military preparedness in the North. Claire Cross's The *Puritan Earl* (London, 1966) is an excellent modern biography that does much to paint the background against which the events described by Eedes transpire, although she did not write about the war scare of 1583 or describe the present conference.

202 Eedes loathed Bishop Barnes on sight, and is presumably attributing to him a discreditable reason for skulking at his Stockton retreat. We shall see that Barnes made an abortive attempt to greet Walsingham and gain his favor by toadying, but was unceremoniously brushed aside (423ff.); afterwards he avoided Walsingham until the end of his visit when he received him at his Auckland estate as Walsingham was quitting Durham (520), when the money issue no longer counted. The subjunctive is used to attribute a motive to someone other than the speaker: Barnes did not see how he could turn a profit on entertaining Walsingham, but could very well imagine that it would cost him money. Thus he earns the derisory adjective *sapiens* (196), and his visitors were surprised that the stingy Bishop offered them a decent meal (205). On another occasion he did not (cf. 523).

203 Mathew and his friends struck northeast from Northallerton to find Bishop Barnes at his country retreat, a distance reckoned by the *Atlas* as 14.3 miles. This was located at Stockden, in the extreme southeastern corner of co. Durham. It is situated on the north bank of the Tee, about seven miles upstream from Tee Mouth and (according to the *Atlas*) 21.8 miles southeast of Durham. As observed by Eedes at 194f., this served as an eminently satisfactory bolthole for Barnes. For a history and description of Castle Stock-den, the episcopal manor, cf. Surtees, *History and Antiquities of Co. Durham* III.170f.

204 The town in question is variously called Stockden and Stockton. Eedes' whimsical etymology presumes the former name.

207 The son is Emmanuel Barnes, who matriculated from Magdalene College, Oxford, in 1577 and incepted for the M. A. in 1581 (Foster, *Alumni* I.74).[1] He then took a D. D. at the University of Basle (478ff.). He was installed as Canon of the fifth stall at Durham in 1585 (Mussett, *op. cit.* 43) and died in 1614. His Basle doctorate, with its implication of Calvinism, was enough to earn Eedes' dislike.

It is regrettable that Eedes did not leave us a portrait of Bishop Barnes' third son, the future poet Barnabe Barnes,

---

[1] At Magdalene he associated with John Florio. According to Frances A. Yates, *John Florio* (Cambridge U. K., 1934) 27, Florio tutored him in Italian and French beginning in 1576; on p. 53 it is also stated that after Florio himself matriculated at Magdalene in 1581 he acted as Barnes' servant.

who was still only a lad—he matriculated from Brasenose College, Oxford, in 1586. Barnabe was, as his *D. N. B.* article indicates, a gifted minor poet. But he inherited a streak of rather farouche eccentricity from his father, manifested in his sometimes bizarre choice of imagery. For example, Sonnet lxii from *Parthenophil and Parthenope* (1593) contained the poet's extraordinary wish to become wine to be consumed by his darling,

> ...*which down her throat doth trickle,*
> *To kiss her lips, and lie next at her heart,*
> *Run through her veins, and pass by Pleasures part.*

Understandably, this earned the attention of humorists. For example, Thomas Campion wrote in *Epigram* I.17 of the 1619 collection:[1]

> *in vinum solvi cupis Aufilena quod haurit,*
> *basia sic faelix, dum bibit illa, dabis;*
> *forsitan attinges quoque cor; sed (Barne) matella*
> *exceptus tandem, qualis amator eris!*

["You crave to be dissolved in Aufilena's wine, so that you may happily bestow a kiss on her as she drinks. Perhaps you will also arrive at her heart. But, Barnes, what kind of lover will you be when you land in her piss-pot!"]

In fact, anybody who reads Mark Eccles' biography of Barnabe Barnes in *Thomas Lodge and Other Elizabethans* (ed. C. J. Sisson, Cambridge U.. K. 1933, repr. New York, 1966) 165 - 241 will find plenty of evidence to support the idea that there was a deep streak of eccentricity, or perhaps something a good deal more sinister, engrained in the

---

[1] See also Nashe's *Have with you to Saffron-Walden* (III.103 McKerrow) and Marston's *The Scourge of Villainy* VIII.126f.

Barnes family. Barnabe was, among other things, a poisoner who tried to slip some mercury sublimate in the lemonade of John Brown, Recorder of Berwick, in 1598 (Eccles 175 - 91). He was arrested, broke jail, and fled to Durham. As Eccles put it (p. 196), Brown's body, "if Barnes had had his way, would soon have lain mouldering in the grave." The reader is referred to this study for a great amount of extra lore about the Barnes family. Note too, as a further example of ecclesiastical standards at Durham, the wife of another Dean who appropriated some Cathedral gravestones to decorate the Deanery and its font for her kitchen, described on p. 221.

209 This translation presumes Eedes was thinking of Seneca, *Thyestes* 609, *ponite in-flatos tumidosque vultus.* But maybe he is describing the Bishop's bloated face. Later he hints that he was an alcoholic (524ff.).

212 Bishop Barnes seems to be going out of his way to demonstrate that he is unimpressed by his distinguished visitor. Always sensitive to slights to the Dean, Eedes perceives this and is annoyed. Thus the tone of Mathew's Durham sojourn is set at the very beginning.

214f. The son, Dr. Emmanuel Barnes, was married to Anne, daughter of William Barnby of Skipton, Yorkshire. Cf. the Barnes pedigree at Foster, *Visitation of Yorkshire* 50 (there is also an inferior one at Surtees, *History and Antiquities of Co. Durham* I. lxxxii). Anne's age cannot be ascertained from the information provided.

215 B's sidenote is a bit garbled, but evidently the Bishop included explanatory rhymes in his paintings.

216f. Bishop Barnes' second wife was Jane Dyllycote (*neé* Jerrade), native of the Duchy of Anjou; her present age cannot be determined. This is taken from Foster's pedigree. Surtees, *History and Antiquities of Co. Durham* I.lxxxii note m, uncritically—or at least with a straight face—quoted an entry from the register of St. Oswald's church, Durham, "Richard Barnes, Bp. of Durham, and Jane Dyllycotes, a French woman, were married at his castle in Durham, upon Wednesday the second week of Lent, being the 20th of March 1588." 1588 is an error for 1582 (cf. Eccles, *op. cit.* 168)—Barnes died on August 24, 1587.

218f. Eedes' point can be adequately explained by quoting *O. L. D.* "emblem" definition 2a: "A drawing or picture expressing a moral fable or allegory; a fable or allegory such as might be expressed pictorially." The first half of this definition pertains to the Bishop's painting, the second half to the Bishop.

220 The barbarous short *u* in *domus* is remarkable and does not appear to result from textual corruption. M. W. Haslam suggests to me that this might be a parody of the Bishop's versification.

225 This line = Horace, *Ars Poetica* 139, with *mus* altered to *sus* contrary to expectation. The reason for this change quickly becomes apparent.

226ff. Although Eedes reacts to this painting with disgust, he seems to be describing an interesting early specimen of political cartooning. Eedes was no doubt especially offended because he detected a whiff of Puritanism in Barnes' vitriolic anti-papism.

229 This line = Horace, *Ars Poetica* 5.

227 The words *inopem me copia fecit* come from Ovid, *Metamorphoses* III.466.

241 The *praebendarii* or Canons of the Cathedral chapter. When Eedes states that they came to greet Mathew because they were duty-bound to do so, he may be implying that their appearance was grudging.

243ff. Eedes succinctly describes Durham. The city is situated at a sharp loop in the River Wier, by which it is surrounded by on three sides.[1] As a result, the city assumes the aspect of a southward-facing peninsula, at the tip of which is a high rocky prominence upon which are built the castle and the Cathedral close. The sight of these imposing structures is what first strikes the visitor approaching from the south. Thus the eighteenth century traveler William Hutchinson enthused about its:

> ...elegant situation, and the grandeur of some of its public buildings. A few paces from the south road, this English Zion makes a noble appearance. In the centre, the castle and cathedral crown a very lofty eminence, girt by the two streets called the Baileys, enclosed with the remains of the ancient city walls and skirted with hanging gardens and plantations which descend to the river Were, in this point of view exhibiting the figure of a horse-shoe.[2]

To continue the Jerusalem analogy, to the north of this hill the ground levels off so that for defensive purposes it was necessary to construct a wall across the peninsula's neck. Within this wall, sandwiched between the hill and the Clay-

---

[1] See the 1611 map by John Speed reproduced on p. 239 of Margaret Bonney's *Lordship and the Urban Community* (Cambridge, U. K., 1990).

[2] Quoted *ib.* p. 1, where other comparisons of Durham with Jerusalem or Zion are also cited: the craggy hill tended to reminds visitors of what they had read in such writers as Josephus about the Temple Mount in Jerusalem and the disposition of the city walls.

portgate, is the market place. The principal north-south road skirts the city, but the east-west road (which has to cross the river twice) cuts through the market. Eedes' point is that this was the only imposing street in town, but because Durham was a crowded and jumbled medieval city the eye could not trace its course. For that one had to climb the Cathedral's steeple and enjoy a bird's-eye view.

251 *Ascensu...primo* because the Deanery, being within the Cathedral close, is atop the hill mentioned in 238.

There is a detailed description of the Deanery at *The Victoria History of the Country of Durham* (London, 1968) III.132 - 5.

255f. Eedes dryly notes that Harrison ate with the dignitaries, not the servants.

258f. Harrison's Furze was the predecessor of another and more famous Christ Church bear, Tiglath Pileser or "Tig", owned in the nineteenth century by Frank Buckland (whose jackal ate the guinea pigs under the sofa). Christ Church students used to dress Tig in a cap and gown and produce him on social occasions, or present him to important visitors.[1] See the passage from G. Bompas' *Life of Frank Buckland* (1885) quoted by Thomas Seccombe and H. Spencer Scott, *In Praise of Oxford: An Anthology in Prose and Verse* (London, 1910) II.647f. The way that Eedes confers academic titles on Furze, if **R**'s sidenote is to be trusted, suggests that this bear performed a similar function.

According to this sidenote Eedes humorously writes as if it were Furze rather than Harrison who is the *fundator* of The Bear. Here *fundator* must mean "landlord," as neither Harrison nor his bear could be described as the founder of

---

[1] Such as Mr. Moncton Milnes, the future Lord Houghton, who attempted to mesmerize him. This made Tig furious but he at last fell senseless to the ground.

an establishment founded in 1432.[1] But **CW**'s sidenote suggests a different interpretation. Anthony à Wood (*Survey of the Antiquities* I.149), records that it was once called "Furres Inne" and in a note added "The Furreses lived at the Bear tempore Henry VIII." According to this reading, Harrison is as dignified as that erstwhile landlord (as memorialized in a portrait hanging in The Bear?); then we must also suppose that Harrison named Furze after that individual. But the animal could have earned this name by dint of being furry: cf. the *O. E. D.* entry, and it may be that Wood's source for this information was in fact nothing more than a fanciful inference based on **W**'s sidenote.

260f. Robert Bellamy M. D. was Canon of the third stall 1573 - 89 (P. Mussett, *Lists of Deans and Major Canons of Durham 1541 - 1900*, Durham, 1974, 25). He matriculated from St. John's College, Oxford, in 1555 and received the D. Med. in 1571 (for his full academic record cf. Foster, *Alumni Oxonienses* I.104). We have a letter of May 30, 1581 from Lord Hunsdon to Walsingham printed by Boyd, *Calendar of the State Papers* VI.12 (cf. the similar letter of July 31, 1581, reproduced *ib.* p. 42, which makes it clearer that Bellamy was Bishop Barnes' candidate, but omits the insinuation that his candidacy was also supported by Archbishop Sandys):

Postscript.—Understands that Mr. wilson is dead. Requests him to move her majesty for Mr. Bellamy to be dean of Durham, who is the vice-dean there, and is accounted a very honest and learned man and a good housekeeper, and one whom he understands both the Archbishop of York and the Bishop of Durham like very well.

---

[1] Previously operated as Le Tabard, this establishment stood on the site once occupied by Parne Hall.

Bellamy, perhaps put forward by the forces of corruption, not only failed to gain the Deanship, but was also replaced as Sub-Dean by Ralph Tunstall (326ff.). In a footnote to the Introduction I have already cited a 1581 letter from Mathew to Burleigh designed to undermine Bellamy's candidacy.

If we assume that Bellamy preached on a Sunday, then he did so on August 24, and Mathew's arrival in Durham can be fixed to the 23rd.

261 *Impar Achilli* comes from Vergil, *Aeneid* I.475.

262 With **R**'s *alte*, Eedes would appear to be describing that unfortunate high-pitched singsong still affected by many C. of E. clergy. Or we could select the variant *alter*, but what would this mean: that he behaved like a changed priest as the result of his defeat? But that setback was two years in the past.

264f. An excellent example of Oxford superciliousness, no doubt noted and resented by the Durhamites.

266 Deer Park Hall, the Dean's manor, is about three miles due west of Durham.

269 The Canons were called *Praebendarii* because their duty was to offer assistance to the Bishop (*praebeo*); in the present case, they have not exactly been *offering*.

Though Eedes does not name all the Canons, I may as well do so here. In the order of the stalls they occupied, in 1583 they were (1) Robert Swift, (2) John Pilkington, (3) Robert Bellamy, (4) Henry Naunton, (5) Ralph Lever, (6) Peter Shaw, (7) Leonard Pilkington, (8) Francis Bunney, (9) Richard Fawcett, (10) Ralph Tunstall, (11) Adam Holiday, and (12) George Cliffe.

272 *Terra ferax* is an Ovidian tag (*Amores* II.xvi.7, *Fasti*

I.68, *Metamorphoses* I.314).

285ff. These line describe the installation ceremony on Sunday, August 31 and a subsequent reception. It may reflect on the Durhamite clergy's attitude toward him that this reception was given by Mathew rather than for him; or this may have been part of his strategy for winning over the Durhamites outlined in a letter to Burleigh quoted in the Introduction.

288f. Cf. Sallust, *Bellum Iugurthinum* xix.2, *nam de Carthagine silere melius puto quam parum dicere.*

292 For *vena* = "talent," *Oxford Latin Dictionary*, article *vena* def. 7, citing Horace, *Ars Poetica* 409 (the source of the tag *divite vena*), *Odes* II.xviii.10, Ovid, *Epistulae ex Ponto* II.v.21, and perhaps with a slight difference of meaning, Juvenal, *Satire* vii.53. In the examples cited the talent in question is literary.

312f. Particularly, the Dean had to remain at Durham until he had sorted out the question of his income (cf. 508ff.).

316 See the Commentary note on 149.

320 Boyd, *Calendar of the State Papers* VI.691 reproduces a document entitled "A note of certaine spoiles committed by the Scotts in the Middle Marches," in which the Elwood (or Elwet) family loom large. Two such complaints were both filed on August 30, 1583:

> Michael Walles, of Stew ward Sherles in Ridsdall, complains upon Archi-bald Elwett, of the Hill, James Elwett his brother, young John Elswett of the Park, and "Hob" Elwet, of the Park, with their accomplices for 400 kine and oxen, six horses and

mares, and household stuff, value 41*l*. and slaying Roger Wales and John Wales.

Percivall Hall and John Hall, of Haueacres, complain upon John Elwet and "Hob" Elwet, of the Park, Archibald of the Hill, "Jocke" Elwet, called "Scottes Hobbe," Jock Eddeich [*sic*], with their accomplices for 100 kine and oxen, 100 horses and mares, household stuff value 60*l*., slaying five [people] and hurting divers others.

These documents were submitted the day before Mathew's installation as Dean and it is not hard to imagine that the Elwoods' large-scale looting was the talk of Durham.

323ff, The boy may have entertained the company with hair-raising border ballads. If he had wanted to chill their blood, he could have sung ballads about the rising of 1569, led by the Earls of Northumberland and Westmoreland, during which the rebels took over Durham Cathedral and caused the Mass to be said: "The Rising in the North", "Northumberland Betrayed by Douglas", and "The Earl of Westmoreland" (Child 175 - 77). Plenty of others describe behavior of the Jock the Scot variety.

326 Ralph Tunstall, Canon of the tenth stall, recently appointed Sub-Dean (Mussett, *op. cit.* 78). Tunstall matriculated from Trinity College, Cambridge, in 1555, and died in 1619 (for his academic career cf. Venn, *Alumni* I.iv.272). Readers of Eedes' disparaging appraisal will be surprised to learn that Tunstall served as Cambridge University preacher for the year 1568, so the man cannot have been altogether devoid of talent. Although **BCW** give his name correctly, **R** may reflect what Eedes actually wrote, if he deliberately mangled it for the sake of the Tall Dunce joke.

From the allusion to the passage of five days in line 299,

we can deduce that Tunstall preached on Sunday, September 7.

327 In using the word *pinguedine* Eedes seems to convey that Tunstall spoke drearily, or even coarsely: cf. *Oxford Latin Dictionary* entry *pinguis* 7b, citing, *inter alia*, Horace, *Epodes* II.i.267.

333ff. *Matthew* 11: 24, *Come unto me, all ye that labour and are heavy laden, and I will give you rest.*

337 Cf. Terence, *Heauton Timorumenos* 877, *quae sunt dicta in stulto, caudex stipes asinu' plumbeus.* In the dedicatory epistle for the first edition of his *Nero* (1603) Matthew Gwinne wrote *recitari nonnunquam frigide, perabsurde, intelligo: sed ab eo cui latera, cui manus, cui cerebrum, non plumbeo, non stolido, non asino, sic recitari vix concesserim.* He was probably thinking of this Terentian tag, but since he was a member of the same circle as Eedes and Gager, he may have read the *Iter Boreale*, and so it is not inconceivable that he remembered the present line.

341 This line = Juvenal, *Satire* I.79.

348f. More charitably, one could translate "he did not fail in one iota of his duty, nor (saving the name of Dean) will he ever fail in it." But Eedes is *not* charitable. *Decani nomine salvo* means "so long as the Deanship itself isn't available to him."

351 At this point two prominent figures from York come up to Durham, raising Eedes' hopes that they will soon escort Mathew southward. The first is Dr. Robert Lougher, an eminent civilian of Welsh extraction, and Vicar General in Spiritualities to Archbishop Sandys. Cf. the *D. N. B.* biography. Lougher was the author of a letter announcing Mathew's appointment as Dean of Durham mentioned in the Introduction. (Wood, *F. O.* I.165, wrongly gives the date of his death as June 3, 1583—this is a misprint for 1585).

The other is Mistress Jane Young, daughter of Thomas Kynaston of Staffordshire, was the widow of Thomas Young (1507 - 68), a former Archbishop of York, who haled from Llanfey in Pembrokeshire: cf. the *D. N. B.* life As we shall see later, she now maintained her own establishment at York, obviously on a rather grand scale. Both here and when she reappears later in the poem there is plenty of flattering punning on her surname. **R**'s *dominum Yongham* and similar sidenote evidently reflects a misunderstanding that the individual here is her son Sir George Young—the *D. N. B.* mistakenly calls him Sir William, but for the family pedigree cf. Foster, *Yorkshire Visitations* 593. But this identification is excluded by 352 *digna.* We are told 569 that Mistress Young had previously invited Mathew's party to stay with her on their return journey through York; presumably she issued this invitation during her visit to Durham.

The only problem with this identification is how Eedes could have transmogrified the name Young into "Youngham." Probably he did so for metrical convenience, but one wonders whether he misheard Northern pronunciation.

354 There is a special point to this comment. Mathew was Bristol-born, and evidently used to congratulate himself jokingly on having narrowly avoided being a Welshman: so Gager, *Musa Australis* 22f. Therefore two passages in Gager's poem contain humor at the expense of Wales, which were subsequently crossed out. The poet probably realized that these unflattering references to Wales would offend his fellow Welsh Christ Church students, the brothers Richard and Oliver Haklyut: in his notebook this poem is immediately preceded by one written to patch up a quarrel with Oliver, or possibly their chronological order is reversed and Gager felt it necessary to soothe his angry friend for what he had written about Wales here.

365ff. Since we have already been told about Tunstall's sermon on the 7th, it would appear that Eedes is describing a remarkable occasion on Sunday, September 14, on which no less than seven sermons were delivered (by Holiday, Naunton, Mathew, Robson, Brown, Bunney, and Ewbanke). I do not know whether such preaching marathons were ever held, but it would seem intrinsically more likely that for dramatic convenience Eedes is combining an account of sermons delivered at various services on this day, or perhaps more generally. This theory would explain an ostensible slip in line 379, when Eedes, after caustically reviewing the sermons of Holiday and Naunton, states that Mathew spoke in the *second* position. Probably Holiday preached at one service and then Mathew spoke after Naunton at another, just as he preached after Eedes on the 21st (cf. 469 below).

365 Adam Holiday was Canon of the eleventh stall (Mussett, *op. cit.* 84). He had received a Cambridge B. D. in 1572 (Venn, *Alumni* I.ii.392). The Greek word ἀμνησίαν can stand in the text if we assume it is wrongly scanned as one short and three long syllables; otherwise, it is a corruption of some other Greek word.

374 Henry Naunton, Canon of the fourth stall (Mussett, *ib.* 33). He matriculated from Trinity College, Cambridge, at the age of twelve in 1561 and incepted for the M. A. in 1570 (Venn, *Alumni* I.iii.232).

372 This image would have been fresh in the minds of Eedes and his audience, for in Gager's *Dido* produced earlier the same year it was said of Elizabeth (345f.):

> *Cynthiae qualis nitor inter astra,*
> *talis in terris decor est Elisae.*

380ff. Gager echoes these lines at *Musa Australis* 69ff.

380 Cf. Vergil, *Eclogue* ix.36, *sed argutos inter strepere anser olores.*

382 This line = Vergil, *Eclogue* i.26.

385 For *Iunonius ales* cf. Ovid, *Amores* II.vi.55.

386 Simon Robson, who had matriculated from St. John's College, Cambridge, in 1569, was admitted to the B. A. in 1573, and incepted for the M. A. three years later (Venn, *Alumni* I.iii.476). At the moment he was rector of Stainton-le-Street, co. Durham. From 1598 to 1617, the date of his death, he was Dean of Bristol Cathedral.

389 Eedes is thinking of the passage in Horace's *Ars Poetica* that begins (408f.) *natura fieret laudabile carmen an arte, / quaesitum est.* His point is that Naunton is deficient in both.

393 Presumably the idea is that such an orator is a mere effigy of a man, not a real person.

394 For *invita...Minerva* cf. (appropriately) Cicero, *de Officiis* I.cx.10, *ad Familiares* III.i.1, XII.xxv.iv, and Horace, *Ars Poetica* 385.

398 I cannot identify this individual with certainty: perhaps he was the Edward Browne who took an M. A. from Brasenose College in 1576, or the similarly-named individual who took an M. A. from Christ Church in 1580 (for both cf. Foster, *Alumni Oxonienses* I.193).

400 For *more fluentis aquae* cf. Ovid, *Ars Amatoria* III.62.

401 I guess the idea is that when he was dealing with an issue of substance he just muttered, but when he had nothing to say he waxed emptily eloquent.

402 Francis Bunney (1543 - 1617), a Perpetual Fellow of Magdalene College, born at Chalfont, St. Guiles, Bucks., had been inducted as a Canon in 1572 and occupied the eighth stall (Mussett, *op. cit.* 63). He is not to be confused with his brother Edmund, a celebrated itinerant preacher who ranged the North country at this time. In his biography of Francis at *A.. O.* II.199f. Wood wrote "This person was very zealous in the way he professed, was a great admirer of Jo. Calvin, a constant preacher, charitable, and a stiff enemy to Popery." See also Claire Cross, *Puritan Earl* 267f. For his academic record and references to genealogy cf. Foster, *Alumni Oxonienses* I.75. The fact that he subsequently published several theological tracts, itemized by Wood, confirms Eedes' appraisal of his comparative intellectual merit among the Durhamites.

405 Henry Ewbanke, former Fellow of Queen's College, Oxford (academic record at Foster, *Alumni Oxonienses* II.475), and destined to be a Canon of Durham when Mathew was elevated to the bishopric (as of 1596). Although he is dealt with by Eedes no less disdainfully than most other Durhamites, we may gather that he was an ally of Mathew, since he was the only clergyman in the diocese to offer him hospitality on the return journey (532f.). Another reason for regarding him as a supporter is **B**'s sidenote, which says that he prayed for Mathews in his sermon; the implication is that the other Durham preachers did not (**W**'s sidenote *A follower of the Deane of Durham* probably points to the same conclusion). A friendly attitude towards the Dean is also suggested by the fact that his son Tobie, born in 1588, who matriculated from Broadgates Hall, Oxford, in 1605 (Foster, *Alumni* II.475), was named after Mathew, no doubt his godfather. In his May 1582 letter to Burleigh Mathew had written "many good men of that church and country were earnest with him to do what in him lay for expedition...For that he was credibly informed that many things there went to wrack." This implies he already had supporters and informants within the diocese. Was Ewbanke one of these? He was installed as rector of Washington parish, co. Durham, on December 23, 1583, and it is tempting to see Mathew's hand in this appointment. See further the Commentary note on 539.

418 B's more specific variant *vix ter* cannot be evaluated Eedes is reckoning days from some indeterminable date on which Mathew's companions had planned to quit Durham. I have selected *vix ter* merely because it is Eedes' habit to be precise about chronology.

419 Cf. Ovid, *Fasti* VI.717, *at pater Heliadum radios ubi tinxerit undis*. Walsingham arrived at Durham on Saturday, September 20, and stayed until the 26th (cf. letters reproduced by Boyd, *Calendar of the State Papers* VI.617 and 621). This intelligence agrees with Eedes' testimony that he spent the first night with Heath at Kepier and came into Durham the next day to hear Mathew preach.

425 For *pluvialibus...Austris* cf. Vergil, *Georgics* III.429.

427 Compare the assessment at William Page (ed.), *The Victoria History of the County of Durham* (London, 1968) II.37, "[Barnes] certainly copied [his predecessor] in his servility to the queen, carrying the alienation of parcels of the bishopric to an outrageous extent."

429 Cf. Plautus, *Poenulus* 332, *tum pol ego et oleum et operam perdidi.*

432 Robert Devereux, Earl of Essex (1566 - 1601). While at Cambridge Essex had run up such huge debts that his guardian Lord Burleigh pulled him out of the University. It used to be thought (for example by the author of the *D. N. B.* biography) that he lived in seclusion at his house in Lamphey (Llanffydd) in Pembrokeshire prior to his introduction at Court by Leicester in 1584. In fact he was placed in the wardship of the Earl of Huntington at York for a year and a half, and was doubtless present at Durham as a member of the Earl's train (Cross, *Puritan Earl* 54f.). Mention of Essex would be of special interest to a Christ Church audience, since his younger brother Walter Devereux was currently a highly popular student there.

434 Henry le Scrope, ninth Baron Scrope of Bolton (1534 - 92), Lord Warden of the West Marches and a member of the Council of the North. Cf. the *D. N. B.* biography.

435 Sir John Foster, Lord Warden of the Middle Marches.

437 Francis Russell, second Earl of Bedford (1527? - 85) had three sons, John, William, and Francis, two of whom were present on this occasion.

440 Sir Walter Mildmay (1520? - 89), Chancellor of the Exchequer, was originally nominated as the leader of this embassy but had been unable to come (cf. the *D. N. B.* biography). He had instead been sent as Elizabeth's ambassador to Mary Queen of Scots in mid-August (Boyd, *Calendar of the State Papers* VI.583), and was probably at Durham now because the closer guarding of Mary was an agenda item at this meeting, as can be inferred from a postscript of a letter by Walsingham printed *ib.* 595. In the following year Mildmay would found Emmanuel College, Cambridge.

Perhaps the other gentleman mentioned in this line is Sir Henry Neville, a protégé of Lord Burleigh and a future diplomat and parliamentarian, who had matriculated from Merton College, Oxford, in 1577. Cf. the *D. N. B.* life.

441 Sir Richard Lowther (1529 - 16076), Lord Warden of the West Marches. Cf. the *D. N. B.* biography.

436 Sir Henry Widdrington (Woodrington), an English diplomat with a history of service in Scotland (see Boyd, *Calendar of the State Papers* VI, index s. v.—his despatches from Scotland cease in July 1582). A good deal about him and Fenwick—the villians of the ballad *Chevy Chase*—and of chaotic conditions in the Middle Marches in the 1590's can be gleaned from Eccles, *op. cit.* 192 - 211. Eccles also gives us a glimpse of Mathew, now elevated to the See of Durham, sitting on the bench of assizes, trying to make sense of these squabbles.

442 Sir Simon Musgrave, Constable of Newcastle, and his son Christopher (cf. Boyd, *Calendar of the State Papers* VI, index s. vv.).

Sir William Fenwick of Wallington, Northumberland (cf. the *D. N. B.* article on his son Sir John). For his father's death in a skirmish with the Scots cf. the letter of Henry Killigrew to Walsingham of July 17, 1575, reproduced at Boyd, *Catalogue of the State Papers* V.168.

450 A Scots eyewitness says that Walsingham had eight score of horse in his train: cf. Sir James Melville, *Memoirs of His Own Life* (Edinburgh, 1827) 310. When the members of the Council of the North and their retinues and also members of the defensive commission established in mid-August are added, one can readily imagine that Durham was full to the bursting-point.

451 John Heath (d. 1590), a merchant and Warden of the Fleet, owned a manor at Kepier in the parish of St. Giles,

Durham, about a mile north of the city center: cf. William Page (ed.), *The Victoria History of the County of Durham* (London, 1968) III.185 as well as Surtees, *History and Antiquities of Co. Durham* I.38 and 158. He had acquired the dissolved Hospital there by purchase and so was styled Lord of Kepier or "Heath of Keeper," as is imperfectly reflected in **R**'s corrupt sidenote.

Heath was a strong supporter of Bishop Barnes' critic Bernard Gilpin. One cannot help noting that when Walsingham spent his first night at Durham under Heath's roof the anti-Barnes, pro-Mathew forces would have had an admirable opportunity to fill his ear with their views.

454 In 1583 St. Matthew's Day fell on Sunday, Sept. 21.

460 Eedes alludes to the 1569 Catholic rising in the North.

467 The words *dominumque domus* indicate that Mathew found a Major-Domo awaiting him at Durham after all.

474 Cf. the Commentary note on 416.

475 Walsingham may understandably have been exhausted, as he had undertaken the Scottish embassy although he was in poor health. His chief reason for lingering at Durham was nevertheless the Scottish crisis.

483ff. Dr. Emmanuel Barnes, the Bishop's son. His Basle diploma must have been very recently conferred: he did not receive his first church appointment (the Rectorship of Houghton-le-Spring, co. Durham) until the following year, and became a Canon of Durham in 1585. Eventually he became a Canon of York (1602), and died in 1614. These lines contrast the son, who for all his faults is a genuine D. D., with his father, whose academic credentials appear to be represented as faintly bogus (see the next note).

487 Barnes had been "actually created doctor of divinity by certain persons appointed by the members of the university, but whether at London, or elsewhere, it appears not" (Wood, *F. O.* I.215—he also uses the words "actually created" at *A. O.* II.826). Eedes seems to be sneering at this transaction, honorific or slightly dishonorable—I do not understand what "actually" means in this context.

This is as good an opportunity as any to note that Surtees, *History and Antiquities of Co. Durham* I.lxxxii, recorded that in his deathbed will Bishop Barnes appointed Mathew and John Heath (for whom cf. the Commentary note on 445) his co-executors. Surtees likewise reports that Dr. Emmanuel Barnes' firstborn son was named Toby. Like Henry Ewbanke, he named the boy after Mathew, in all probability his godfather. Are these signs of eventual reconciliation, or further evidence for Barnesian obsequiousness? The same question might be asked about Barnabe Barnes' subsequent dedication to Mathew of his *Divine Century of Spiritual Sonnets*.

489 The allusion is to Lucretius' famous axiom (I.156f.) *nil posse creari / de nihilo*.

495 Eedes possibly had in mind the situation described by Cicero, *de Oratore* II.lvii. 233, *eorum impudentiam qui agunt in scaena gestum spectante Roscio*. Or more precisely, he may have been thinking of the quotation of this phrase in Edward Forsett's recent comedy *Pedantius* (p. 120 of the printed edition): see the next note.

497 Cf. Persius, *Satire* I.28, *at pulchrum est digito monstrari et dicier "hic est."* Note the echo of this line at Gager, *Musa Australis* 81.

In Edward Forsett's highly successful comedy *Pedantius*, produced at Trinity College, Cambridge, in February 1581, the title character (whom Nashe claimed to be a lampoon of

Gilbert Harvey), a self-important rhetorician with a grossly inflated opinion of his abilities, exclaims at one point (p. 120 of the printed edition), *me (dum in curia versabar) praetereuntem demonstrabant omnes digito, insusurrantes, hic est ille, (quod nisi Demostheni olim contigit mortalium nemini).* Eedes may have had this passage in mind, or even expected his audience to recognize the allusion.[1]

492f. **R**'s sidenote can be interpreted as referring to a proposed return, but why say towards Matthew Hutton, the Dean of York? Although Mathew did meet him while on his return journey through York (609), Eedes scarcely represents this as the high point of his visit. Probably **R**'s copyist abridged a note that originally stated that Mathew returned to York where he met Mrs. Young, Archbishop Sandys, and Dean Hutton.

504f. Evidently Walsingham paid off the debts Mathew had incurred in entertaining him. Bishop Barnes, who had shunned Walsingham to avoid such expenses, must have found this galling. If only because of Mathew's letters to Burleigh Walsingham would have been aware of the financial problems in the Deanery.

510ff. Diocesan income largely derived from rents and other revenues from its landholdings. A certain share of these rents were set aside to support the Dean (cf. 231f., where he is greeted by his tenants); while the Deanship lay

---

[1] *Pedantius*, to be sure, was not printed until 1631, but other cases can be demonstrated in which unprinted plays performed at one of the Universities found their way to the other in manuscript form. The first acts of both *Pedantius* and William Gager's *Meleager* of 1582 are largely devoted to a debate about the comparative values of celibacy and marriage, and although these debates are pitched very differently one wonders whether Gager and Eedes had had the opportunity of reading Forsett's comedy.

vacant his rents had been abstracted by the Chapter, just as his deer park had been depopulated. See further Mathew's letters on the subject quoted in the Introduction.

512 Gager seems to have been thinking of this line when he wrote *Musa Australis* 47ff., a passage which tends to conflate the thieving Jock the Scot with the Durham clergy! We may note in passing the similarity of this Gager passage to a description of the Irish by Michael Wallace (Valesius), *In Serenissimi Regis Jacobi...Liberationem Foelicissimam Carmen* Ἐπιχάρτικον, printed by John Field at London in 1606, pp. 4f.:

> *Hibernosque feros, montosaque tesqua colentes,*
> *queis pro lege fuit vis, queis mos vivere rapto.*

517 The date of their departure cannot be fixed. It was not before Sunday, September 18, when Mathew wrote a letter to Lord Burleigh dated from Durham, reproduced by Strype, *Annals of the Reformation* III.ii 266 - 68.

518 There was another grand episcopal manor at Bishop's Auckland, situated upstream on the Were, perhaps fourteen miles to the southeast of Durham as the crow flies. Our friends crossed the Were at Sunderland, then were obliged to travel southeast rather than due south on the great London-Berwick road.

524 There is no such word as *immediate* in the classical Latin lexicon. Either this is an error for *immoderate* or it is a neologism meaning "without interruption."

525 Cf. Vergil, *Aeneid* I.738f.:

> *ille impiger hausit*
> *spumantem pateram et pleno se proluit auro.*

528 The point of the pun is that Germans were notoriously boorish (and young Dr. Barnes had finished his education at Basle, which at the time was reckoned a part of Germany).

529 C's sidenote implies the friends in question were acquired during Dr. Barnes' Magdalene days.

530 For *cane peius et angue* cf. Horace, *Epistulae* I.xvii.30 (also echoed at Forsett's *Pedantius* p. 99).

534f. To preserve the pun I use the word "mundane" in an unusual sense, = Fr. *mondain* (*O. E. D.* def. 1c).

536 Cf. Camden's geological note at *Britannia* p. 591, *montes vero ipsi plumbo, carbone fossili, nec non aere gravidi...quod in eorum autem summitatibus, ut etiam alibi lapides nonnunquam fuerint reperti cocheleas marinas, et alia aquatica referentes, si nonsint naturae miracula: refusi in omnem terram sub Noe diluvii certa esse indicia, cum Orosio Christiano iudicabo.*

536 Cf. Leland's *Itinerary* IV.24ff., "Richemont is pavid. Richemont towne is waullid, and the castel on the river side of Swale is as the knot of the cumpace of the waulle...The toun is set on a hille side. The greate hil above hit more then a mile of is cawllid Penhil, and is countid the hiest hille of Richemontshire." This arrangement reminds Eedes of Homer's descriptions of Ithaca in the *Odyssey*, both because of its general cragginess (IX.20ff.) and because of the way Mt. Neritos dominates the landscape (XIII.351).

539 For Henry Ewbanke cf. the Commentary note on 400. He had not yet received his own parish at Washington, co. Durham, and presumably held some subordinate or temporary ecclesiastical post at or near Richmond. To judge by *patria* in the next line, he was native to the region. Or is *patria* used for "parish" in either the ecclesiastical or the British colloquial sense of the word?

543 It is impossible to imagine that Mathew would have lugged along a water-clock on his travels. Eedes wrote *clepsydra* because the three successive short syllables in *horologium* cannot stand in a hexameter line. Doubtless the timepiece in question was one of those traveling-clocks described by Elizabeth Burton, *The Elizabethans at Home* (London, 1958) 115. Such instruments were still a sufficient novelty to inspire an apostrophe by Thomas Campion, *Epigram* I.cli of the 1595 collection, *de Horologio Portabili*:

> *temporis interpres, parvum congestus in orbem,*
> *qui memores repetis nocte dieque sonos:*
> *ut semel instructus iucunde sex quater horas*
> *mobilibus rotulis irrequietus agis:*
> *nec mecum quocunque feror comes ire gravaris,*
> *annumerans vitae damna, levansque meae.*

["Time's interpreter, packed in a tiny globe, who day and night recalls the hour with a chime, how cheerfully, when once wound up, you tirelessly transverse twenty-four hours with your little moving wheels. Nor do you complain that I carry you as my comrade wherever I go, counting out the loss of my life, but also lightening its burden."]

544 Cf. Plautus, *Amphitruo* 282, *credo edepol equidem dormire solem*, and Seneca, *Phoenissae* 394, *vide ut atra nubes pulvere abscondat diem*.

546 Cf. the Commentary note on 153.

553 The sidenote indicates that Harrison thought this landlord looked like Furze the bear (or like Furze the erstwhile landlord in his portrait?).

555 Cf. Vergil, *Aeneid* I.723, *postquam prima quies epulis mensaeque remotae* (cf. also *ib.* I.216).

566 *Verecundum...pudorem* is an Ovidian tag (*Ars Amatoria* II.572, *Tristia* IV.iv.50).

567 For Jane Young cf. the Commentary note on 351.

573 Cf. Vergil, *Aeneid* I.597, *o sola infandos Troiae miserata labores* (as if Mistress Young were Dido, welcoming the shipwrecked Trojans).

574f. Cf. Ovid, *Metamorphoses* VIII.677f.:

> *super omnia vultus*
> *accessere boni nec iners pauperque voluntas.*

595 *Bis mille* is the preferable reading, since this is the approximate distance from York to Bishopthorp.

597f. *Utrisque academicis* refers to Blenkowe and Eedes.

609 I cannot identify this individual: nobody named Parsons, Person, Persons, or Pierson who took a doctorate from either University was a member of the Yorkshire clergy, or a lay officer of the diocese, at this time. Hence my retention of **R**'s *Parsons* in the text has no more to recommend it than the seeming support of **W**'s *Persons*.

617ff. In view of his sentiments, Eedes would have been gratified to learn that she survived until 1614.

619 The eagle in question is the Phoenix.

623f. Eedes now discovers why the Tadcaster bridge was so large.

628 Mathew's company returned on a road several miles eastward of their outbound journey, about nine miles from Aberford, and stayed at the market town of Pontefract or Pomfret. Pontefract Castle, with its sinister memories of the murder of Richard II and the execution of Anne Neville's kinsmen by Richard III, was not pulled down until the Civil War.

630 Leland (*Itinerary* I.39) appears to have shared Eedes' lack of enthusiasm for Pomfret, for he says much about the Castle but nothing about the town beyond "the fairest parte of Pontefract stondith on the toppe of the hille." Camden (p. 566) was more enthusiastic: *loco sedet peramoeno, aedificiis excultum nitibus.*

642 Eedes alludes to the fact that Blenkowe haled from Cumberland.

644ff. From Leicester the travelers took a track westward of Northampton, to reach Aston-on-the-Walls (or Aston-le-Wall) in the Warden Hundred of Northamptonshire, situated near the headwaters of the Cherwell eight miles north of Banbury. They stayed with George Butler, whose son Alban matriculated from Magdalen Hall, Oxford, two years later (Foster, *Alumni* I.222). For the family cf. Walter C. Metcalfe, *The Visitations of Northamptonshire made in 1564 and 1618-19* (London, 1887) 8. To enjoy their hunting the party had bypassed Northampton to the west, and intended to follow the road paralleling the Cherwell down to Banbury and hence to Oxford. There was no direct road from Leicester or Northampton to Aston, hence Eedes' remark about *multis ambagibusque usi.*

654ff. The first lines of Gager's *Musa Australis* were written in response to this passage.

647 Cf. Ovid, *Metamorphoses* XIII.641, *cum primum haec moenia vidi*. The city wall of Oxford had last been repaired in the reign of Richard II and was an advanced state of disrepair, save for those portions incorporated into collegiate walls, and it is these which Eedes must be describing: cf. Wood, *Survey of the Antiquities* I.242f.

651 For *rustica Musa* cf. Vergil, *Eclogue* iii.84.

653f. Cf. the Commentary note on 380.

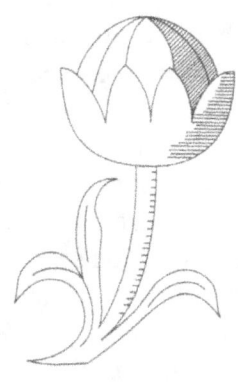

AD ORNATISSIMVM ET DISERTISSIMVM VIRVM DOMINVM
DOCTOREM MATTHÆVM DVNELMIÆ ATQVE ÆDIS CHRISTI
OXONIÆ DECANVM
ANNO DOMINO 1583, NOVEMBRI 11

totum ornavit iter gelidas Aquilonis in oras
    Musa Aquilonaris, culta sciensque tamen.
nunc reditum in terrae partem melioris, et Austrum
    Australis canerem Musa Thalia tuum.
digna etenim res est et debita gratia tanto   5
    in quo cui dives vena deesse potest?
instar veris enim rediisti gratus ab Arcto,
    et caepit subito laetior ire dies.
sed nec opis nostrae est Borealem aequare Thaliam
    et reditum in reditu iam meditare tuo.   10
iste quidem reditus non est, neque gaudia portat,
    ni constans nobis perpetuusque foret.
Australisne ergo Boreales ibis in oras?
    tam longinqua tibi terra petenda fuit?
ecquid te nostri ceperunt taedia caeli?   15
    quod te detineat nil tuus Auster habet?
quid, Matthaee, tibi est dura cum gente Brigantum?
    quid cum Matthaeo, barbara terra, tibi est?
ecquid in exilium iam te non sentis abire?
    exilii paenam cur tibi sponte creas?   20
si tu Cambrorum natus de stirpe fuisses
    (quam quod sic aegre fugeris ipse soles
laetari tecum) minor haec iactura fuisset,
    nec de te talis nostra querela foret.
te tulit ingeniis subtilior aura creandis   25
    Bristolii, et partu nobilitata tuo.

TO THAT MOST DISTINGUISHED AND LEARNED MAN, DOMINUS DOCTOR MATHEWS, DEAN OF DURHAM AND OF CHRIST CHURCH, OXFORD, NOVEMBER 11, 1583

A northern Muse, but nevertheless one elegant and learned, has already adorned your journey to the frigid northerly climes. Now I, the southern Muse Thalia, would sing of your return to the better part of the world, the southland. For the subject is a worthy one, and what well-earned gratitude can be lacking towards such a man in anybody who has a rich vein of poetry? So you have come from the North, welcome as the springtime, and immediately our days begin to pass more happily. It is not my task to match the northern Thalia, and as you come back to us you are already planning your return journey. So your returning here is no homecoming, and brings us no gladness, unless it could be permanent and enduring. And so will you, a man of the South, depart for northern regions? Must you seek such a distant land? Did your climate grow boresome? Does your southland have nothing to hold you?

What, Mathew, do you have in common with these northmen? What, you barbaric land, do you have in common with Mathew? Do not see that you are going off into exile? Why voluntarily penalize yourself with exile? *If you had been born of Welsh stock (and you are in the habit of congratulating yourself on barely escaping this fate), the loss would have been less, nor would we have such a quarrel with you.*[1] But the air of Bristol, more refined in the

---

[1] These lines were written and then deleted so as not to offend Gager's Welsh friends; see the Commentary note on *Iter Boreale* 354.

Oxonium instituit. rapiet Dunelmia fructum?
    haud locus ingenio convenit ille tuo.
fasne latere tibi est? num te spelunca decebit?
    tu media solis luce carere potes?   30
ota tuam poscit cum principe curia vocem,
    Paulinae efflagitant rostra diserta crucis.
ore tuo mater pendere achademia gestit,
    ad nati dotes obstupefacta sui.
te schola divinae decet usurpata palaestrae,   35
    haec sunt ingenio digna theatra tuo.
tanta diu nequeat scenae persona deesse,
    usuramque tui quilibet actus habet.
pace tua dicam nunquam tanti ipse fuisses,
    ingenium lucis si caruisset ope.   40
tu poteris tolerare nives, caelique ruinas?
    frigora tam gracili corpore tanta feras?
quid minor et maior quantum facit Ursa timorem?
    et trux, Angligenis gens inimica, Scotus
quos faciet tibi Iocche metus? noctuque latrones   45
    in lectis hominis qui iugulare solent?
res ibi vi geritur. non certant lege, sed ense,
    et nisi lex illic Martia, nulla valet.
vivitur ex rapto, et veteri de more Scytharum;
    haud furtum facies nullum ibi pondus habet.   50
quicquid habes commune putant, nec vespere clausum
    usque ad mane tuum dixeris esse pecus.
raptor eques praedas abigit, famamque latronis
    quaerit, et a furtis nobile nomen habet.
quid Musis cum Marte? tibi cum milite duro?   55
    tu gere facundae praelia digna togae.
quid quod ibi facile cuivis licet esse disertus?
    oratoris ibi nomen habere leve est.
solus ibi ornate, nullo rivale, loquaris,
    et tibi, non secus ac rauca cicada, canas.   60
ruricolas inter nihil est facundus haberi,
    inter facundos gloria summa viros.

creation of talent, produced you and was ennobled by your birth. Oxford reared you—is Durham to steal the fruit? That place scarcely matches your nature. Is it proper for you to lie hidden? Will a cave befit you? Can you do without the noontime sun? The whole Court, together with the sovereign, requires your voice; the learned pulpit of St. Paul's Cross[1] clamors for it; your mother, the University, is eager to hang from your lips, astonished at the gifts of her child; your empty place in the School of Divinity suits you. These are worthy theaters for your talent. Such a character cannot long remain offstage, and each act has its need for you.

Pardon me for saying so, but you would never have been worth so much if your talent had lacked the benefit of the light. Will you able to withstand blizzards and torrents? Can your slender frame bear the freezes? What about the fear which Ursa Major and Minor inspire? And what of the terrors that fierce race, hateful to the English, and Jock the Scot will create for you? What about the thieves who are accustomed to strangling men in their beds of nights? There business is conducted by violence. They do not contend at law, but with the sword, and no law prevails save for the law of warfare. They live by thievery, and the old customs of the Scythians. THOU SHALT NOT STEAL carries no weight there. They think that whatever you possess is common property, and the flock you lock up at nightfall you can't call your own by morning. A robber baron carries off his booty, seeking to make his reputation as a bandit, and acquires a noble name by his depredations. What business have the Muses with Mars? What business have you with harsh campaigning? You wage wars suitable for the eloquent gown. What of the fact that there anybody at all can be eloquent? There a reputation as a speaker is accounted a trivial thing. You may alone speak ornately there, unrivaled, and yet you will sing for yourself not otherwise than does the shrill cicada. It is nothing to be reckoned eloquent among hayseeds, but in the company of eloquent men it is the height of glory.

---

[1] A celebrated open-air pulpit in front of St. Paul's Cathedral.

oppiduli primus quam vel Romae esse secundus
    quod malles, Caesar, vox ea stulta fuit.
est victi vincentis honor. nisi strenuus Hector,   65
    Pelidis nunquam gloria tanta foret.
si Cato, si Catulus, si non Hortensius essent,
    laus esset magno de Cicerone minor.
inter apes summam, non fucos inter inertes,
    Attica apis laudem sedulitatis habet.   70
non miror proceram inter viburna cupressam,
    sed quae prospectat desuper omne nemus.
ad vada Maeandri qui nomen quaerit olores
    non inter corvos concinat albus olor.
dicere quae Humfredus, Westfalingusque, paresque   75
    Thorntonus, Iamsus, cultaque turba probent
haec laus, hoc decus est. quid quod facundia languet
    quam non expectat docta corona fori?
suscitat ingenii gravis expectatio vires,
    saepe vicem virtus aemula cotis habet.   80
ingens calcar habet laudari, et dicier "hic est,"
    et subdit studiis gloria iusta faces.
utque habeas quocum possis contendere (quanquam
    in pugna eloquii te minor omnis erit),
est tamen hoc satius quam nulla vincere lucta,   85
    ultro cedentes sternere nullus honor.
vilis Olympiaca est nullo certamine palma
    et laudem victo victor ab hoste capit.
haud clypeum tanti fecisset Achillis Ulysses
    rivalis fuerat ni Telamone satus.   90
scilicet ingenua est aegre superare voluptas,
    difficili quiddam dulce labore latet.
rostra disertus amat, quae te subducis in antra?

Caesar, that saying of yours was foolish, that you would prefer to be the top man in a small village rather then even the second man at Rome. Honor is gained for the conqueror from the nature of the man he defeats. Unless Hector was a mighty man, Achilles' glory would never have been so great. If there had been no Cato, no Catulus, no Hortensius,[1] great Cicero's praise would have been diminished. The Attic bee gained praise for its industry among other bees, not among idle drones. I do not admire a cypress tall among viburnums, but one that overtops the entire forest. On the waters of the Maeander, the white swan does not sing among crows. To say the things of which Humphreys, Westfaling, their peers Thornton and James,[2] and the learned throng approve, this is praise, this is glory. What of the fact that eloquence fails when the learned congregation does not expect it? For such keen expectation stimulates one's talents, and rivalry often performs the office of a whetstone. Praise is a mighty stimulus, having it said "this is the man," and glory well won kindles the fire of industry. For even if everyman is your inferior in the battle of eloquence, it is better to have someone to compete against than to win without a contest, there is no honor in laying low those who voluntarily yield. An Olympian palm gained without a contest is a cheap thing, and a victor gains his praise by overcoming his rival. Ulysses would scarcely have put such value on Achilles' shield if Ajax had not vied with him. Surely there is a natural pleasure in winning with difficulty, a certain pleasure in hard endeavor. The eloquent man loves the pulpit. In what caves are you hiding yourself?

---

[1] Cicero's leading contemporaries.

[2] Some of the other great Oxford preachers of the day. Until assuming the Deanship of Winchester in 1580, Laurence Humphrey had been President of Magdalene College. Harbert Westfaling (Eedes' future father-in-law) and Thomas Thornton were Canons of Christ Church. William James was currently the Master of University College and was about to be selected as Mathew's successor as Dean of Christ Church.

solus ubi sapias devia lustra petis?
quanquam ibi si sapias, quae non intelligit, odit   95
    et ridet doctos rustica turba viros.
barbarus ille tibi locus est, tu barbarus illi
    cum nemo sapiat qui bene dicta siet.
cum non perciperis, tacuisse loquique perinde est,
    totus nequiquam sumitur ille labor.   100
aura levis vapulat cum non intelligor ulli,
    et purum in vacuo littore spargo salem.
nec plane indoctos tutum est nimiusve scientes
    censuram de te iudiciumve dare.
utque statim fera turba stupet, sic invidet excors.   105
    in Scotia livor concomitare solet.
exitio multis fuit ignorantia vulgi,
    quam semper culti pertimuere viri.
Orphea cantando sylvasque ferasque trahentem
    in partes Ciconum diripuere nurus.   110
Orpheus admoneat, sed in hac tibi parte timendum
    ne linguam inficiant barbara verba tuam.
scilicet est quaedam gelidi contagio caeli,
    nec refert, ubi quis vixerit usque, parum.
rare Aquilonarem vidi Cambrumque disertum,   115
    idque reor fieri conditione loci.
aere Thebano non gaudet natus Athenis,
    hinc finxit mores natio quaeque sibi.
est virtus vitiumque loci. pars altera fertur
    aurae Bristolii crassior esse tuae.   120
quin tu si gelido morerere sub axe (quod absit),
    proh scelus, ossa locus tam ferus ille tegat?
sed frustra. cur haec? ibis nobisque relinques
    quam desiderium triste avidumque tui?

Are you seeking some out-of-the-way lair where you can be wise by yourself? And even if you are wise there, the rustic crew hates that which it does not understand and jeers at learned men. This place is barbaric for you, and you are a barbarian as far as it is concerned, when nobody can discern what is said well. When you are not understood, it's all the same whether you speak or remain silent, all of that endeavor is undertaken pointlessly. I am just stirring the air in vain when I don't make myself understood to anybody, I'm just scattering my pure salt on an empty beach. Nor is it quite safe to give ignorant illiterates power and judgment over yourself. As soon as the savage crowd is amazed, it goes wild with envy. Ill feeling is your constant companion in Scotland. The ignorance of the common man has been the ruin of many, and the educated have always feared it. The women of Thrace tore Orpheus apart limb by limb as he was leading the trees and beasts by his singing. Let Orpheus serve as a warning.

And in this part of the world you have to feel anxiety lest barbarian words infect your style. For there is a certain contagion under a northern sky, and it scarcely matters where you have lived up to now. *I have rarely meet an eloquent northman or Welshman, and I imagine this is to be blamed on the nature of the place.*[1] An Athens-born man takes no pleasure in the climate of Thebes, and on this basis each nation acquires its own character. There's virtue and shortcomings in a place, and another location has heavier air than does your Bristol. But if you are to die beneath a frigid sky (and may this not happen!), oh the shame of it, is this savage place to cover your bones?

But all is in vain. Why say all this? You will go, and what will you leave us save sadness, as we hungrily long for you? How can I hope that my entreaties can hold a man whom

---

[1] In the manuscript these words were written but subsequently deleted for the same reason as the lines above.

147

quem non detineat maerens achademia mater,   125
  qui sperem nostras posse tenere preces?
scilicet auspiciis et divae numine fretus,
  quamque iubet carpes Elizabetha viam.
i decus, i nostrum, nec te dirum oscinis omen
  traiiciensve tuos terreat anguis equos.   130
non canis occurrat praegnans, faciatque timorem,
  nec caeptum vulpes faeta retardet iter.
i decus, i nostrum, vanoque timore Thaliae.
  ter faelix opto sis ubicunque placet.

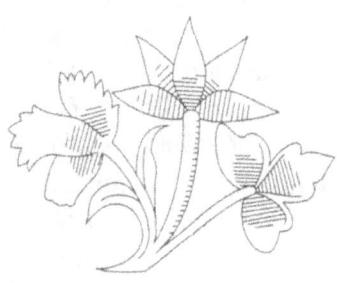

our mournful mother, the University, cannot restrain? Assuredly, relying on that divine lady's auspices and holy authority, you will travel wherever Elizabeth commands. Go, our glory, let no bird of ill omen or slithering snake frighten your horses. Let no pregnant bitch run out before them and create a panic, let no pregnant fox delay your journey once you have begun it. Go, glory, and I hope that my Muse's fear be in vain, and that you may be happy wherever you chance to be.

GEORGE PEELE,

PAREUS

1585

Introduction

he following mini-epic about William Parry's conspiracy against Elizabeth, issued anonymously in 1586 by Joseph Barnes, printer to the University of Oxford, merits our attention for at least three reasons: it was evidently written by George Peele, a former student of Christ Church; it and some related works on the same subject seem to have been highly significant for the foundation of what evolved into the Oxford University Press; and it exerted a rather surprising influence on a number of subsequent writers.

The case for attributing *Pareus* to Peele, made by Tucker Brooke,[1] is worth quoting in full:

> The name of this none-too-modest author is not stated. It might at first be supposed that he was William Gager of Christ Church, who was writing and publishing admirable Latin odes on similar subjects at this time; but I see little suggestion of Gager's manner, and the opening lines point in another direction. They are in the style of the inscription prefixed to the *Aeneid, ille ego, qui quondam gracile modulatus avena*...which Spenser, also, imitated in the first stanza of the *Faerie Queene*, and may be rendered:
>
> *Lo, I, the man who sportingly once writ*
> *The goddess-contest on Mt. Ida's top,*

---

[1] C. F. Tucker Brooke, "A Latin Poem by George Peele (?)," *Huntington Library Quarterly* 3 (1939 - 40) 48f. This attribution was endorsed by Leicester Bradner, *Musae Anglicanae* 65.

> *The apple, Trojan fire, and rape of Helen,*
> *Harping in tutelage to Grecian Homer,*
> *Address myself to sing another theme.*

The foregoing is an accurate summary of the contents of George Peele's *Tale of Troy*, an English poem of about the same length as *Pareus*. The *Tale* was not printed till 1589, but was then published by Peele as "an old poem of mine own," and has been shown to be earlier in composition than his *Arraignment of Paris* (printed in 1584), which handles some of the same material. Peele was capable of Latin verse, though it has not been known that he wrote more than short bits in that language; he was a friend of Gager, and had been in Oxford in June, 1583, assisting in the production of two of Gager's plays. I suggest that it was Gager who arranged for the publication of *Pareus* by the Oxford Press, in a form similar to that in which Gager's odes were appearing. Gager probably revised the text and cut it to the precise limits of a sixteen-page pamphlet. There is, of course, a possibility that Gager translated the entire poem out of English verse into Latin, for that was an art in which he had much skill and practice; but in that case one would have expected Peele to publish the English original, and I doubt whether Gager was ever guilty of as bad a verse as the twelfth in this poem, *artibus, et sacro late loca fervere bello.*

Although this attribution is only noted in passing in one footnote in the biography and edition of minor poems that counts as the first volume of the Yale edition of Peele's complete works,[1] it deserves to be taken seriously: nobody

---

[1] David H. Horne, *The Life and Minor Works of George Peele* (New

has ever challenged Brooke's diagnosis. In introducing the text of *Pareus* Brooke alluded to two passages in which the author writes of himself, at the beginning and the end of the poem. He did not consider whether a third might contain a clue about the writer's identity (210 - 12):

> *nec enim verba aspera terrent,*
> *illa, quibus quondam regno demissus Ibero*
> *in nostris dulcem terris mihi laesit amicum.*

These lines are very hard to understand—they are discussed in a Commentary note *ad loc.*—but it is tempting to think that the allusion is to Peele's presumptive Oxford friend, Alberico Gentili. Mattaeo Gentili and his two sons Alberico and Scipio had been hounded out of Italy by the Inquisition, and had found temporary refuge in Austria, which because of current political alliances could reasonably be called a *regnum Iberum*.[1] Ejected from Austria, the Gentilis came to England armed with letters of introduction to the Earl of Leicester, Sir Philip Sidney, and Tobie Mathew, and through Mathew's agency he was granted an Oxford doctorate and appointed to a law tutorship (in 1587 he would be made Regius Professor of that subject).[2] At Oxford he belonged to the same intellectual and literary circle as did Eedes, Gager, and Peele. Although Peele had incepted for the M. A. in 1579, he stayed on at Oxford for two more years, during

---

Haven, 1952) 42 n. 48. Did Horne fail to evaluate this attribution because he knew no Latin?

[1] The allegation that Cardinal Como was personally responsible for the persecution of the Gentili brothers—if this surmise about the identity of the writer's nameless friend is correct—does not seem to be anything more than hyperbole.

[2] For Alberico, cf. Gesina H. van der Molen, *Alberico Gentili and the Development of International Law, his Life, Work, and Times* (2nd ed. Leiden, 1968), D. Panizza, *Alberico Gentili, Giurista-Ideologo nell' Inghilterra Elisabettiana* (Padova, 1981), and Binns, *Intellectual Culture* 338 - 57.

which time he probably wrote *A Tale of Troy*. He therefore had every opportunity of forming a friendship with Gentili. And so this passage scarcely discourages the conclusion that Peele wrote *Pareus*.[1]

Neither, of course, does it serve to confirm the attribution. But to question it one would have to suggest a plausible alternative: an Oxford man who had previously written a piece about the Trojan War. The objection that, save for scraps embedded in his vernacular works, Peele is not known to have composed any Latin poetry, is not fatal. Latin prose and verse composition was standard fare in the secondary school curriculum,[2] so any University man can be assumed to have had at least a modicum of ability at the art. Gager's 1583 tragedy *Dido*, which had to be written at remarkably short notice, shows strong internal signs of multiple authorship,[3] and Peele is known to have collaborated in the production of this play and may well have lent a hand in its writing. All in all, at least until someone can propose another possible author for the piece, Peele's responsibility for *Pareus* ought to be provisionally accepted.

---

[1] Another consideration possibly favoring attribution to Peele is admittedly subjective: some of the speeches (notably those of Cardinal Como to Parry) are fine examples of ethopoiia, such as one would expect of a writer with considerable talent as a dramatist. And the author's admission that he conceived the work in a series of Aristotelian episodes shows that he thought like a playwright, blocking out his narrative into scenes.

[2] Baldwin, *op. cit.* Vol. II, Chapter XLI.

[3] See the Introduction to this play in Volume I, pp. 247 - 9, of Gager's *Complete Works*, where Peele's involvement with the play is described. But, as I have noted in an earlier context here, the possibility that Gager's collaborator was Richard Eedes cannot be ignored.

Pareus is interesting for another reason, having to do with the foundation and early operation of the Oxford University Press.

Printing presses had existed at both Oxford and Cambridge before the 1520's, but had been closed down soon after the rift between England and Rome. The Tudors were strong on the subject of press censorship, especially on matters of religion and morals, and the Universities were regarded as hotbeds of Papists and nonconformists. Therefore the government adopted an adamant policy against academic presses. This meant that academics who desired to publish were obliged to submit to the inconvenience, and perhaps the humiliation, of dealing with London printers; for although there were printers at London who could set type in Latin, Greek, Hebrew, and even languages using more exotic alphabets, the necessity of relying on them may well have been galling to academic self-esteem.

Therefore in 1584 Convocation petitioned the Earl of Leicester, Chancellor of the University, for permission to operate a press. Such permission being rapidly granted, Convocation then voted to advance a loan of £100 to Joseph Barnes, a local bookseller and wine merchant, to set up a press, permitting him to designate himself Printer to the University and to use the University seal as his personal printer's mark.[1] Save for a broadsheet designed to flatter Leicester, Barnes' first publication was *Speculum Moralium Quaestionum in Universam Ethicen Aristotelis,* by the philosopher John Case, issued in 1585. *Pareus* and William Gager's cycle of poems about Sir William Parry presently to be mentioned appear to have been Barnes' next publications. Between then and his death in 1617, he published just about 300 books; the title of Printer to the University passed to others, and thus the arrangement continued until well into

---

[1] Or so it is usually said. Not all books issued from Barnes' press bear the seal, and the reasons for its use or non-use could perhaps be clarified by further investigation.

the seventeenth century, when Dr. John Fell employed the Clarendonian Grant to establish a press owned and operated by the University itself.

Such is the standard account of the foundation of the O. U. P., as set forth in its official history.[1] In one crucial respect this story looks incomplete, for it fails to answer what at least should be an obvious question. Why did the government suddenly reverse its long-standing policy against University presses?

Indeed, the question is even more puzzling, for until 1604 Barnes was not required to join the Stationers Company, the primary instrument by which the government controlled the printing of books. In the case of the new press at Cambridge, founded at the same time as that of Barnes, the Archbishop of Canterbury was empowered to exercise censorship, and did so on at least one occasion in what looks like a trial case designed to affirm his authority.[2] One does not hear of any similar control imposed on Barnes. Thus at one moment a press at Oxford was forbidden; then, at a stroke, one was not only sanctioned but also, evidently, exempted from any censorship at all during the reign of Elizabeth.

It is tempting to suppose that the reason for this sudden *volte-face* was a new awareness on the part of the government that University presses could play a useful role in disseminating war propaganda and organizing educated public opinion. More particularly, Eleanor Rosenberg[3] has shown how Leicester used literary patronage to foster writers who advanced his own anti-Catholic, aggressively anti-Spanish, and somewhat pro-Puritanical program. Probably Leicester and like-minded members of the government, suddenly perceived that academic presses could be put to use in the same effort, and that some sort of bargain was struck whereby, in

[1] Harry Carter, *A History of the Oxford University Press* (Oxford, 1975) Chapter II.

[2] Strype, *Annals of the Reformation* III.i 650f.

[3] Rosenberg, Eleanor, *Leicester, Patron of Letters* (New York, 1955).

exchange for permission to operate, they would agree to publish a certain amount of propaganda.

Shortly after the foundation of Barnes' press, there appeared a series of small sixteen-page pamphlets of politically-oriented poetry. These were printed anonymously in 1585 and 1586: *Pareus*; a cycle of odes (padded out with some epigrams) on the attempt of Dr. William Parry to assassinate the Queen, *In Guil. Parry Proditorem Odae et Epigrammata* (1585); a pamphlet of odes on the Babington Plot, *In Catilinarias Proditiones ac Proditores Domesticos Odae 6* (1586); and an expanded second edition of this work issued later in the same year, *In Catilinarias Proditiones ac Proditores Domesticos Odae 9*. The last three of these are demonstrably Gager's work.

It would therefore seem that in the early days of the Press Gager and Barnes had some special relationship. Further reason for thinking this is that in 1587 Gager was hand-picked by Leicester's chaplain Dr. James, the current Dean of Christ Church—which probably means by Leicester himself—to edit the University's memorial volume on the death of Sir Philip Sidney, as we know from its dedicatory epistle to Leicester.[2] This is the first of a considerable series of such academic anthologies, many of which had some distinct political or propagandistic angle. So Gager did not only write pro-Establishment poetry on national themes himself, he also extracted it from other Oxford men, assembled it, and saw it through press. Tucker Brooke has suggested that he played a similar role in the case of *Pareus*. Did Gager act as a kind of intermediary between Barnes and the University, and as the organizer of the press's propagandistic activities?

These poems appear in Volume III of *Wiliam Gager: The Complete Works* (New York, 1994) as poems II - XXVI. The grounds for attributing them to Gager are set forth in the Introduction to that volume (p. vii).

[2] *Exequiae Illustrissimi Equitis D. Philippi Sidnaei, Gratissimae Memoriae ac Nomini Impensae*; the dedicatory epistle appears in Volume IV of Gager's *Complete Works* (pp. 250 - 6).

In the dedicatory epistle to Leicester prefacing the Sidney anthology he rather mysteriously writes as if Leicester was his strong supporter, although there is no evidence that he ever enjoyed a standard patronage relationship with the Earl. What this all amounts to is far from clear, but one gains the general impression that, with the blessing of Leicester, Gager played an important role in the early days of the press. *Pareus* has interest as a further specimen of the same kind of propaganda aimed at an educated and at least largely academic readership. Of course, since works of this type appeared bearing the University seal, which lent them a quasi-official character, they also performed a secondary function of displaying the University's loyalty to the government and its policies.

Peele invented a highly effective propagandistic formula, appropriated by a number of subsequent writers. The source of this formula can be located in the infernal council at the beginning of Canto IV of Tasso's *Gerusalemme Liberata*.[1] Tasso, doubtless with Dante in mind, was responsible for creating a hybrid Pluto-Satan, described in Edward Fairfax' 1600 translation as *The ancient foe to man and mortal seed.* This Pluto, an inveterate enemy of Christianity, is distraught by the French presence in Palestine and convokes a council

---

[1] This has been observed by Leicester Bradner, *op. cit.* 38, and Walter R. Davis, *The Works of Thomas Campion* (New York, 1967), 359.

There is no need to ask whether Peele knew enough Italian to read Tasso in the original. It is likely that he read this portion of Tasso's epic in the Latin translation of the first part of Canto IV of *Gerusalemme Liberata* published by Scipio Gentili at London in 1584 under the title *Plutonis Concilium*, printed as an Appendix here.

of his followers. But he himself hatches no scheme for their ruination: he only intervenes when he is summoned by the Syrian wizard Hidroart, who seeks his counsel. Peele modified Tasso's dramatic situation to suit local English requirements, by converting Pluto into an enemy of Protestantism. At the same time, he attributes to Pluto a fertility of invention and a dynamism absent from his Italian model: this new Pluto devises his own scheme for England's subjugation and, through the agency of his lieutenant Deception, actively recruits human agents to execute his plan.

The ploy of having Pluto or one of his henchmen appear to someone in a dream has no basis in Tasso. Its inspiration comes from quite a different source. In Book VII of the *Aeneid*, Aeneas' great enemy Juno commands the Fury Allecto to fly to Italy and fill the hearts of Turnus and his mother Amata with hatred of the Trojans, and Allecto appears to the sleeping Turnus to rouse him to action: hence the war between the Trojan immigrants and the native forces of Italy. Peele adapted this narrative move to the present situation.

The reader will doubtless be impressed by the striking resemblance of the first part of *Pareus* to Milton's Latin poem on the Gunpowder Plot, *in Quintum Novembris, Anno Aetatis 17* (1626). Both poems begin with the same literary creation, introducing as ruler of the Underworld a hybrid Pluto-Satan (named Summanus by Milton), who conceives a violent dislike of the English, expressed in a ranting monologue: Satan's speech at *Pareus* 10 - 31 is quite comparable with *in Quintum Novembris* 25 - 44 in terms of both style and contents. Peele's Satanic Pluto summons Deception and bids her fly to Rome. A suitably sinister description of her journey is provided (53 - 6). In Milton Summanus makes the flight himself, coming in for a landing at the same place (45 - 7, 53). Both Deception and Summanus then appear to the sleeping Pope and plant a malevolent impulse in his mind. In Peele, the Pope sends for Cardinal Como and instructs him to find a sympathetic expatriate to assassinate Elizabeth. Milton's pontiff sends for various otherworldly agents lurking about Rome (Murder, Treason, Discord, Guile, Quarrels, Calumny, Fear, and Horror) and orders them to hasten to England and launch the Gunpowder Plot.

These resemblances between *Pareus* and *in Quintum Novembris* are sufficiently striking that we are entitled to wonder whether Milton was writing under Peele's influence. More likely, he was following what had become a traditional narrative pattern instituted by Peele and copied by a succession of later writers, the last of whom was Milton. With individual variations, these poets reproduced Peele's Protestant reinvention of Tasso's Pluto and imitate Tasso's Hellish council; most of them also appropriated Peele's plot device of having Pluto or one of his lieutenants enlist a human agent, usually the Pope, to carry out his great scheme for England's defeat. Often (although not in *Pareus*) this scheme is defeated by some manner of divine intervention, and these poems routinely end with praise of the sovereign, sometimes coupled with the advice that a harder line should be taken against England's enemies. I shall now provide brief summaries of the items in this series standing between *Pareus* and Milton's poem, in their approximate chronological order.[1]

---

[1] Two other works appear to be influenced by Gentili's translation of Tasso, and in one case by *Pareus* as well, since they contain equivalents of Pluto's aggrieved and angry speech, although they do not reproduce *Pareus'* narrative pattern: Eclogue IV from Thomas Watson's *Amintae Gaudia* (1592) and Thomas Campion's epyllion *ad Thamesin* (1595). For the influence of *Pareus* on the latter see the Commentary note on *Pareus* 339ff. Additionally, a number of works described here imitate Tasso in having Satan or a distinctly Satanic Pluto make his speech in the context of an infernal council, and it may be possible that this literary tradition exercised influence on John Donne's *Ignati Conclave* (1611). Cf. the edition of this and of Donne's parallel English work *Ignatius his Conclave* by T. S. Healy S. J. (Oxford, 1969).

1. William Alabaster's abortive attempt to write an *Aeneid* for his times, the *Elisaeis*,[1] composed prior to 1592 since it is praised by Spenser at *Colin Clout's Come Home Again* 400ff. (printed in 1595, probably written three years earlier). In Book I—all that Alabaster ever wrote—Satan gives an angry speech about the progress of the Protestant cause in England, and then goes to Rome to goad Papacy (the Church personified) into action. Papacy in turn goes to England, where she appears to the evil Bishop Stephen Gardiner in a dream and inspires him to fill the newly-enthroned Queen Mary with fear and hatred of her younger sister Elizabeth. Mary responds by having Elizabeth put under arrest, and at the end of the Book she is brought to the Tower.

2. A poem with the lengthy title *In Serenissimi Regis Iacobi Britanniae Magnae, Galliarum, Hiberniae etc. Monarchae ab Immanissima Papanae Factionis Hominum Coniuratione Liberationem Faelicissimam Carmen* Ἐπιχάρτικον by Michael Wallace (Valesius), Professor of Philosophy at the University of Glasgow, printed at London in 1606.[2] Angry at the peace and prosperity of England under

---

[1] Unprinted until modern times but preserved in manuscript form, this poem has been edited by Michael O'Connor, *"The Elisaeis" of William Alabaster (Studies in Philology* monograph 76, 1979). Its intended *Aeneid*-like character is indicated by the statement on the title page that its author proposes to write it in twelve Books and by its many strategically-placed quotations from Vergil, a number of which are pointed out in sidenotes. Thus, for example, the reader is informed that Satan's anger against England is based on the wrath of the Vergilian Juno (The historical parts of the work closely follow Holinshed).

[2] Edited by Estelle Haan, "Milton's *In Quintum Novembris* and the Anglo-Latin Gunpowder Epic, Part II" *Humanistica Lovaniensia* 42 (1993), 368 - 401.

the rule of King James, Pluto convenes a hellish council where he makes his complaint. The devil Abaddon responds with the advice that Pluto should employ the services of the Jesuits to rectify the situation. Abaddon, disguised as a Jesuit, appears at Rome, where he recruits Guy Fawkes with a speech remarkably like that of Cardinal Como to Parry in *Pareus* (175ff.), urging him to explode Parliament when the royal family is present. Fawkes complies, but the Gunpowder Plot is foiled when God perceives it and intervenes. A mysterious letter is sent to the Catholic peer Lord Monteagle; he discloses it to the government; James in his wisdom deciphers the letter, and the Plot is foiled. The poem concludes with praise of the King and an exhortation to exterminate the Anglo-Catholics.

3. Francis Herring's *Pietas Pontifica*, also printed at London in 1606.[1] Lucifer sired the devil Falsus on the Great Whore (the Church). Now that Falsus has grown to maturity, the Whore delivers a speech to him complaining about having lost England to Protestantism. She urges him to go to England to rectify the situation. Arriving there disguised as Guy Fawkes, he recruits many men to his cause, and (much like Peele's Parry) insinuates himself at Court. Ultimately he plants among his confederates the idea of blowing up Parliament; the plan goes forward until God looks down, sees it, and sends an angel to set in motion the train of events that unmasks the Plot. The poem ends with an exhortation to James similar to that of Wallace, including the advice that Anglo-Catholics should be extermi-

---

[1] Edited by Estelle Haan, "Milton's *In Quintum Novembris* and the Anglo-Latin Gunpowder Epic," *Humanistica Lovaniensia* 41 (1992) 221 - 95.

nated.

Unlike Wallace's work, Herring's poem proved popular and went through several printings and an English translation. Evidently inspired by his literary success, Herring issued a much more ambitious version in 1609, dedicated to Prince Henry, and prefaced by a long prose essay about the Plot, and accompanied by a sequel (really a Book II with a separate title), *Venatio Catholica*, about the apprehension of the conspirators. The most important alteration is that the names of Falsus and Sir William Catesby have been exchanged at a crucial point, giving to Catesby the proposal to explode Parliament, and Falsus an answering speech in praise of this suggestion. This change was presumably made in the interest of historical accuracy, for Catesby was the prime mover of the Plot. But it was ruinous to the literary effect Herring originally strove to create. Since the Plot's central idea is now hatched by a mortal rather than by the agents of Hell, Fawkes-Falsus is now demoted from a demon to the status of a minor imp and, although Herring's infernal machinery is retained, it is rendered largely pointless.

4. Phineas Fletcher's *Locustae* was originally written in 1611, put through several revisions preserved in various manuscripts, and eventually printed at Cambridge in 1627 together with a loose English adaptation entitled *The Apollyonists*.[1] Dis (whose

---

[1] Originally edited in *The Poems of Phineas Fletcher B. D., Rector of Hilgay, Norfolk* (ed. the Rev. Alexander H. Grosart, privately printed, 1869). II.3 - 58. On pp. 177 - 86 of the same volume Grosart reproduced a "spirited if somewhat periphrastic translation" by a Mr. Sterling that had appeared in a volume entitled *Miscellaneous Poems, Original and Translated by several hands, viz., Dean Swift, Mr. Parnel, Dr. Delany,*

home, interestingly, is in Virginia)[1] convenes an infernal council and complains of the lapse of Catholicism around the world. A devil named Aequivocus[2] responds by urging Dis to rely on the Jesuits. Aequivocus himself volunteers to go to Rome to inspire the Pope. There follows an excursus in which the effects of the Jesuits' subversive activities on various nations is recounted. Aequivocus comes to Rome and finds the Pope. Another excursus traces the rise of the papacy.

The Pope, himself distraught by the decline of Catholicism, convokes a council and delivers a complaining speech, placing especial emphasis on the situation in England. Inspired by Aequivocus, a senior Jesuit speaks up and advises the Pope to work by stealth. He then sketches a plan for blowing up Parliament and the royal family. This advice is greeted with cheers. The Pope agrees to adopt the plan. The Jesuit recruits the members of the Gunpowder Plot, who set about their work. God looks down, sees the crime about to occur, and sends one of His eagles down to earth to intervene. The Plot is revealed thanks to the Monteagle letter, and the poem ends with praise of God and King James.

5. Thomas Campion's *de Pulverea Coniuratione*

Mr. Brown, Mr. Ward, Mr. Sterling. Mr. Concawen and others. Published by Mr. Concawen. 1724. A superior edition, with a collation of the manuscripts, appears in the second volume of Frederick S. Boas *The Poetical Works of Giles Fletcher and Phineas Fletcher* (Cambridge U. K., 1909). I am informed that a critical edition by Estelle Haan is in preparation.

[1] Likewise Thomas Campion places his Satan in America, conceived as a mysterious oceanic island, in *ad Thamesin.*

[2] A name calculated to evoke the doctrine of Equivocation preached to the Gunpowder Plotters by Father Henry Garnet, the Jesuit Superior for England.

has recently been discovered in a Cambridge manuscript.[1] The poem is articulated into two Books that correspond in their contents to the revised version of Herring's *Pontificia Pietas* and *Venatio Catholica* in that Book I recounts the origins of the Plot, its discovery, and the arrest of Guy Fawkes, and Book II narrates the subsequent capture of the Plotters who remained at large. The principal characteristic of this work its far greater fidelity to historical fact—uniquely, Campion shows that Catesby and Percy were the head plotters and Fawkes only a demolitions expert—coupled with interesting and lifelike characterizations of the principal actors. Only the contents of Book I are relevant to the present investigation.

Satan, angry at the decline of Catholicism, calls an infernal council and delivers his now-familiar speech. A nameless hooded devil urges him to employ gunpowder to destroy King and Parliament. At Satan's instigation False Religion appears to Sir William Catesby as he is sleeping and recruits him to organize the Plot. He in turn recruits the other Plotters. They become involved with the Jesuits, who second their efforts. Fawkes is brought into the conspiracy. They make their preparations and the Plot moves forward. In a scene set at Elizabeth's tomb in the Abbey true Religion prays to God to preserve Britain from the Plotters. God responds by inspiring James to prorogue Parliament. After a delay, when the day for Parliament's convocation is at hand, God sends an angel, who delivers the mysterious letter to Lord Monteagle, James deciphers its

---

[1] It has been edited by David Lindley with the help of Robin Sowerby, *Thomas Campion: de Puluerea Coniuratione* (Leeds Texts and Monographs n.s. 10, Leeds, 1987).

meaning, and steps are taken to foil the Plot.

It will be seen that, in their several ways, each of these poems replicates narrative and thematic elements first found in *Pareus*. The commonest of these is the initial wrathful speech, in every case but one (Herring's *Pietas Pontifica*) this speech is delivered either by Satan or by a Pluto to whom distinctly satanic attributes are given. Often this harangue is made in the context of an infernal council. Satan-Pluto's anger at England then sets in train a narrative sequence, the end result of which is some sort of subversive plot launched against England and her sovereign.[1] The sequence in question often takes the form of a more or less elaborate chain reaction in which Satan-Pluto or his agent recruits the Pope or some other personification of the Catholic Church, who in turn recruits human agents to commit the wicked deed in question. In *Pareus*, and also in Alabaster's *Elisaeis* and Fletcher's *Locustae*, as well as Milton's *in Quintum Novembris*, the arrival at Rome of Satan-Pluto or his agent provides the occasion for a more or less satirical description of the Vatican and its denizens. The poems in this group often conclude with praise of the sovereign coupled with the advice that she or he should adopt a harsher policy towards England's external or internal Catholic enemies.

The similarity of these works is thematic as well as narratological. Peele invented a formula which involved the mythologization of historical episodes and the literal demonization of Protestant England's enemies, and imparted greater significance to contemporary events by making them part of an ongoing cosmological struggle between the forces of good and evil. Likewise, internal Catholic opponents to the government are portrayed as agents of Rome, itself the instru-

---

[1] In the case of Alabaster's *Elisaeis*, against her future and rightful sovereign.

ment of Satan's empire on earth. This formula invented by Peele proved remarkably successful and enduring. It is after all, a powerful one, that works by exactly inverting the claims of Britain's Catholic enemies, so that the self-professed agents of God on earth are revealed to be doing the work of the devil. Obviously, it was calculated to stimulate and give shape to the reader's paranoia by encouraging a Manichaean view of contemporary history and by manufacturing "conspiracy theories" to explain current events.

The question of the relation of *Pareus* to Milton's *in Quintum Novembris* can now be considered in its proper perspective. Estelle Haan has recently studied the interrelationship of some although not all of the relevant Latin epics written on the subject of the Gunpowder Plot.[1] Her highly interesting and illuminating exposition is incomplete, first, because did not know of the discovery and publication of Campion's *de Pulverea Coniuratione*, and, second, because she was unaware that the cluster of Gunpowder Plot poems she examined was part of a larger tradition of Anglo-Latin epic poetry with its roots in the Elizabethan period. The exact relationship of the individual items within this series remains to be worked out, and doubtless will repay further study,[2] but on the basis of what has been written two things are tolerably clear. The origin of this tradition is to be located in *Pareus*, but by the time Milton wrote in *Quintum Novembris* its narrative and thematic contents were well established. The resemblance between these two poems would appear to be generic rather than specific.

---

[1] In the earlier of her two articles cited above.

[2] I shall offer a few preliminary observations in an Appendix.

Dr. William Parry M. P. was executed in Westminster Palace Yard on March 2, 1585 (new style).[1] This put an end to the chequered career of a man who was at least accused of planning the queen's assassination. Born William ap Harry at Northop, Flintshire, Parry had something of a genius for getting in trouble. In 1570 he married a wealthy widow and thus acquired a number of manors in Linconshire and Kent. But he soon managed to squander this fortune, and rumors circulated that he had debauched his wife's daughter by a previous marriage.

Facing penury, he entered government service as a spy, and spent much time in Italy—where he could conveniently dodge his creditors—reporting on the activities of Anglo-Catholics. But his time abroad had an effect on him and he secretly converted to Catholicism. During a sojourn in England in 1580, he stabbed one of his creditors, Harry Hare, in an affray at the Temple, was convicted of burglary, and condemned to death. But because of irregularities in the trial Elizabeth commuted the sentence.

A couple of years later we find him back on the Continent, ostensibly spying once more. In fact, his Catholic sympathies were coming to the fore, and he cultivated the acquaintance of various notable English expatriates. Beginning as an advocate of greater tolerance of Anglo-Catholics, by degrees he persuaded himself that more violent remedies were needed, and was deeply impressed by Cardinal Allen's arguments that the assassination of Elizabeth was lawful. After trying, evidently without much success, to gain the support of Church authorities, he left Italy and, after passing through Paris, landed at Rye in January 1584.

Upon his return he hastened to Court, where he revealed the sensational news of an alleged plot to murder Elizabeth,

[1] The following facts are primarily drawn from the *D. N. B.* biography. Cf. the sources cited there and also John Strype, *Annals of the Reformation* III.i. 360 - 82.

invade via Scotland, and set Mary, Queen of Scots, on the English throne. In November he was elected to Parliament to represent a Kentish borough, and made sensational speeches in favor of religious toleration. Meanwhile he was conspiring with his "cousin" Edmund Neville about assaulting Elizabeth. His delays and vacillations were such that nothing came of all these conversations, and early in 1585 Neville turned Queen's evidence. In the Tower Parry first wrote a confession, then a retraction and various appeals for mercy, none of which did him any good.

Was Parry a man acting out of genuine conviction, though vacillating, or was he perhaps mentally disturbed? Although Peele represents his choices as rational and stage-managed by the Machiavellian Cardinal Como, his tendency to work both sides of the street at once are disturbingly reminiscent of the behavior of Lee Harvey Oswald in his dealings with Cubans. But if a modern does not know quite what to make out of Parry, or how seriously to take the threat he ostensibly posed, Elizabeth's government experienced no such difficulty. Here was a golden opportunity for an exercise in anti-Catholic, xenophobic propaganda, a kind of dress rehearsal for the similar exploitation of the 1586 Babington Plot that led to the execution of Mary Queen of Scots. Parry was transformed into, if not exactly a human fiend, at least the catspaw of sinister overseas forces bent on England's subjugation. This was all the more plausible and easy to do since the Prince of Orange had recently been assassinated by a Jesuit agent. This viewpoint was expressed in a pamphlet quickly printed at London, *A True and Plaine Declaration of the Horrible Treasons Practiced by William Parry*, a kind of governmental "white paper" on the subject.[1]

---

[1] Printed by C. B. at London, no date; the pamphlet largely consists of source documents (the confessions of Parry and Neville, Parry's retraction, Como's letter to Parry, and summaries of speeches at Parry's trial, linked by a disapproving narrative tissue. All the discreditable features of Parry's career mentioned by Peele (his change of name, his

Loyal subjects with a literary bent picked up the theme. The official interpretation is replicated, for example, in Holinshed's account, tricked out with a piece of contemporary doggerel on the topic that shows a similar propagandistic cooption of poetry at the low end of the literary scale.[1] Gager's volume of odes and epigrams on the subject does the same thing at a higher level, directed towards a more sophisticated kind of readership, but the viewpoints adopted by the chapman and the *doctus poeta* are exactly congruent. So too with *Pareus*. Like Gager, Peele refers to the various embarrassing episodes in Parry's past, such as his supposed incest with his step-daughter and his assault on Harry Hare; both writers even manage to hold his Anglicized surname against him. But since Peele's work is narrative by nature, he could go farther. Parry's ambivalent behavior is interpreted as the sign of a master intelligence: not his own, but that of his puppeteer, Cardinal Como. The factual basis is slender indeed. Parry had written a letter to the Pope and, when in England, received an answer from Como. The Cardinal's response was at best ambiguous. In the letter he said that he approved of Parry's intentions but, since we have no idea what intentions Parry had revealed, we cannot be sure that this letter constitutes any kind of Church approval of his assassination plans. Certainly Peele's version of events, that the Pope had been seeking a volunteer assassin, and that Parry had been recruited and pre-programmed by Como, is manufactured out of whole cloth.

The relation of *Pareus* to the governmental "white paper" just mentioned is not without historical interest. As founders of the modern British state, the Tudors and early Stuarts were confronted with a characteristic problem of national

---

profligacy, his seduction of his step-daughter, the Harry Hare affray) are touched upon, with suitable clucking.

[1] Raphael Holinshed, *Chronicles of England, Scotland, and Ireland*, printed by Henry Denham, London, 1587; cf. the London edition of 1807 - 8 (reprinted New York, 1965) IV.536f.

governments, the need to orchestrate public opinion by manipulating the written and printed word. One way in which this was done was press censorship largely achieved via the Stationers Company and the limitation of presses to London.[1] But governmental attempts to manipulate literature and presses for purposes of opinion management took a positive as well as a negative form. I have already had cause to mention Eleanor Rosenberg's study of Leicester's politicized use of literary patronage; this was a single case history of the widespread employment of patronage to elicit writing congenial to governmental views. Then too, it is probably no historical accident the issuance of governmental "white papers" designed to set forth the orthodox interpretation of current events and the licensing of academic presses occurred at the same time. Before long, by a development not entirely unrelated, the world was treated to the unusual spectacle of a pamphleteer-sovereign sitting on the British throne, avidly condescending to engage in polemical exchanges with his opponents.

If *Pareus* foreshadows similar literary effusions on the subject of the Gunpowder Plot, so too the "white paper" issued on the subject of Parry distinctly anticipated two books printed in 1606, *A true and perfect relation of the proceedings at the severall arraignments of the late most barbarous Traitors* and *A Discourse on the maner of the discouery of this late Intended Treason* (the latter printed as an appendix to James' 1605 address from the Throne). Both of these works distinctly resemble *A True and Plaine Declaration of the Horrible Treasons Practiced by William Parry*, being an assembly of documents such as confessions of the accused and prosecutorial trial speeches linked by a running narrative. It looks very much as if the white paper about Parry served as a model for later publications of the same kind.

---

[1] A strategy of limited success since both Catholic and nonconformist presses on the Continent kept issuing a steady stream of publications for English consumption.

The various Gunpowder Plot poems described above[1] stand in much the same relation to these two "white papers" as *Pareus* does to *A True and Plaine Declaration*, taking many of their narrative details from these works, as well as giving embroidered literary shape to the officially sanctioned version of events.

Pareus was printed at Oxford by Joseph Barnes in 1585. A transcription of the text has been printed by Tucker Brooke, as noted above, with no translation supplied. Otherwise it appears to have eluded any serious study. Like most of the poetry volumes issued by Barnes, *Pareus* is a rare book: the two extant copies are owned by Winchester College and the Huntington Library of San Marino, California.

---

[1] And also other Plot literature that does not conform to *Pareus'* narrative formula, such as William Gager's *Pyramis* of 1608.

AD LECTOREM

Ne quis error alicui obiiceretur, lectorem hoc loco prae-
monendum censui, me in hoc Pareo describendo summam
argumenti fideliter retinuisse; sed tamen ornatus et delect-
ationis causa ἐπεισόδια quaedam, ut Graeci vocant, excogi-
tasse et affinxisse. quod quidem et Aristotelis praecepta, et
optimorum poetarum exempla secutus feci; atque ut nihil
attexuerim, quod non esset verisimile,[1] aut ab argumenti
natura abhorreret.

1 *virisimile* lib.

TO THE READER

Lest any blame be imputed to me, I have decided that here the reader should be advised that in describing Parry, I have faithfully adhered to the general outline of events. But for the sake of elegance and delight I have invented and inserted some episodes, as the Greeks call them. And indeed in so doing I have followed the precepts of Aristotle and the example of the best poets, thus writing that I have added nothing inconsistent with verisimilitude, or the nature of my story.

Pareus

qui Phrygio quondam certantes vertice divas
et malum, Troiae cinerem, raptamque Lacaenam,
auspicio lusi vatis modulatus Achivi,
nunc aliud canere adgredior, remoque paludem
Cocyti tranare meo: iuvat alta videre   5
Tartara, et hinc saevam Parei deducere fraudem
reginam immeritam contra, gentemque Britannam.
tu mihi per dumos, atque aera lucis egenum,
Musa, praei, et pavido cunctantem dirige gressu.
    viderat inferna laetus regnator ab unda   10
affictas pietatis opes, atque omnia foedis
artibus, et sacro late loca fervere bello.
solam autem immunem scelerum cladisque iacere
insulam Oceano in magno: hic nam virginis altae
imperium, et laetos pacem florere per agros.   15
tum vero invidia mentem suffusus amara
sic secum. "meane hanc unam modo temnere gentem
numina? nec diras quicquam curare sorores?
heu sortem invisam, quid tot mihi dextra Latini
profuit Albionum in dominam iaculata tyranni   20
fulmina? quid caecae moles? quid classis Iberum?
totque ducum validae per bella horrentia vires,
si tamen hinc animos et opes interrita ducit?
mene igitur fessum, victumque residere tanto
fas erit incaepto? nostrasque impune per aras   25
mortales ierint dextrae? Plutoniaque eheu
regna tot ereptis patiar lugere trophaeis
unius ob merita, et iussum Teutheris Elisae?
consiliis, ferroque nefas hanc vincier? esto:
at fraude unius potero superare Britanni,   30
ni me fata vetant, ni mens improvida fallit."

Parry

I, who once wrote sportively of the goddesses holding their contest on the Phrygian mountain,[1] of the apple, Troy's ashes, and the abducted Spartan lass, singing under the auspices of Greece's poet, now undertake to sing another song, and to row my skiff over lake Cocytus. I crave to visit dark Tartarus, hence to bring forth Parry's savage scheme against our undeserving queen and the British nation. Pray, Muse, lead the way through the thornbrakes and the lightless air, and direct me as I hesitate with fearful step.

The ruler of the Underworld was cheered to look up from his infernal waters and see Piety's forces oppressed, to see every region widely aboil with foul contrivances and religious war. But he perceived a single island set in the great sea to remain free of crimes and slaughter: for here peace and a high virgin's reign flourished throughout the land. Thereupon, his mind suffused with bitter envy, he addressed himself: "Is this one nation to scorn my power? Have the dire Sisters no concern? Alas, unhappy fate! What has it profited me that my hand has cast so many of the Latin tyrant's lightning bolts against the mistress of the English? What of those blind masses? What of the Spanish fleet? What of so many captains' mighty strength in terrible battle, if she, undaunted, retains lives and powers intact? And so will it be allowed me to sit here, exhausted and overcome, in the midst of such an enterprise? Shall mortals lay hands on my altars with impunity? Shall I, alas, suffer Plutus' realm to be plundered of so many trophies by the efforts of a single woman, and the bidding of Elizabeth Tudor? For this lady to be defeated by steel and stratagems? Let it be so—but I shall be able to prevail thanks to the deceit of a single Englishman, if the Fates do not forbid, if an imprudent mind

---

[1] Mt. Ida.

sic ait, atque imis excita Acheruntis ab oris
evocat ad sese Fraudem. venit illa vocantis
ad nutum, et celeres per noctem concutit alas.
cui crines Lyciae fallentia colla columbae   35
assimulant, ostroque genae minioque rubescunt.
flores laeva gerit, rigidum tenet altera ferrum
veste tegens guttis maculosa, et pellibus atris,
qualis in Euboeae campis notissimus ille   40
humani generi insidias, mortemque parare,
mille notis lucet stellatus tergora serpens.
hanc ergo alloquitur Pluton, ac talibus infit.
"vade age, et hunc proprium patri fer, nata, laborem.
Romuleas, i, scande arces, atque atria nota   45
pontificis, saevumque inspira in pectora virus,
communi ut caedem maturet callidus hosti,
reginae Britonum caedem, populoque ruinam.
tu potes insidiis invictos tollere reges,
natorum et iugulo laqueos innectere patrum,   50
lethaeosque manu latices miscere marita.
i foelix, i sola meos ultura dolores."
    illa nihil contra refert, motisque per amplum
aere findit iter pennis, qua turbidus halat
Taenarus, invisique patent spiracula Ditis.   55
et tandem Ausonia nitens super astitit aede.
ut limen tetigit thalami, multoque solutum
pontificem somno vidit. sub pectora nullo
influit attactu, et circum praecordia serpit,
fraudis agens animam, fraudisque immite venenum.   60
agnovit solitam mentem, Stygiamque sororem
primo mane senex, oculosque per omnia volvit
ardentes igni, et suffusa caede rubentes.
continuo fidum custodi ad limina mandat
accersi fratrem ipse suum, tristemque colonum   65
urbis Iulaeae, quam Lari margine Caesar

does not deceive me."

Thus he spoke, calling to himself Deception from Acheron's deepest shores. She came at the behest of her summoner, plying her swift wings through the night. Her hair resembled the neck of a tricksy Lycian dove, her cheeks were reddened with purple dye and rouge. A smile played on her rosy mouth and in her shifting eye. In her left hand she bore a garland, while the other held unyielding steel, which she concealed with a blood-spattered garment and with dark pelts, just as the serpent from Euboea's fields, notorious for contriving plots against humanity and preparing its death, shines with its star-spangled back. And so Pluto addressed her, starting with these words: "Come now, child, and convey your father's special work. Go, mount Romulus' citadels and the courts of the Pope, familiar to you; breathe a savage venom into his heart, so that in his cunning he may speed the demise of our common enemy, the murder of the queen of England, the ruination of her people. By your wiles you are able to bring down invincible kings, coil fathers' nooses around the necks of sons, and mix lethal potions with wifely hands. Go, fortunate one, go, you are uniquely destined to avenge my sufferings."

She made no answer, but forged her way, her wings beating the vast air, by the route where turbid Taenarus breathes its fumes, where the vents of hateful Dis lie open. And by striving she finally alit atop the Ausonian[1] palace. As she stepped on the chamber threshold and saw the Pope plunged in great slumber, without touching him she poured herself into his breast and stole around his heart, bringing the spirit of deception and deceptions' cruel poison. At day's dawning the old man recognized this familiar spirit, this Stygian sister, and he rolled his eyes in all directions, red as they were shot with blood. Straightway he bade a guard standing at his door go fetch his trusty brother, that baleful inhabitant of the

---

[1] Roman.

181

condiderat, Graioque vocarat nomine Comum.
nec mora: iussus adest, thalamoque assistit eburno,
fausta salutantum primum de more precatus.
isque ubi consedit, tali pater incipit ore.   70
"me super Europae rebus, nostroque putantem
multa super regno, et veteri ditione meorum,
arctior in noctem pressit sopor; hic ego mentem
infusam superis aliam de sedibus hausi.
mentem, qua vires nostri heu tot per loca fractas   75
colligere imperii possim, rursumque sub alta
mole locem, unde hominum foede furor impulit audax.
unius hic animae petitur cruor, unius Anglae
excidium, neque enim ignoras, carissime, (teque
saepe meo memini mecum ingemuisse dolore)   80
Romanas ut opes sola e tot regibus ausa
proruerit, pedibusque meos calcarit honores.
quid memorem infandos ritus? turpique madentem
caede recens terram, atque appensos turribus artus
sanctorum, et pilis praefixa trementibus ora?   85
in regnis agit ista suis tamen, atque agat, opto.
(quanquam o, sed sancti, quaeso, mihi parcite manes)
quid terram petit ignotam, et sceptra extera tentat?
quid Gallos tegit auxilio, Belgamque rebellem,
et coniuratos in nostra incendia Pictos?   90
huius in auspicio, Stygiis emissa tenebris
relligio nova per terras caput altius omnes
extulit, et, ceu flamma Euro vivescit eundo.
hanc ego non validis regum, quae despicit, armis
evertam, aut caeco populi gliscente tumultu,   95
fraude nova adgrediar. ne te morer: Anglus adiret
huc aliquis modo, cui praesens in pectore virtus
adsit, et infidi mores, animique sequacis
ingenium, multusque lepos et gratia linguae,
nec bene contentum parvo, maculave notatum.   100
ambitio caeca, ac tabes exurat habendi,
ausit ut in quasvis animo procurrere formas,

Julian city founded by Caesar on the bank of Lake Larius, which he had named by the Greek name of Como. Without delay, as bidden, he presented himself and stood at the ivory threshold and, according to etiquette, was the first to wish well to the other. When he had taken his seat, the Holy Father began in such wise: "A heavier sleep than usual overcame me as I was deeply pondering on Europe's affairs, my kingdom, and my ancient authority; here I received an inspiration from Heaven, by which I can regain the powers of my empire, which (alas) have been shattered in so many regions, and place them once more under the weight of my dominion, whence men's bold madness has foully driven them. Only the blood of a single soul is sought for, the downfall of one Englishwoman. Nor are you unaware, my dearest fellow (and I recall how you have often shared my grief over this sorrow) how she alone among so many sovereigns has dared expel Roman forces, trampling my honors underfoot. Why recall her unspeakable rites, the land lately drenched with blood, Saints' limbs hanging from towers, heads on quivering spikes? But she works these things in her own realm—and I hope she may thus continue working. But (o pray spare me, blessed shades!) why does she seek alien territory and make attempts against foreign scepters? Why does she put the French and rebellious Belgium under her protection, and the Picts, sworn to our conflagration? Under her auspices a new religion, let loose from the Stygian darkness, raises its head higher throughout all the lands, lively as a flame fanned by the East wind. I shall not overthrow this woman by kings' mighty weapons, which she despises, or by the mob's blind rioting tumult. I shall attack her with a novel deceit. Let me not detain you: would that some Englishman were to approach us now, a stout-hearted fellow, having a character of bold audacity, with much charm and eloquence, not well content with little, nor branded with infamy! Let him burn with blind ambition and acquisitiveness, so he might dare hurl himself into any

ingenti precio, pulchrove inductus honore.
hunc equidem compulsum auro, palmaque virenti
in mea nunc traherem vota, et clam fraude iuberem   105
officiis illam affectans sub Tartara ferro
truderet, et metui nostro medeatur, et irae.
quod fore, ni visi in somnis me fallit imago,
et spero, adnitarque libens." sic fatur: at ille
pauca refert contra. "mecum, o pater optime, tantis   110
hoc opus insidiis, hic erit labor. exue curas,
atque omnes seclude metus: ego funera faxo
certa dolis, nec te divina insomnia ludunt."
     haec fatus, veniam poscit, propriosque penates
multa animo volvens repetit: cui munera tanta   115
committat, quibus illum animis, quibus instruat armis.
forte aderat Romae Cambrus, cui nomen Ilermo
Graecum est, antiqua missus de gente Britannum,
sed qui vix alium primo a genitore cieret.
huic facies insignis erat, praelargaque fandi   120
copia, tum varii mores, sed rebus egenis
asper, avens animus, facibusque incensus amaris
haustae vulgo ignominiae. nam coniugis olim
ipse suae natam, castos scelerans hymenaeos,
invasit, matrisque thoro geniale recepit.   125
atque idem claro maiorum sanguine cretum,
impius ante larem, patriaeque in limine Vestae,
incautum ferro iuvenem transfixit acuto.
pro quibus informi letho damnatus, Elisae
(o quid agis nimium clemens, nimis inscia Parei?)   130
servatus fuit imperio, vitaeque sibique
redditus. hunc igitur Romae tum forte morantem
Tartareus Pluton Comensi obiecit alumno.
hic vultu cunctantem hilari, blandisque vicissim
vocibus accepit, votisque ut credidit aptum   135
esse suis, paulum semotas duxit in aedes.

fancy at all, led on by hope for great rewards and fair honor. I would draw this fellow into my plans, compelled by gold and the verdant palm of sainthood so that, while feigning to do his duty to her, he would use his steel to drive her deeper than Tartarus, thus curing me of my dread and my wrath. And I both hope this will come to pass and shall eagerly strive to accomplish it, unless the vision I saw in my dream was deceptive."

Thus he spoke, and the other man briefly replied: "This work, requiring such wiles, this effort, will be done with my help, oh greatest Father. Set aside your cares, abandon all fears. By my schemes I shall assuredly accomplish her death, nor does your heaven-sent dreams deceive you."

Having thus spoken he excused himself and besought his own home, pondering much in his mind: to whom could he charge such great tasks, how to buck up his courage, with what to arm him? It chanced that present at Rome was a Welshman going by the Greek name of Ilermo, sent from the ancient nation of the Britons, but a man who would scarcely call another by his ancestral name. His appearance was distinguished, he had a never-ending fund of things to say, and his manners were compliant, but in financial adversity his mind was harsh and grasping, inflamed by the bitter torches of the public infamy he had endured. For once he had violated his own wife's daughter, defiling chaste wedlock and taking her into her mother's marriage-bed. Likewise, this impious man took his steel and ran through a youth of good blood on the threshold of the nation's Temple of Vesta. When in return for these adventures he was condemned to a disgraceful death, he was spared at Elisa's behest (oh what were you doing, too merciful, too unknowing of Parry?), and given back to himself and to life. And so Tartarus' Pluto put this fellow, who happened to be tarrying at Rome, in the way of Lake Como's child. With pleasant mien and friendly words, Como received him, albeit hesitant, and as he believed Parry to be suitable for his plan, he

mox prior haec. "nisi me multum tua nobilis ista
effigies, iuvenis, tuaque illa exordia fallunt,
haud geris absimilem tuam pulchro corpore mentem,
vulgaresve animos spiras, nec tu mihi iussus   140
femineos, aut sceptra queas imbellia ferre.
unde ego, quem tali nuper dignatus honore est
omnipotens, voluitque suis incumbere sacris:
magnum animo facinus, magnum, sed pulchrius ipsi
utiliusque tibi, atque adeo proclive volenti   145
concepi. sine me tantam spem ferre futuri,
virtutisque tuae, et nostris bonus annue votis.
illam etenim nosti, et, credo, indignaris Elisam
in summos rabie indomita, atque cupidine ferri
pontifices, et sacra Dei, ritusque parentum,   150
et nostros premere, adversos attollere coelo."
   hic autem subito ex imo suspiria Cambris
corde trahens, "equidem novi, nec gratulor," inquit.
"et me, si laevum quando mihi numen adesset,
iuravi ultorem patriae, vestrique futurum.   155
sed tu, quis tantis modus, et quae sit via coeptis,
ede, precor, venerande pater. te plurimus usus
erudiit rerum, nec te sanctissimus orbis
necquicquam summis dominus praefecit habenis.
atque equidem tales crebro sub pectore curas   160
sollicitus volvi mecum, multumque diuque
omnia versavi frustra. tum me ista parantem
facta, pavor, non supplicii, neque luminis huius,
quorum animus mihi contemptor, sed me acer habebat
inferni metus ignis, et irremeabilis orae.   165
hunc mihi, si poteris, quaeso, convelle timorem."
ille autem: "nimium, o iuvenis clarissime, vanus
te metus."inquit, "habet; tantumque hoc accipe contra,
non nos reginae pestem meditamur Elisae:
verum illi, quam regno olim Pius ipse paterno   170

gradually drew him into his private apartments. And soon he was the first to speak: "Young man, unless I am greatly misled by your noble appearance and opening remarks, you are possessed of a mind scarce dissimilar to your body, and are inspired by no ordinary spirit. Nor do you seem to me able to suffer a woman's rule or her unwarlike scepter. Hence I, whom the highest has lately enlarged with such honor, wishing me to apply myself to his holy affairs, have conceived in my mind a great crime, a great crime but one that is good and useful for you, for which reason you ought to fall in with it with enthusiasm. Allow me to offer you great hope for your future, for your virtue, and be so good as to agree to my wishes. For you are familiar with Elisa, and I imagine you are outraged by her, a woman indomitable in the flood-tide of her madness, in her zeal to use the sword to put down high Popes, God's sacraments, the rites of her forefathers and of ourselves, raising our enemies to the skies."

But at this point the Welshman suddenly issued a deep sigh and said, "Indeed I am aware and scarce happy; if a friendly spirit were to support me, I would be my nation's sworn avenger and yours. But, reverend Father, pray explain the ways and means of such great undertakings. You have been instructed by your greater experience; not for nothing has the world's most holy master placed the reins of power in your hands. I for my part have been vexed, turning over such concerns in my heart. But I have turned them all over in vain, for when I was making ready to do these things I was gripped by a great fear— not of punishment or for this life of mine (for my mind is contemptuous of these things), but fear of Hell's fire and of that shore from which one cannot row back. Free me of this fear, I beg, if you are able." And the other responded, "Oh most excellent lad, your dread grips you quite in vain. Learn this much instead: *we* are not contemplating the destruction of queen Elisa. Indeed, this was done to her by Pius, who once interdicted her from her

exuit, atque hostem iussit famulamque vocari.
immo ego te dignum coelo, sanctoque deorum
concilio hanc unam ob mentem nunc auguror esse.
quod si tam clarum incoeptum fortuna sequetur
(ut reor, et firment superi), quae praemia vivus   175
a nobis, et quanta feres! sin te atra (sed omen
in ventos disperge Deus), sin te tamen atra
sors tulerit, quali nobis donabere palma!
quam tua laus nostris semper celebrabitur aris!
nunc age, quae coeptis fuerit via tutior, edam.   180
insidiis opus esse vides, ferroque latenti;
insidiis sed non solitis, nec qualibus usi
hactenus et regni proceres regesque fuerunt,
frustra omnes: alias poscunt haec tempoa fraudes,
diversosque dolos, et non vulgaria furta.   185
tu vero, si qua est nobis prudentia rerum,
hac insiste via, atque tuo haec sub pectore fige.
non ulli te crede hominum, nullumque vocato
in partem laudis. tibi mens tua sola senatus
conciliumque esto: dubiis hanc consule rebus,   190
huc consulta refer, mutoque incide sub aere.
nec satis hoc. quaerenda via est, qua mollis in aures
influere, ac procerum possis arrepere victu,
atque ipsi te etiam dominae insinuare loquendo.
hoc duplici, aut una potius ratione tenebis,   195
si nostri simules odium, cupidumque tuorum
te fingas, dominaeque tuae. quare omnia prudens
vestiga, semperque aliquam circumspice causam,
et rape, qua fidus patriae regique putere.
quin etiam (si tanta animis constantia surgit,   200
si tantum de te fides) per mollia fandi
tempora reginae sensus tentabis, et ultro
illusum nobis, caedemque fatebere pactam.
interdumque illude volens: nam talia sanctus
ignoscit pater, et portis indulget apertis."   205
sic effatus, eum sponte haec in foedera pronum

ancestral rule and bade her be designated an enemy and a handmaid. Moreover, how I deem you worthy of Heaven and the holy company of the saints for this one scruple! And if good fortune attends this fine enterprise (as I predict, and may the powers of Heaven confirm it), what great rewards you will reap from us! But if a dark fate should take you off (God scatter this omen to the winds), what a palm we will award you! How your   praise will always be celebrated at our altars! Come now, let me explain how the path of our enterprise may be rendered safer. You perceive the need for devices, for the hidden blade—for devices, but not the usual ones, nor the kind hitherto employed by peers of the realm and by kings. Those have all proved fruitless, these times demand novel wiles, uncommon deceptions. And so, if we are to exercise any prudence, you must take this path and store these things in your heart: entrust yourself to no man, invite nobody to share your glory. Let your mind be your only forum and council chamber. Consult it about uncertain matters, report your decisions there, and inscribe them on its silent brass. But this is not enough. A way must be sought by which you may gently gain her ear, steal your way into her courtiers' routine, and insinuate yourself into your mistress' conversation. You will cling to this duplicitous, or rather this *single* program, if you feign hatred for us and pretend to be most zealous for your fellow citizens and for your mistress. Wherefore you must shrewdly examine each sign, each issue, and seize the means by which to be thought loyal to state and sovereign. And indeed (if such great constancy, if such trust in you grows in their minds), by gentle occasions for talk you will make trial of the royal attention, saying you have been tricked by us and confessing a plot for her murder. And all the while be willing to deceive her. For the Holy Father forgives such things and indulges them, Heaven's gates remaining open." Thus saying he enmeshed

impulit, accepitque fidem, scelerisque tabellas
liventi spuma, sanieque obsignat et angui.
  hic ego te porro, fraudum caput, impie cultor
arguerim Comi (nec enim verba aspera terrent,   210
illa, quibus quondam regno demissus Ibero
in nostris dulcem terris mihi laesit amicum:
ten' ait, o iuvenis, ten' amentissime, patrum
purpureos ausum calamo strinxisse galeros?)
verum ego compellem porro te: quid petis istis   215
saeve modis? num regna pia florentia pace?
anne caput sacro perfusum regis olivo?
proh crudele nefas, uno Pacisque Fideque,
et ducis et populi cervicem abscindier ictu!
at non ille pii pastor gregis, et sacer omnium   220
interpres, cuius frater mentiris et haeres,
haec docuit, vobisque dolos in morte reliquit.
non generis vestri princeps urbisque creator
talis erat, talesque suos amet esse colonos.
hunc etiam (priscis si quicquam credere dignum est   225
carminibus vatum, et curant mortalia manes)
Elysio in nemore, aut umbrosa valle sedentem ingemere,
et tales nunc credam fundere questus.
"hei mihi non liquido auspicio, ductosque sinistra
urbis avi muros, quam ferro barbara quondam   230
evertit manus, et duro disiecit aratro,
non sine dirarum precibus vocum, et sale multo.
atque utinam segetes illis, et gramina campis
nunc etiam starent, nec tu foedissime noster
audires tanta pollutus labe colonus.   235
nunc petis insontem furto ferus. anne ego magnos
Albionas sic quondam adii? primusque Quiritum
reclusi populo? quum me Neptunia ab imis
ira excita vadis classemque haurire pararet,

---

211. *dimissus* potius legendum?   218. *unon'* lib.   219. *ictu?* lib. I   pro
Fideque vid. Comm not.

the eager youth in this compact and received his pledge: he signed the contract for this crime with livid foam and snake's blood.

At this point, you leader of schemes, you wicked citizen of Como, I will further accuse you (nor do these harsh words daunt me, these words by which he, having been sent from Spanish territory, worked harm to my sweet friend in this country—did he say that you oh youth, oh great fool, dared wound the Fathers' red caps with your pen?), I shall go yet farther and press you: what are you attacking by these savage means? A realm flourishing with sacred peace? The anointed head of a ruler? Ah, the cruel crime, That with one blow you strike at the neck of Peace, Loyalty, sovereign and state? But the shepherd of your pious flock,[1] the holy interpreter of all things, whose brother and heir you feign to be, did not teach you these things, bequeathing you treachery in assassination. The head of your race, the founder of your city,[2] was not that kind of man, not the sort to wish his citizens to be such. If the songs of the old poets are trustworthy, and if the shades have any concern for our mortal affairs, I even believe him to be sitting in the Elysian grove, in that shadowy vale, moaning and issuing such complaints as these: "Alas, how a barbarian's hand once used steel to overthrow this city's walls, erected with ill auspices and sinister omens, plowing them under with a harsh plow, not without dire curses and much salt! Would that crops and grass stood in the fields in their stead to this day! Then, most foul inhabitant, polluted with such ignominy, you would not be so bold. Now you savagely seek out an innocent woman with your blade. Thus have I ever visited great Albion? Did I thus reveal her to the people of Rome? When, roused out of her oceanic waves by wrath, she made ready to destroy me and my fleet, I dodged the threat and raised my standards

---

[1] Numa Pompilius.
[2] Julius Caesar.

191

evasi tamen, atque adverso littore signa,   240
caeruleam contra pubem, currusque tremendos,
constitui, multum et limo luctatus, et unda.
hic ego vi vera, et socium virtute Britannos
aggresus vici, ac iussis parere coegi.
quin etiam placidas pacis conversus ad artes,   245
Troigenum populo, demissaeque ab Phryge gentis,
imposui, gaudens cognato sanguine, regem.
cuius nunc solio divam, sceptroque potitam
perdere per summum tendis scelus. o utinam tu
exilio, virgisque fores multatus, et ulmo,   250
non novus ille alter civis Comique meusque
Aemathii qui causa mihi non ultima belli.
quid queror? aut quisquam nostris hos sedibus ortos
Romanosve putet? nostra occidit, occidit ingens
gloria, et Italiae fatis desedit iniquis."   255
sic ait illachrimans, et se luco abdidit alto.
at Pareus turpi perfecto foedere laetus
(o infanda caput fleturum) moenia Romae
deserit, et duras Ligurum trans avolat Alpes.
donec Sequania Gallorum constitit urbe.   260
hanc sibi fallendo sedem legit: hic sibi multos
relligione viros, patriaque adiungit eadem.
horum animis furtim illabi, sanctusque videri
magnarumque capax rerum, cui credere tuto
omnia, et arcanos possent committere sensus.   265
ipse animi catus, et levi mage lubricus angui,
Anglorum primis, regni rerumque magistris
cuncta aperit, quae rem summam spectare videret
consilia, atque ipsam dominam. fraudemque retecta
fraude tegit, scabrisque viam, quo mollius iret,   270
sentibus obducit, clypeo, quam vulneret, armat.
    iamque ubi se charum patriae, fidumque potenti

against her woad-smeared youths and her huge war chariots, struggling greatly with her marshland and water. At that time I attacked the Britons and overcame by genuine might and the valor of my allies, compelling them to heed my commandments. And then, having converted them to peace's tranquil arts, I imposed a king on this Troy-born folk, a king of the race descended from Phrygia, rejoicing in a kindred blood-line. And now you are attempting to destroy a queen on his throne, mighty with his scepter, by the worst of crimes. Oh, would that you would be punished with exile, scourges, and the elm, not that other new citizen of mine, and of Como, who was not the ultimate cause for Emathian war for me. Why do I complain? Or who imagines these people to be Romans, sprung from my home? My great glory and that of Italy has faded, faded thanks to the unfriendly Fates."

Thus he tearfully spoke and hid himself in a deep pool. But Parry, glad that the foul pact had been struck (oh you fellow, destined for unspeakable lamentations!) departed the walls of Rome and flitted across the Ligurians' harsh Alps until he established himself in France's Paris. He chose this as headquarters for working his deception, and here he joined to himself many men of his same religion and nationality. Being adroit at managing great affairs, he was able stealthily to insinuate himself into their minds and appear holy, the sort of man in whom they could safely place all their trust and reveal their inmost thoughts. But he, shrewd and more slippery than a gliding snake, revealed everything to the leading men of England and the magistrates of the realm, the counsels he saw to be aimed at England's most vital concerns and at the queen herself. And by revealing one deception he concealed his own, he made his path through the rough brambles so that it would go the smoother, he armed England with a shield designed for her wounding.

And now, after he had portrayed himself as loving towards

reginae finxit, nec quicquam obsistere vidit
imbelles praeter curas, animique pavorem,
huc reditum parat, et magnis insuescere coram   275
insidiis optat, nexosque expandere casses.
solvitur infoelix, infaustaque alite navis,
et tandem patriis hominem deponit in oris.
ille pedem titubans fulva prolapsus arena
dicitur, et capiti corvi obstrepuisse loquaces: 280
"quo tendis, miser, o miser? hic te dira manebunt
supplicia, et laeva tetigisti littora planta.
hic tibi pro tali scelere, atque immanibus ausis
praemia iusta dabunt superi, quum carcere tetro
eductus humili ad mortem raptabere crati;   285
quum tua terribilis laqueo colla impia lictor
inseret, impelletque cruci, nodoque reciso
semianimem distendet humi;quum viscera cultro
discludet; quum cor trepidum vivo, atque videnti
eruet, impingetque oculis, ignique cremabit,   290
membraque sanguineo manabunt dissita tabo."
  ille nihil casus, obscaenarumque volucrum
omine commotus, fatalem pergit ad urbem,
quam quondam Brutus Thamesini fertur ad amnis
florentes ripas, udoque in gramine campi,   295
Ilio ab incenso profugis posuisse colonis,
et patriae dixisse novam de nomine Troiam.
forma antiqua manet, periit nomenque genusque.
parva olim, nunc Anglorum domus ardua regum,
et totum penitus fama celebrata per orbem.   300
haec nunc te recipit, Pareu, natosque laremque,
coniugiumque tibi reddit, neque redderis illi
exul adhuc, aliasque animo proiectus in oras.
  saltem incusanti similem, similemque precanti
aspiceres patriam. "quid de te, perfide Pareu,   305
sic merui? patriaene adiges in viscera telum
crudelis? neque enim telo, quam credis, Elisam

his nation and loyal to his puissant sovereign, and saw no obstacle in his way save for cowardly cares and a mind's fear, he prepared his homecoming from Paris, hoping to become a familiar figure in the midst of this great scheming and to cast his nets more widely. So his unhappy ship cast off with its ill-omened sail, and at length deposited the man on his ancestral shore. And he, catching his foot, fell headlong on the sand. Some raucous crows are said to have screeched: "Where are you headed, you poor, poor man? Here dreadful punishments await you, and you have alighted on shore with your left foot. Here the powers of heaven will give you the rightful rewards for such a crime, for your monstrous undertakings: when on a lowly hurdle you will be conveyed from a dark cell to your execution; when the dread hangman throws the noose over your impious neck and makes you mount the scaffold; when he cuts the rope and stretches you out on the ground, half-alive; when he takes his knife and lays bare your guts; when he shows you your beating heart as you are still alive and able to see, then burns it in his fire; then your lopped-off limbs will drip with gore." But he, undeterred by his fall or the foul birds' prophecy, hastened towards the fatal city which Brutus is said to have founded by the flowery banks of the river Thames, on grassy marshland, for refugee settlers come from fire-ravaged Ilium, naming it Troynovant after his homeland. Its ancient shape remains, though its original name and population have perished. Once it was small, but now it is the high home of English sovereigns, world-famous. Now, Parry, he received you, she who had given you sons, a hearth, and a wife. But you had not repaid her, being until now an exile, cast by your own choice on foreign shores.

Indeed, you could have seen your nation accusing you in this wise, in this wise beseeching you: "How have I thus deserved of you, traitorous Parry? Are you cruelly planting your sword in your nation's bowels? Your are not, as you

appetis, aut unum duces in funere corpus.
illa quidem superis celsum caput inseret astris,
unde genus ducit, perque omnia viva feretur   310
ora virum, victrix meritis atque auspice fama.
illa tuas coelo furias spectabit ab alto,
horrentes facibus furias, atrisque colubris.
ast ego tam dulci genetrix orbata parente
(namque parens est illa mihi) lugubria rursum   315
(quod potius nostros omen vertatur in hostes)
fata feram, canibusque dabor laceranda Latinis,
quae nunc flaventi frugum redimita corona
purpureos vultus sub candida sidera tollo,
orbis amor, saeclique auro florentis imago.   320
mene petis? per ego has auras vitamque, meo quas
hausisti primum gremio, per numina tantum
damnatura scelus, fundoque ultura sub imo,
parce precor, parce: haud duro de semine quercus
te genui, Hircanave alui Britannia tygri.   325
fallor? an invitum maior, fatique rapit vis,
et male vitatas expendes sanguine poenas?
sic eat o potius, nostro quam terra cruore
manet, et immeritum letho caput, improbe, sternas."
has equidem credo voces nunc patria Pareo   330
mitteret, ipsa loqui Pareo si patria posset.
sed quid verba iuvant, animos ubi caeca peredit
proditio, et scelerum coquitur mens impia flammis,
assiduoque vias infanda ad crimina versat?
ergo aut nobilium mensas, coetusque virorum   335
arripit insinuans, summisque in rebus agendis
versatur. quid lentus Arar, quid cogitet Ister,
quidque pater Tyberinus, et auro flavus Iberus,
et qua cunctorum tacitis Nereius undis
occurrat Thamesis, fluctusque infringat apertos,   340

fancy, making an attempt against Elisa with this weapon, or striving to bring a single body to the grave. She indeed will raise her head high to the stars, whence she derives her lineage. She will be borne before the faces of all mankind, triumphant in her accomplishments and high renown. From on high she will witness the Furies hounding you, Furies horrid with their torches and black snakes. But I, who created you, bereft of such a sweet parent (for she is my parent) shall for my part suffer this lugubrious fate (but this omen would better be turned against our foemen), I shall be given over to Latin hounds for the rending, I who now raise aloft my rosy countenance under the shining stars, girt with a golden crown of my crops, the world's darling, the image of our age that flourishes with gold. Are you making an attempt on me? I pray you by this breath of life, this existence which you first enjoyed while on my lap, by the gods, bound to condemn such a crime and to avenge it by thrusting you beneath Hell's foundations, spare me, pray spare me. I did not give birth to you as an oak, grown from a hard seed, nor did I, England, nourish you with the aid of a Hircanian tiger. Am I deceived, or does the overwhelming power of fate seize you against your will, and will you unfortunately pay with your blood ill-avoided penalties? Oh, better abandon this, rascal, rather than have our land drenched with blood and lose your worthless head in death."

I imagine the nation would have such things to Parry, had she been able to address him. But what help is there in words, when purblind treason destroys a man's senses and his impious mind is burned by the flames of evildoing, industriously placing him on a path that leads to monstrous crimes? Thus he insinuated himself at the dinner-tables of the nobility and the congregations of men, becoming involved in high matters of state. What the sluggish Saône or the Danube were thinking, or father Tiber, or the Ebro, tawny with gold, and the means by which the oceanic Thames might counter the silent currents of each or shatter

mille suo volvens aeratas flumine puppes,
omnia nec Pylio peius, nec Pallade narrat.
aut placidis animum studiis oblectat, et ipsas
invisit iuvenum choreas, mollesque Caemoenas,
inque dies tota volitans nitet aureus aula.   345
saepe etiam humanam dictis adgressus Elisam,
grandibus aut monitis, aut dulci detinet ore,
obsequioque fidem, nec inani pignore firmat.
namque illam fertur, cultos dum sola per hortos
pubentes legeret formoso pollice flores,   350
talibus affatus Pareus: "fuge gramina velox,
heu fuge, diva; latet tumidus sub floribus anguis."
  sic ait, atque anguem dextra protendit, ut uda
(pontificis signum) cera, levique papyro
alte pressus erat. videas ardere veneno   355
turgentes oculos, trifidisque micantia linguis
ora, et sublatam squamosa in tergora caudam.
illa iocum risit, causamque petivit eiusdem.
cui Pareus: "fidei, fidei cape pignora nostrae,
en," ait, et caedem diram, nomenque resignat   360
purpurei patris, et promissa ingentia pandit.
obstupuit subito, turbataque pectore virgo est.
non secus, ac, caulas cum vespertinas oberrat,
audito visoque lupo, tremit artubus agna
illa licet clathris, et amica septa canum vi,   365
sic virgo, quamvis circum sit fusa corona
fidorum procerum, Latii praedonis ut atras
auribus insidias oculisque micantibus hausit;
extimuit tamen, et placida sic voce locuta est.
  "at tu sanctorum custos mitissime regum,   370
si iustis regno imperiis, si pectore puro
te colui, semperque colam, si nescia falsi

---

349. *nanque* lib.   365. i. e. *clatris* (nisi error typotheti)   366. *quanvis*
lib.

their undisguised waves, swirling their myriad gilded hulls
in its riverine current—all this he recounted no less ably
than a Nestor or an Athena. Or he would bewitch the mind
with his quiet pursuits, being present at the young men's
choruses, the gentle Muses, daily shining golden throughout
all the Court. And often he made his suit to our kindly Elisa
with his conversation, detaining her either with important
warnings or with his sweet address, affirming his devotion
by his humility—no empty pledge, for Parry is supposed to
have said to her such things as these, as in her solitude she
was in her well-ordered garden, plucking the blossoming
flowers with a comely thumb: "Swiftly flee the grass, divine
one, alas, flee! A puffed-up snake lies concealed beneath the
flowers."

Thus he spoke, and produced a snake in his hand, impressed in wax (a Papal seal!) on a thin sheet of paper. You
could see its bulging eyes glittering with poison, its mouth
gleaming with a forked tongue, and its tail raised above its
scaly spine. She laughed at his joke, and inquired of its
meaning. And to her Parry made reply: "Lo, receive these
pledges of my faith." And he spoke of foul murder,
mentioning the name of the purple-clad Father, and
disclosed monstrous pacts. Of a sudden the virgin fell silent,
disturbed of heart. Not otherwise than when a lamb at
eventide roams through her fold, and at the sight of a wolf
trembles in her limbs, albeit she is protected by fences and
the strength of the sheepdogs, so the virgin, though ringed
about by trusty lords, nevertheless grew afraid as she
absorbed the Latin thief's plots; with her ears and flashing
eyes, she grew afraid and thus she spoke with her tranquil
voice:

"But You, most kindly Protector of pious sovereigns, if I
rule by a just government, if I have worshipped You with a
pure heart and always shall, if our religion, ignorant of

te colui, semperque colam, si nescia falsi
relligio, positis hominum templa incolit aris,
si non digna fero, penitusque insueta, neque ullum
aut sceleri locat ille modum, aut mansuescere novit,   375
huc ades o, meque infando, pater, eripe letho,
eripe, et Ausonii telum perfringe latronis.
tu vero, tali lucis pro munere, Pareu,
non unquam mihi parvus eris, nec tempore in ullo
immemorem meriti tanti maerebis Elisam ."   380
    dixit, at ille suum dictis mitescere pectus
praesensit, dulcemque animis illabier auram.
nec iam se duro divae tam mollia ferro
rumpere membra velit. manibus namque effluat ensis
conanti timet, et pavidos stupor alliget artus.   385
nec tamen incaeptum penitus dimittere possit.
unde aliquem sibi sufficere, atque asciscere tantae
decernit fraudis socium, caedisque ministrum,
oblitus Comi monitorum, artisque Pelasgae.
ut qui nubiferam demens attingere rupem   390
exesum per iter quaerit, dum proximus imo
correpit pendetque solo, securus et audax
urget opus miserum. postquam subnisus in altas
est cautes, et summa manu fastigia prensat,
tum vero subita mentis vertigine raptus   395
in praeceps ruit, et scopulis revolutus acutis
purpuream effundit disiecto corpore vitam.
sic Pareus, ubi res summam deducta sub oram est,
defecit trepidus, coeptisque audacibus amens
excidit, atque animam sparsos super edidit artus.   400
fama est, cum socio pepigisse haec foedera Cambrum
Nevilio,. ipse aditus molles causasque morandi
praeberet per pura suis violaria rivis,
quo cum regina crebro secedere suetus.
ille latus furtim ferro recluderet atro   405
virgineum, et mediis moribundam linqueret herbis.

falsehood, maintains churches with the established altars of mankind, if I suffer unworthy and altogether strange things, and if that man puts no limit on his wrongdoing, or learns to moderate himself, then be present, Father, and rescue me from an unspeakable death; rescue me and shatter the Ausonian bandit. And you, Parry, in exchange for your gift of life, will never in my sight be paltry, nor will you ever have cause to complain that Elisa is forgetful of such a favor."

She spoke, and he felt his heart melting at her words, a sweet breeze wafting into his spirit. Nor did he any longer crave to rend asunder the divine lady's soft limbs with his hard steel, for he feared that the sword would slip from his hand as he made the attempt and paralysis would bind his terrified limbs. But he still could not complete abandon his enterprise.

Wherefore, forgetful of Como's admonitions and Greekish cunning, he decided that some ally and partner in murder must aid and abet such a great scheme. Like a fool who aspires to climb to some cloud-bearing pinnacle by an eroded path, while he stays at ground level boldly and self-assuredly presses his ill-starred endeavor, but after he has scaled the heights and is clutching at the summit, his mind is overwhelmed by sudden vertigo and he plunges headlong and, tumbling down the jagged cliffs, spills out his crimson life's blood, his body torn asunder, thus Parry, when the matter was brought to the verge, grew fearful and failed. Out of his mind, he recoiled from his bold enterprise, yielding his quartered limbs as well as his life. The story goes that our Welshman struck a bargain with his confederate Neville, that he was to arrange an easy encounter at the undefiled violet-beds along his streams, where he had often been accustomed to retire with the queen. Neville was to plunge his blade stealthily in her virginal side and leave her to die among the flowers. And Parry was to expostulate: "Where is your wickedness leading you?" And at the same time,

clamaret Pareus, "quo te scelus abripit?" una
evasuro illi mortem intentaret, et ensem.
et fors mactasset prudens, sanctisque dedisset
manibus inferias, factum ut crudele lateret,   410
principis et magnus clareret sanguinis ultor.
quicquid erat, postquam capiti res turbida coepit
et timida esse suo, multis impellere dictis
est socium, multisque minis adgressus, acerbum
maturaret opus: corrumpi talia namque   415
cunctando, longoque animos languescere tractu.
aut si tam eximiae laudis caeptique pigeret,
vadat, et in tutas celeri trabe naviget oras,
seque metu indicii, se mortis liberet aura.
ille autem, seu mentem egit terrorve Deusve,   420
seu strinxit patriae dominaeque cadentis imago,
iam non stare loco patitur, sed foedere rupto
prosilit, indiciique volans prior emicat albam
ad metam, summoque haerentem carcere linquit
mactandum prodens immiti Parea letho.   425
haec finis fraudum, hic illum tulit exitus aevi.
   at vos, qui late Europam ditione tenetis,
et finem miseris optatis ponere rebus,
obtestor, tenuis magnos; si vestra per arva
Romani auspicio flagrum Bellona tyranni   430
sanguineum quatit incedens, populosque quietos
arma iubet rapere, et fines vastare beatos,
si fraudes, saevique doli, medicataque viru
pocula, et intenti vestris cervicibus enses,
si quicquid miseri est usquam, si quicquid acerbi,   435
hinc prodit, totoque (malum) diffunditur orbe.
foedere quin iuncto hanc, paribusque invaditis unam
urbem animis? ut quondam acies Telesinus oberrans,
Marsus homo, et magnis Samnitum ductor in armis,

---

407. *abripis* lib. | *unaque* lib.

drawing his sword he was to make an attempt on Neville as he sought to escape. And perhaps in his wisdom he would have killed the man and given him as a sacrifice to the blessed shades, so that the foul deed would remain concealed and he would gain great distinction as the supposed defender of the royal blood. However it transpired, after the confused affair took on the aspect of a capital crime, yet one fearful for its own existence, with many speeches and threats Parry pressed his friend to hasten the bitter task, for such things are undermined by delay and spirits grow faint-hearted if things drag on. Or if he was ashamed of great praise and of this enterprise, let him take a swift ship to safe shores, thus freeing himself from fear of betrayal and the shadow of death. But Neville, either because terror or God affected his mind, or because he was moved by a vision of his nation and his falling mistress, would not allow this business to continue. Rather, he broke his word and hastened to be the first to attain the shining goal of turning Queen's Evidence, leaving Parry marooned in the deepest of dungeons, by his betrayal dooming him to be hacked apart in pitiless death. This was the end of his deceptions, this ending of his life took him off.

But you, who hold Europe under your widespread dominions and hope to put an end to these miserable affairs, I appeal to you, a humble man addressing the great: if under the auspices of that Roman tyrant Bellona strides through your fields, brandishing her bloody scourge, bidding your peaceful citizens snatch up arms and lay waste to your happy territories; if plots, savage schemes, cups tainted with poison, and swords are aimed at your persons; if there be any suffering, any hardship, it emanates from this source (oh the evil!) and spreads throughout the whole world. Why not form an alliance and, being of like mind, assault this single city? Just as Telesinus prowled the battle-line, a man of the Marsi,[1] a

[1] An Italic tribe.

dicitur haec multum Roma iactasse sub ipsa: 440
illa dies, qua Romae arces, qua corruat ingens
imperium: vos has latebras, silvasqueluporum
libertatem Italae praedantum excindite gentis.
non alia illorum vobis vitare licebit
incursus. agite, et tutos prohibete receptus." 445
haud aliter (nec tu magnis frustrabere votis,
nec fas) Europae clarae gens, inclyta bello
progenies, non Romulidas, arcemque superbi
imperii, sed bustum atrum virtutis, et illos
fraudum invade specus, regnataque vulpibus antra. 450
non alius dabitur finis, requiesve malorum.
tuque o magnanimum virgo sata sanguine regum,
Europaeque decus, quam fata ad tanta reservant
munera, trigeminos curru subiunge leones,
sublimisque incede tuis stipata Britannis, 455
et tandem invictum coelo caput effer aperto.
tunc ego felici praecinctus tempora lauro,
per medios Italum populos tua dicere facta
adgressus, numerisque sacros memorare triumphos,
venturo forsan vates tuus audiar aevo. 460

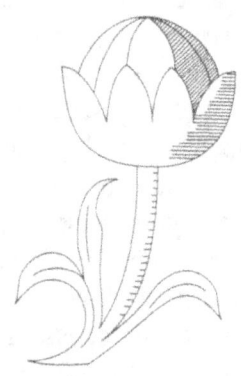

great Samnite battle-leader, and is said to have boasted thus beneath the very walls of Rome: "Come now, comrades. Now the appointed day is at hand on which Rome's citadels, her wide empire must fall. You must destroy these lurking-places, these forests belonging to wolves who despoil the race of Italy of its freedom. Not otherwise will you be permitted to avoid their incursions. Come, deprive them of their safe refuges." In no other wise, great race of Europe, famous children of battle (for you will not be cheated of your high hopes, nor will this be allowed), you must assault, not the people of Romulus and the capital of a proud empire, but rather Virtue's dark pyre and the caverns of deception, caves governed by foxes. No other ending will be granted, no other respite from these evils.

And you, oh virgin born from the blood of great-minded kings, glory of Europe, reserved by the Fates for such high responsibilities, hitch triple lions to your car and advance, encircled by your British subjects; at length, raise your invincible head under a clear sky. Then I, my temples girt with the gladsome laurel, undertaking to proclaim your achievements among the peoples of Italy, and recall your sacred triumphs in my verses, in after years perhaps shall acquire the reputation of being your bard.

Commentary

1ff. The beginning of *Pareus* is modelled after the alternate proem of the *Aeneid* preserved by Donatus and Servius:

> *ille ego, qui quondam gracili modulatus avena*
> *carmen, et egressus silvis vicina coegi*
> *ut quamvis avido parerent arva colono,*
> *gratum opus agricolis, at nunc horrentia Martis*
> *arma virumque cano...*

3 Homer, of course.

8 Peele was perhaps thinking of Statius, *Thebais* IV.804f.:

> *illi per dumos et opaca virentibus umbris*
> *devia.*

10ff. This passage is modeled after Ovid, *Metamorphoses* 787ff., in which Envy catches sight of Athens:

> *illa deam obliquo fugientem lumine cernens*
> *murmura parva dedit successurumque Minervae*
> *indoluit baculumque capit, quod spinea totum*
> *vincula cingebant, adopertaque nubibus atris,*
> *quacumque ingreditur, florentia proterit arva*
> *exuritque herbas et summa cacumina carpit*
> *adflatuque suo populos urbesque domosque*
> *polluit et tandem Tritonida conspicit arcem*
> *ingeniis opibusque et festa pace virentem*
> *vixque tenet lacrimas, quia nil lacrimabile cernit.*

17ff. In a general way, this speech is modelled on that of indignant Juno at Vergil, *Aeneid* I.37ff., which begins:

> *mene incepto desistere victam*
> *nec posse Italia Teucrorum avertere regem?*
> *quippe vetor fatis, Pallasne exurere classem.*

19f. Cf., perhaps, Ovid, *Metamorphoses* II.61, *qui fera terribili iaculatur fulmina dextra.*

28 There seems to be no classical basis for the epithet *Teutheris*. Evidently it is merely a poetic form of "Tudor."

35 Peele was probably thinking of Lucretius II.801 - 5 (but why state that the dove was a Lycian one?):

> *pluma columbarum quo pacto in sole videtur,*
> *quae sita cervices circum collumque coronat;*
> *namque alias fit uti claro sit rubra pyropo,*
> *inter dum quodam sensu fit uti videatur*
> *inter caeruleum viridis miscere zmaragdos.*

39 Since Deception is described as looking like a raddled old whore, perhaps *pellibus atris* are grubby furs.

40ff. This epic simile is slightly defective insofar as such a comparison would normally have a verb for Deception that would match *lucet* for the snake. The points of comparison are obviously that a.) both Deception and the snake were deceptively attractive and b.) both were enemies of humanity.

40 Presumably the beast in question is the great serpent killed by Cadmus at the Castalian Spring, who in one versions of the myth was Draco, the son of Ares. Cf. Robert Graves, *The Greek Myths* § 58 (g).

41 In my translation I assume *parare* is epexegetic, to be construed with *notisssimus.*

46 Cf. Ovid, *Metamorphoses* VIII.819, *seque viro inspirat*. This echo indicates that the operation Deception is about to perform is based on the rather similar one of Famine (at the bidding of the offended Ceres) in Ovid when she visits the sleeping Erysichthon (*ib.* 815 - 22):

> *peragit perque aera vento*
> *ad iussam delata domum est, et protinus intrat*
> *sacrilegi thalamos altoque sopore solutum*
> *(noctis enim tempus) geminis amplectitur ulnis,*
> *seque viro inspirat, faucesque et pectus et ora*
> *adflat et in vacuis spargit ieiunia venis;*
> *functaque mandato fecundum deserit orbem*
> *inque domos inopes adsueta revertitur antra.*

54 It was thought that there was an entrance to the Underworld beneath Mt. Taenarum in Laconia. This and the next line are suggested by Seneca, *Hercules Furens* 662 - 7:

> *Spartana tellus nobile attollit iugum,*
> *densis ubi aequor Taenarus silvis premit;*
> *hic ora solvit Ditis invisi domus*
> *hiatque rupes alta et immenso specu*
> *ingens vorago faucibus vastis patet*
> *latumque pandit omnibus populis iter.*

58 The Pope in question is that great enemy of Protestantism and champion of the Jesuits, Gregory XIII.

65 Tolomeo Galli, Cardinal Como, "the first papal secretary of state in the modern sense" (J. N. D. Kelley, *The Oxford Dictionary of Popes*, Oxford, 1986, 271). Peele presumably is using *fratrem* figuratively (as is suggested by the use of *frater* at 221), if he was not confusing Cardinal Como with Gregory's nephew Filippo Cardinal Boncompagni, who was responsible for administration of the Papal States.

67 According to Strabo, *Geography* V.213 Julius Caesar in effect refounded Comum (Como) by settling three thousand veterans there. Strabo implies that the name of the town was derived from *komos*, the Greek word for "village."

84f. Peele is no doubt thinking of the English habit of publicly displaying the heads and limbs of traitors executed by the process he describes below.

90 I. e. Presbyterian-dominated Scotland.

93 Peele was evidently thinking of the image at Horace, *Odes* IV.iv.42 - 4:

> *ut Italas*
> *ceu flamma per taedas vel Eurus*
> *per Siculas equitavit undas.*

97 Cf. Vergil, *Aeneid* V.363f.:

> *si cui virtus animusque in pectore praesens,*
> *adsit.*

106f. Cf. *Aen.* IX.496, *invisum hoc detrude caput sub Tartara telo.*

117 This detail is evidently Peele's invention: no contemporary source I have seen mentions any such pseudonym.

119f. I. e., he would not call a son of his by his father's name, since he had changed his name by Anglicising it from ap Harry to Parry. In one of his printed epigrams on Parry, William Gager also twitted him on this name-change (poem *XI.1 - 4):

> *cui patris obscurum nomen, genus, omnia, mater*

> *plane ignota foret, ni notha nata foret.*
> *Parry sibi nomen finxit, patris illud ap Harry*
> *non placuit.*

120f. Cf. Vergil, *Aeneid* XI.378, *larga quidem semper, Drance, tibi copia fandi.* It appears to have been commonly agreed that Parry was a man of considerable parts. Gager's verdict (poem V.51f.) was to include him among that category of men,

> *cuicunque dotes dii dedere*
> *ingenuas, pietate cassas.*

121 Cf. *Aeneid* VIII.365, *rebusque veni non asper egenis.*

123f. Gager also alluded to Parry's seduction of his daughter-in-law, and likewise to his attempted murder of Harry Hare, in poem III (25 - 31):

> *quis iste mos est, barbare, virginum*
> *libare saevo pectora vulnere?*
> *privigna sensit mitiorem*
> *cum gravidam tibi ferret alvum.*
>
> *praelusit olim pugio qui tuus*
> *in creditoris sanguine subditi*
> *iam victimam spernens minorem*
> *imperii caput expetebat.*

125 *Geniale* is the alternate ablative form.

126ff. In 1580 Parry had stabbed Harry Hare, a creditor who was suing him, in the Temple. In this context I scarcely know how to translate the fancifully Romanizing *ante larem.*

Gager also made this episode the subject of an epigram

(poem *VII):

> *non explere sitim poterat tibi sanguinis Harus,*
> *sanguine reginae quod cupis esse satur?*
> *in leporem quicquid poteras audere, leonem*
> *irritare tua non sine morte potes.*

130 Parry's royal pardon was the subject of Gager's poem
*VIII:

> *usuram vitae damnato quae dedit, illi*
> *usurum vitae, quam dedit ipsa, negas?*
> *sic bene latrones faciunt: qui liberat illos*
> *carcere, latrones experietur eos.*

167ff. The arguments in this passage are written to echo
those advanced by Cardinal William Allen in *The True,
Sincere and Modest Defence of English Catholics* (1584); in
his confession, Parry admitted to having been inspired by
this work. Its contents are summarized by Claire Cross, *The
Royal Supremacy in the Elizabethan Church* (London - New
York, 1969) 62 - 4.

170 Cardinal Como alludes to Pius V's decree of 1570
placing England under interdict, and pronouncing anathema
on Elizabeth. This papal bull released English Catholics
from their obligation of loyalty to their sovereign and imposed on them the duty of opposing her. Its text is given in
translation by Cross, *Royal Supremacy* 152 - 54.

189 The conceit of convoking a private mental senate is
taken from Plautus, *Epidicus* I.ii.56, *Mostellaria* III.vii.158,
and *Miles Gloriosus* II.ii.41. It also figured prominently in a
comedy produced at Cambridge in 1581, Edward Forsett's
Pedantius (IV.i), that seems to be echoed in a couple of Oxford works emanating from the literary circle to which Peele

belonged, William Gager's tragedy *Meleager* (1582) and Richard Eedes' *Iter Boreale* (as suggested in Commentary notes on lines 170, 495. 497, and 530 of that work).

211f. As stated in the Introduction, these lines seem to refer to the expulsion from Austria of Peele's friend and a prominent contemporary Oxford figure, the Humanist and legal scholar Alberico Gentili. But they are somewhat obscure, since they refer to an unknown incident, and also because the book's *demissus* is hard to understand; it is not unlikely that we should *dimissus*. Then they would mean that somebody was sent from Spain, or at least from Spanish-held territory, to do some kind of injury to Peele's friend.

Evidently this unnamed man got in trouble for writing a tract against the Church hierarchy. The item in question may have been Gentili's *de Papatu Romano Antichristo Assertiones ex Verbo Dei et SS. Patribus* preserved in the D'Orville ms. in the Bodleian Library and signed *Alberico Gentili Italo*, but I have not had the opportunity to see this work and so cannot confirm this surmise. (In 1603 all of Gentili's works were placed on the Index.)

213f. The meaning of these lines is not exactly self-evident: perhaps it refers to the second expulsion of Catholicism upon the death of Queen Mary.

218 The book's reading *Fideque* can be retained according to the assumption that this is the alternative form of the genitive found at Ovid, *Metamorphoses* III.341 etc.

220 Numa Pompilius, Romulus' peaceful successor, established Rome's religious institutions and was the first Pontifex.

225f. Caesar was deified after his death; the allusion to "ancient bards" probably refers to the account of his apotheosis at Ovid, *Metamorphoses* XV.746ff.

246f. Geoffrey of Monmouth and other writers fostered a tradition that New Troy (London) had been founded by a Trojan refugee, Brutus, the grandson of Aeneas, who was thus the eponymous hero of Britain.

250 Eutropius, *Breviarium* vii.ix, described the Roman method of executing traitors: *quae poena erat talis, ut, nudus per publicum ductus, furca capiti eius inserta, virgis usque ad mortem caederetur, atque ita praecipitaretur de saxo.* I would suppose that the elm mentioned here supplies the *furca* in which the traitor's head is inserted.

251f. *Non novus ille alter civis Comique meusque / Ae-mathii qui causa mihi non ultima belli* requires a bit of un-ravelling. *Aemathii...belli* refers to the Civil War between the forces of Julius Caesar, the refounder of Como (cf. the Commentary note on line 67) and Pompey, brought to a conclusion at the battle of Pharsalus. For *Emathius* (lit. "Thessalian") referring to Pharsalus cf. Lucan I.688 and Silius Italicus, III.400. The speaker is therefore saying, in ef-fect, "Caesar was not the final cause of civil strife in Italy; therefore you deserve punishment more than he did."

261f. In his confession Parry stated that during his Parisian sojourn he had recruited the Anglo-Catholic expatriates Thomas Morgan and Lord Fernehurst as members of a plot to assassinate Elizabeth and set Mary Queen of Scots on the English throne: *A True and Plaine Declaration* pp. 8 and 10.

280 Perhaps this admirably wierd scene was suggested to Peele by the popular ballad *The Three Ravens* (Child no. 24), although admittedly Child's evidence for this ballad is distinctly later than Peele's time.

282 For a classical example of this superstition cf. Petronius, *Satyricon* xxx.5.

305ff. The idea of allowing personified England to deliver this speech is derived from Cicero's *First Catilinarian Oration* xi, a passage introduced by the words *etenim si mecum patria, quae mihi vita mea multo est carior, si cuncta Italia, si omnis respublica loquatur.*

325 Peele was of course thinking of a famous passage from the *Aeneid* (IV.364ff.):

> *nec tibi diva parens generis nec Dardanus auctor,*
> *perfide, sed duris genuit te cautibus horrens*
> *Caucasus Hyrcanaeque admorunt ubera tigres.*

337f. Each of these rivers represents its nation; thus Parry discoursed on the policies of France, Austria, Italy, and Spain, and how England might counteract these.

339ff. These lines seem to have suggested the conclusion of Thomas Campion's *ad Thamesin* (printed 1595), in which the nymph Thames raises the Armada-destroying storm.

349ff. This scene is invented by Peele; it is included both for its symbolic value (the snake-sealed document Parry proffers is as bogus as the assassination threat he reveals to the government, and there may be an insinuation that Parry is the proverbial snake in the grass), and also to show that Elizabeth was wont to walk in gardens with Parry, the setting in which he planned to murder her (cf. 402ff. with the Commentary note *ad loc.*).

352 Cf. Vergil, *Eclogue* iii.93, *o pueri (fugite hinc!), latet* *anguis in herba.*

363ff. Compare the beginning of Gager's poem III:

> *quales columbae vulturis unguibus*
> *vix liberatae, faucibus aut lupi*
> *iam nuper ereptae, pavores*
> *esse solent trepidantis agnae,*
>
> *tales Elisae pectora candidae*
> *sensere nuper vulturis et lupi,*
> *mortisque pulso vix timore*
> *agna pavet trepidatque turtur.*

Both poets seem ultimately indebted to Ovid, *Metamorphoses* VI.527ff.:

> *illa tremit velut agna pavens, quae saucia cani*
> *ore excussa lupi nondum sibi tuta videtur,*
> *utque columba suo madefactis sanguine plumis*
> *horret adhuc avidosque timet, quibus haeserat, ungues.*

365f. In poem V Gager is more explicit about this same point (41ff.):

> *sic bellicosum Clinton avum refert*
> *Lincolniae spes, iamque patri aemulus.*
> *cum fratre Gualterus Roberto*
> *sic minor et Devereux patrizat.*
>
> *quos inter omnes syderis in modum*
> *fulget Philippus (grande equitum decus)*
> *Sidneius, et vires Elisae*
> *ingenii vovet atque dextrae.*

216

367 Like the *Ausonius latro* in line 377, the *Latius praedo* is of course the Pope.

370 Cf. Gager's poem IV.13, *Iupiter regum pater atque custos*. This line epitomizes a good deal of contemporary thinking about the nature of kingship.

379 Cf. Vergil, *Aeneid* IX.256, *meriti tanti non immemor umquam*. Peele presumably knew William Gager's *Meleager* (1582), in which Atalanta says (921f.):

> *ubicunque vivam, nullus oblitam tui*
> *meriti videbit, nullus ingratam dies.*

381ff. This sequence of events and the motives attributed to Parry and Neville are manufactured by Peele. The documents printed in *A True and Plaine Declaration* (including Parry's own confession) do not mention Elizabeth promising her favor to Parry or any resulting vacillation on his part; nor is there any testimony that Parry recruited Neville as a means of bucking up his own courage. Quite to the contrary, Edmund Neville's account of the way Parry had enlisted him seems to attest his resolution (*Declaration* p. 8) was *Not long after viij or x dayes (as I remember) Parry comming to visit me at my lodging in Herns rents in Holborne, as he often used, we walked foorth into the fields, where he renewed againe his determination to kill her Maiestie whome he saide he thought most unworthie to live, and that he wondered I was scrupulous therein.* A remark by Parry in his own confession shows that Neville was scrupulous, not about regicide in principle, but merely about its methodology (*Declaration* p.18): *Master Nevil hath (I thinke) forgotten that hee did sweare to me at divers times...that though hee woulde not lay hand upon her in a corner, his hart served him to strike off her head in the fielde.* But there is an undeniable historical truth to Peele's inventions: by their own admission, the two conspirators discussed the Queen's assassination over the space of no less than five months without achieving anything, and so it is likely that one or both of them was guilty of irresolution. Quite likely Neville peached on Parry out of fear that Parry was about to do the same to him (this is hinted at 423 below), and was all too eager to blacken Parry by representing him as more decisive than he actually was.

383f. Cf. Gager's poem III.21ff.:

> *crudele mentem robur et aes triplex*
> *communiebant et ilices tuam,*
> *tam molle pectus cum parabas*
> *horribili terebrare ferro?*

389 For *artisque Pelasgae* (i. e. the arts of Greek treachery) cf. Vergil, *Aeneid* II.106 and 152.

390ff. This simile may have been inspired by the fate of Oeneus in Act V of Gager's *Meleager* of 1592. Cf. 1849ff.:

> *est turris alta, cuius e fastigio*
> *caelo videtur proxima ostendi via,*
> *despectat omnem regiae partem domus.*
> *furibundus hanc conscendit, et tanquam manus*
> *inferret astris, inde pulsurus deos,*
> *dissiluit amens, pondere illisum iacet*
> *deforme corpus.*

402ff. Edmund Neville (1560? - 1618), Parry's "cousin," co-conspirator, and ultimate betrayer. There is a life in the *D. N. B.* In his confession he stated that the plan was to murder Elizabeth in a Thames-side garden and then escape by barge (though in his own confession Parry alleged that they had planned to make the attempt while she was riding in St. James' Park). Cf. *A True and Plaine Declaration*, pp. 9 and 18 respectively. If the interpretation of the subjunctives in 405ff. is right, in Peele's version Parry was to act so as to conceal his guilt after the assassination. (The quotation marks in 407 are inserted in accordance with this understanding.)

407 One could also retain *abripis* and put *scelus* in parentheses as an expostulation like *malum* at 436. *Unaque* could stand according to the understanding that it is hypermetrical, but such lines seem uncommon in Anglo-Latin verse of the period.

427ff. Similarly, the last of Gager's subsequent cycle of odes on the Babington Plot (poem XXV) is addressed to the Protestant rulers of Europe. It begins:

> *salvete reges, progenies deum*
> *et certa proles, imperium quibus*
> *caelo secundum, vestra virtus*
> *et superi faciles dederunt:*

> *servate cauti sceptra, satellites*
> *fidi coronent, proditio furit.*
> *en sanguinis vestri nefanda*
> *quae subiit sitis hauriendi?*

438ff. Telesinus was a Samnite general during the Social War in the early first century B. C., who fought a battle against Roman forces led by Sulla near the Colline gate. Velleius Paterculus, *History of Rome* II.xxvii, calls him *vir domi bellique fortissimus penitusque Romano nomini infestissimus*. His speech is an expansion of that reported by Velleius: *circumvolans ordines exercitus sui Telesinus dictitansque adesse Romanis ultimum diem vociferabatur eruendam delendamque urbem, adiiciens numquam defuturos* *raptores Italicae liberatis lupos, nisi silva, in quam refugere solerent, esset excisa.*

460 If this sentiment represents anything more than immodest rhodomontade (as thought by Tucker Brooke, in a passage quoted in the Introduction), it perhaps indicates that, like William Alabaster after him, Peele briefly entertained the idea of writing a Great Patriotic Epic in the Vergilian manner.

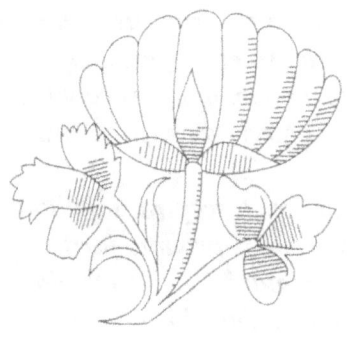

The exact relationship between the various poems enumer-
ated in the Introduction is a subject that no doubt deserves
further investigation. Here I offer only a few observations to
supplement Estate Haan's 1992 article on the subject.[1]

Michael Wallace's *in Serenessimi Regis Iacobi...* and
Francis Herring's *Pontificia Pietas* are so similar in conception, structure, narrative strategy, and particular details, that
one must have been written with awareness (and to a large
extent in imitation) of the other. Hence one of these two
poets must have been the first to adapt Peele's formula to the
new situation of the Gunpowder Plot. But which was written
first? Both are dated 1606, but neither was registered with
the Stationers' Company and so we are denied the evidence
that would allow us to settle the issue beyond doubt. One
consideration appears to suggest the priority of Wallace's
work. He Latinizes Guy Fawkes' surname as *Fauxius*, while
Herring employs the form *Falsus*. The direct transformation
of Fawkes into *Falsus* is neither natural nor self-evident,
but makes good sense if a pun on the French *faux* is involved.[2] So it would appear that Wallace created this initial
bilingual pun, so that Herring's *Falsus* is a secondary elaboration on it. To the extent that this observation is valid, it is
probably safe to assume that Wallace's work is the earlier;
the most important of Herring's alterations is the introduction of a strong Puritanical coloration (it may have been this,
as well as the simplicity of his Latin, that made his work so
popular).

At lines 27f. of Wallace's poem, Pluto summons his

---

[1] Michael O'Connor also discusses the relationship of some of these
works in introducing his edition of Alabaster's *Elisaeis*.

[2] Fawkes is also called Faux in *The Apollyonists*, Phineas' Fletcher's
English version of his *Locustae*, although in the Latin work he uses different punning etymologies of the name (618ff.).

council:

> *infernosque furens ad limina tetra ministros*
> *concilium crudele vocat.*

So Pluto convokes his council at Gentili's *Plutonis Concilium* 11f.:

> *imperat horrendum prima intra limina cogi*
> *concilium, et toto manes Acheronte cieri.*

And likewise at Thomas Watson's Sixth Eclogue from *Amintae Gaudia*, 34f., we read:

> *nec mora, lucifugos ad regia limina coetus*
> *imperat acciti.*

Wallace describes James' reign as a new Golden Age in a passage that begins (43ff.):

> *illius auspiciis en aurea nascitur aetas,*
> *en antiqua redit pax et concordia mundo.*
> *en pietas et cana fides iam libera passim*
> *incedunt, nostraque canunt de plebe trophaea.*

Compare Pluto's alarm at the prospect of a new Golden Age to be precipitated by Elizabeth's birth at Watson's *Sixth Eclogue* 28ff.:

> *ille dies olim divae natalis Elisae*
> *non prius illuxit, quam decertantia pridem*
> *sydera virtutes concordi pace ligabant*
> *oppositas, atque omne novice aspectibus astrum*
> *aurea venturo spondebant tempora seclo.*

The ultimate model for such passages is Vergil, *Eclogue* iv.

Cf. particularly 4ff.:

ultima Cumaei venit iam carminis aetas;
magnus ab integro saeclorum nascitur ordo.
iam redit et Virgo, redeunt Saturnia regna.

The conception of Phineas Fletcher's *Locustae* is sufficiently similar to that of the poems of Wallace and Herring that its author must be presumed to have been familiar with both works. Indeed, the alternative title *Pietas Iesuitica* itself serves to establish familiarity with Herring's *Pontificia Pietas*. On the other hand, the poem begins with an infernal council such as had been portrayed by Wallace, whereas there is no equivalent scene in Herring. Though he might have acquired this idea directly from Tasso (perhaps with a little help from John Donne), there is no similar ambiguity about the indebtedness of his demon Aequivocus to Wallace's Abaddon, a character conceived in very much the same way, and who performs exactly the same function in the story (Campion introduced a similar, unnamed character in his equivalent passage in *de Pulverea Coniuratione* I.75ff.). Likewise, the description of the House of Parliament and the prospective session there, coupled with the speaker's advice about blowing it up at 554ff. resembles *in Serenissimi Regis Iacobi* 202ff. rather more closely than the equivalent passage at *Pontificia Pietas* 168ff. Therefore Fletcher seems to have been familiar with both earlier printed Gunpowder Plot poems. At least in its final form, his work may perhaps be described as an embroidery on those of his two predecessors, with a great deal more interest in showing how the Plot fit in with the strivings of the international Jesuit octopus, and a healthy admixture of satire.

In *de Pulverea Coniuratione* Thomas Campion's insistent denial (II.13ff.) that there was any unusual portent on the night of November 4 - 5, especially one of a celestial nature, invites interpretation as a response to, and quite likely as an implied rebuke of, Wallace's description of a solar eclipse at *in Serenissimi Regis* 279ff. Other signs of familiarity with that workare visible. Campion's nameless hooded Jesuit who advises Satan that Parliament ought to be blown up (I.96ff.) bears a strong resemblance to Wallace's Abaddon, as do the speeches these two figures deliver. Second, Campion's pun on the name of *Ignitius* Loyola at I.305 is borrowed from line 159 of *in Serenissimi Iacobi.* An outburst of indignation at the Plotter's misuse of the rite of Communion at I.282ff. looks like an elaboration on a similar expostulation by Wallace (255f.).

Catesby's speech at I.184ff., in which he reproves a confederate for being insuf-ficiently daring and stresses the need to wipe out the entire royal family, rather than just James, appears modeled on Falsus' similar advice at Herring's *Pontificia Pietas* 148ff. Other details suggest familiarity with that work. The description of Fawkes' trip to Belgium in May 1605 (I.563ff.) finds a match in Herring's poem (116ff.) but is not mentioned in that of Wallace. The unhistorical detail (I.679f.) that the pretext for searching the Whynniard house (whence the Plotters tried to drive a tunnel into Parliament's cellar) was to hunt for some garments that had been stolen from Queen Anne looks indebted to *Pontificia Pietas* 355f. The same may be true of the expression of anxiety that the Abbey might have been damaged in the explosion (II.30ff.), for Herring gives voice to a similar fear (250f.). More generally, the articulation of Campion's poem into two Books resembles that of Herring's expanded second two-Book version. For although Herring gives each portion of his work its own title, it is really a continuous narrative in two parts. The first deals with the hatching of the Plot and the arrest of Fawkes, and the second with the fate of the rest of the Plotters. It is probably no accident that Campion distributes his material according to the same scheme. Though the two works are quite different in detail (Herring's sequel is much more mythologized and, like its predecessor, is largely devoted to anti-Catholic rhetorical excursions) they both contain some parallel episodes: Digby's feigned hunt, and the fate of the Plotters when run to earth at Holbeach by a sheriff's posse.

Like Fletcher's *Locustae*, therefore, albeit in a very different way, *de Pulverea Coniuratione* is an expanded and elaborated rewriting of these two works. In part, this was accomplished by the addition of a welter of additional heavenly and infernal interventions in the course of the story. But the chief new ingredient was a new fidelity to the historical record, coupled with far more detailed and realistic characterizations of the Plot's *dramatis personae*.

Ever since Grosart broached the idea, it has frequently been written that Milton's primary source of inspiration was Fletcher's *Locustae* and perhaps his accompanying *The Apollyonists*.[1] At first sight this idea seems no more than fatuous, inasmuch as Fletcher's volume was not printed until 1627.[2] But plenty of Elizabethan and Jacobean literature circulated in manuscript form, and so the possibility that Milton read this Cambridge work cannot be excluded on *a priori* grounds.

But there are more substantial reasons for rejecting Grosart's theory. There are no obvious verbal echoes or

---

[1] In his edition of Fletcher's complete poetry, I.cccxviii. This is made in the course of a long essay largely devoted to arguing that Milton reflected Fletcher's works in *Paradise Lost*, a claim that need not be considered here. Milton may of course have read *Locustae* and *The Apollyonists* after they had appeared in print.

[2] Grosart tried to anticipate this objection by alleging that "Flecher's poems were published in 1626- 27...and in truth the coincidence of date goes far to shew that the young poet had instantly possessed himself of the volume." But Fletcher's volume is unambiguously dated to 1627, i. e. not prior to March 25, 1627, because the old style calendar was in force, whereas Milton celebrated his eighteenth birthday on December 9, 1626. By the minimum possible reckoning, therefore, Milton must have completed his poem no less than three months before *Locustae* appeared in print.

close imitations of the sort that have allowed the conclusion that Fletcher and Campion had read and learned from the previous Gunpowder Plot poems of Wallace and Herring. And some of the narrative components in Milton's poem are familiar from others in the series under discussion, but are either not to be found in Fletcher or at least not only in Fletcher. In short, Milton's poem bears a certain resemblance to that of Fletcher, but his similarity looks generic rather than specific. I do not think there is any detail in *in Quintum Novembris*, large or small, that is indisputably indebted to *Locustae*. While the possibility that Milton had read this work prior to its publication cannot be disproven, it is hard to think of any way in which the poem would necessarily have been different if Fletcher had never put pen to paper.

It might seem most probable that he would have read works already printed, Wallace's, Herring's, or both, and this possibility can scarcely be excluded. But the strongest points of specific resemblance in fact involve Alabaster's *Elisaeis* and Campion's *de Pulverea Coniuratione*. There is, after all, nothing more far-fetched in the idea that Milton read these works than in the suggestion that he read Fletcher's *Locustae* in manuscript, as he would have had to do. All three poems are of Cambridge provenance.

When Milton's infernal Summanus overflies England and looks down on the white cliffs of Dover (25f.), this replicates the similar view seen by flying Papacy at *Elisaeis* 294f. Other narrative features may very well have been inherited from Alabaster. In introducing *Pareus* I pointed out that there is a plot move devised by Peele and adopted by Alabaster, in which there is a kind of chain reaction beginning with Pluto or Satan, involving either the Pope or at least Papacy personified, and ending with the recruitment of a human agent to do the crime in question. In both poems a rather satirical description of the Vatican is combined with this narrative sequence. Herring employed a rather simplified derivative of this same pattern, but Milton replicates it in a more fully developed form, linked to a description of Rome. The most economical explanation is that he acquired this from Alabaster. In their edition of Milton's poetry Carey and Fowler pointed out the indebtedness of Milton's description of the hideous place to which the Pope summons his agent (139ff.) to Vergil's description of Hell gate surrounded by personified abstractions (*Aeneid* VI.273ff.), imitated by Spenser at *Faerie Queene* II.vii.21ff.[1] Alabaster— demonstrably a friend of Spenser—imitates the same model, with some quite similar details, in his description of Papacy's home at *Elisaeis* 153ff. and the picture of the interior of St. Peter's at *in Quintum Novembris* 60f. resembles that given at *Elisaeis* 203ff.

Hope's bedside speech to Catesby at *de Pulverea Coniuratione* I.162ff. bears a strong resemblance to Summanus' similar speech to the Pope at *in Quintum Novembris* 92ff., considerably more so than the beginning of the only other bedside speech in this series of poems, Alabaster's *Elisaeis* 346ff. When Deception appears to the sleeping Pope in Peele's *Pareus* there is no speech, and the poems of Wallace and Herring do not contain equivalent scenes. And the monkish disguise adopted by Summanus at *in Quintum Novembris* 79ff. distinctly recalls the appearance of the nameless hooded fiend of *de Pulverea Coniuratione* I.85ff.; the physical resemblance is considerably closer to this figure than to Wallace's Abbadon or Fletcher's Aequivocus.[2]

It also seems possible that Milton had read Campion's *ad Thamesin*. This is suggested in the first place by the evident echo of *ad Thamesin* 7, *deus aetherea qui fulminat arce*, at 167 (*despicit aetherea dominus qui fulgurat arce*). Likewise,

---

[1] *The Poems of John Milton* (edited by John Carey and Alistair Fowler, London - New York, 1968).

[2] It is well known that the disguised Summanus is described in language borrowed from the verbal portrait of St. Francis in George Buchanan's *Franciscanus* I do not think this excludes my suggestion.

Milton's description of the tower of Rumor at 169ff. is rather in the style of Campion's Spenserian emblematic creations in that poem: the House of Dis, the House of Avarice, and the Fountain of Envy. His employment of *Hesperia* to denote Spain rather than Italy at 102 is Campion's evidently idiosyncratic usage in both poems (*ad Thamesin* 60, 96, 129, 134, 214, 239, *de Pulverea Coniuratione* I.43, I.249, I.395). But here I must admit that my knowledge of Anglo-Latin literature of the period is scarcely exhaustive, and in the absence of any kind of relevant lexicon I cannot readily verify the truth of this suggestion.

Scipio Gentili (1563 - 1616) was the younger son of the physician Mattaeo Gentili of Castello San Genesio, Ancona. Because of their Protestantism, Mattaeo and his two sons Alberico and Scipio were obliged to flee Italy in 1572. Settling temporarily at Leibach in Austria, they were expelled from there too. Scipio remained on the continent, where he attended the universities at Tübingen and Wittemburg. Then he received an appointment as Professor of Ancient Law at Altdorf. But he must have visited England repeatedly, for he published a series of volumes of Latin poetry at London between 1582 and 1585:[1] renditions of Psalms in Latin hexameters,[2] two translations of selections from Tasso, and *Nereus*, an original poem on the birth of Sir Philip Sidney's daughter Elizabeth (1585). The present short volume is prefaced by an epistle dedicating the work to Sir Philip as a New Year's present (*strena*) and thanking him for the kindness and favor extended both the writer and his brother. Then Gentili presents the first eighteen and a half stanzas of Canto IV of *Gerusalemme Liberata* in Latin hexameters, without

---

[1] Biographical notices about Scipio assert that he stayed on the Continent and acquired a university education in Germany, though he issued this series of small poetry volumes in England in the early 1580's. Binns, *Intellectual Culture* 346f., stated that he lived in England at that time, citing no authority for this assertion, and van der Molen, *Alberico Gentili* 51, wrote that he often visited Alberico in that country, and hence made Sidney's friendship. One or the other of these assertions must be true, but I have been unable to locate anything remotely resembling an adequate biography. The fullest account seems to be the article in the *Allgemeine Deutsche Biographie* VIII.576f., which pays no attention to his literary activities and makes no mention of his English connections.

[2] Poetic paraphrases of Psalms constituted a recognized genre: Thomas Watson did some, now lost, probably in Latin, and Sir Philip Sidney in the vernacular.

imitation of Tasso's eight-line stanzaic scheme. In terms of religious bias, as in other ways, the translation is quite straightforward and faithful. Nor, despite Gentili's Protestant faith, in his dedicatory epistle does he recommend any kind of sectarian reading of the poem.

Tasso's Pluto is compounded from the like-named god of the classical pantheon and the fallen angel Lucifer. As the result of defeat in a previous war against the Olympian gods,[1] he has been branded a rebel and is now consigned to the Underworld where he rages with jealousy, nurses his grudge, and plans a new rebellion. Obviously, therefore this figure is a conflation of the Pluto of classical mythology and the Christian Satan. The degree to which Tasso was influenced by Dante in creating this figure is of no immediate concern for us: it is sufficient to observe that by means of Gentili's translation (and latterly thanks to Edward Fairfax's 1600 translation into English), Tasso introduced him to England. This Satanic Pluto reappears in *Pareus* and many of the poems belonging to the Anglo-Latin epic tradition begun by Peele, including Milton's Summanus. The dictum of the eighteenth century scholar and poet Thomas Warton about *in Quintum Novembris* is frequently quoted,[2] "this little poem, as containing a council, conspiracy, and expedition of Satan, may be considered as an early and promising prolusion of Milton's genius to the *Paradise Lost*." In his important study of this work, Macon Cheek spent considerable effort in pointing out that in several important aspects the Summanus of *in Quintum Novembris* foreshadows in embryonic form our poet's subsequent conception of Satan. As

---

[1] The classical prototype for this earlier episode is the revolt of the giants against the Olympian gods and the ensuing war in which they were defeated: Robert Graves, *The Greek Myths* (New York, 1955) § 35.

[2] Thomas Warton, *Poems upon Several Occasions, English, Italian, and Latin, with Translations, by John Milton* (2nd ed., London, 1791) 497.

he put it,[1]

> ...if one were asked to name the three concepts
> most basic to the character of Satan as he is finally
> portrayed in *Paradise Lost*, he could perhaps find
> none more fundamental than the three following:
> first, the exile from heaven, the fallen arch-angel,
> that is, and, since fallen into a state "where peace
> and rest can never dwell," the forever restless one,
> the eternal wanderer; second, the eternal envier and
> willful destroyer, hating all who possess that state
> of peace and rest which he once knew but can never
> know again, and inasmuch as he can never hope to
> regain it determined that all others shall lose it; and
> third, the wily plotter, "the artificer of fraud," who
> works through deceit to conspiracy and then exe-
> cutes his conspiracy of destruction "under the fair
> pretense of friendly ends." And though but briefly
> sketched here, and with a few lines only for each,
> these are essentially the three chief qualities of
> character which Milton gives this early Satan of the
> "In Quintum Novembris," two of the three indeed
> being couched in phrases which in slightly modified
> form were to carry over into *Paradise Lost*.

Cheek supported these generalizations with a series of detailed observations: "the lines which bring [Summanus] first
into the poem introduce him as the *regnans Acheronte
tyrannus* and, in almost immediate juxtaposition, as the
aethereo vagus exul Olympo thus establish him from the beginning in that dual role of 'Hell's dread emperor' (*Paradise
Lost* II.510) and 'Heav'ns fugitive' (*PL* II.57), an idea in

---

[1] Macon Cheek, "Milton's 'In Quintum Novembris': An Epic Foreshadowing," *Studies in Philology* 54 (1957) 184f. Cf. also his observations about Satan's aerial flights and views from high places in *Paradise
Lost* at 179ff.

paradox, which, though not further developed here, is at the root of all his *Paradise Lost* soliloquies, and a major motivation behind much of his action there. And here, as there, it makes of him the restless wanderer (p. 181)." He also drew such verbal comparisons as 10f. (*dinumerans sceleris socios, vernasque fideles, / participes regni post funera moesta futuros*) with *P. L.* I.571, *Their number last he sums*, and *P. L.* I.606, *The fellows of his crime, the followers rather*, and 16f. (*et quoscunque videt purae virtutis amantes, / hos cupit adiicere imperio*) with *P. L.* V.110f. (*by thee at least / Divided Empire with Heav'ns King I hold*) and *P. L.* IV.121, *Artifcer of fraud*). The Miltonic Satan's literary pedigree is of course rich and complex, but to the extent that Milton drew on previous works in the Anglo-Latin tradition of epic written on episodes of more or less contemporary history initiated by Peele, the portraits of Satan and the satanic Pluto in this series of poems would appear to constitute an important strand in his ancestry, with Gentili's translation of Tasso standing in the background.

Gentili's translation was printed at London by John Wolfe in 1584, and, as far as I know, has never been reprinted. I therefore take the present opportunity to place the text on the record.

PLVTONIS CONCILIVM

ARGVMENTUM

Bello sacro, Christiani pene iam omnem materiam fabricandis machinis
bellicis, quibus Hierosolyma oppugnaretur, in nemore proximo succider-
ant, molemque prae caeteris maximam contexuarant. quod Pluton cum
vidisset, veritus ne continuo urbs caperetur, statuit obviam ire. concilium
itaque fingitur daemonum suorum coegisse, orationemque habuisse, qua
eos ad Christianarum legionum perniciem ultimam cohortatus est.

talibus Hesperiam coeptis insistere pubem,
nigrantem in sylvam liventia lumina torquens
prospexit Pluton: iamque altam surgere molem,
iam pugnare viros, studiisque afflictus ovantum,
labra sibi, palmasque furens utrasque momordit.   5
ac veluti taurus ferro male caesus ad aram
mugitus ciet horrificos, sic ille dolore
infremuit, gemitumque alto de pectore rupit.
inde animis horum in seram conversus iniquis
perniciem pestemque virum, per muta locorum   10
imperat horrendum prima intra limina cogi
concilium, et toto manes Acheronte cieri.
demens, qui superum regi se conferat, et se
posse putet fixas fato convellere leges,
nec memor et quanta ille suos iaculatus in hostes   15
fulmina vi quondam fuerit, quibus arserit iris.
iamque vocans atri cives tuba ferrea regni
murmure Tartareo mugit, quo protinus Orci
intremuit domus, et vastae insonuere lacunae.
nec sic aeriis fulmen regionibus actum   20
discludit celsas stridenti verbere turres,

15. *memo* lib.   20. *fulmem* lib.

233

nec sic obnixu ventorum, animaeque coactae
foeta tremit minitans tellus. haud fit mora: manes
convenere citi, variisque ad regia turmis
undique tecta ruunt, et nigris postibus adsunt.   25
heu quam terribiles formae! qui splendor in ipsis
est oculis! quantos gemitus, clademque minantur!
hic nexus, gyrosque trahit per humum, ille ferarum
unguibus in morem fissis vestigia signat,
implexis horrens humana in fronte colubris.   30
pone autem villisque carens immensaque cauda
porrigitur, longique sinus de more flagelli
evolvitque legitque, et sontes territat umbras.
hic mille aspiceres armatas igne Chimaeras,
Harpyasque, et Centauros, Scillasque voraces   35
succinctas latrante canum nivea inguina turba,
Sphyngesque, Hydrasque, et pallenti Gorgonas ore,
collaque caeruleis Pithonum sibila squammis.
hic Polyphemus adest, hic illa tripectora surgit
Geryonis facies, et centimani Briarei,   40
monstraque diversis aliter connexa figuris,
non unquam usurpata oculis, non auribus unquam.
considunt pars ad dextram, pars altera laevam.
ipse sedet medius Pluton, ferroque gravatum
sustinet, et scabra exesum rubigine sceptrum.   45
nec tantum aerii scopuli, deruptave cautes,
aspera nec tantum Calpe, nec pinifer Atlas
erigitur quin ceu collis videatur ad altum
regnatorem Erebi plano subsidere campo.
sic frontem anguineis vallatam cornibus effert.   50
olli fastum alti maiestas horrida vultus,
terroremque animis, loca sola colentibus, auget.
et gemina in morem lugubris clara comoetae
lumina suffusoque igni, sanieque rubescunt.
at mentum et malas ingens, atque bispida barba,   55
densaque convestit, setisque astantibus hirtum
in pectus proiecta fiuit. patet oris hiantis,

sanguine foedum atro, vastaque voragine guttur.
quales sulfureo commixsti turbine fumi,
atque ignes, atque ater odos e faucibus Aetnae   60
cum gemitu expirant, talis sese halitus ore
effundit foedo, et sonitu commixsta favilla.
quo dicente, sinu Cocytus restitit atro,
et custos ululare canis cessavit, et hydra
muta metu stetit, ac nigrae intonuere cavernae,   65
murmureque hoc ingens verborum immugit antro.
    "Tartarei proceres, digni melioribus oris,
et complere alti gemmata sedilia coeli,
unde genus trahitis, quos mecum casus in ista
horrida claustra olim regnis felicibus egit.   70
conatus nostri ingentes, adversaque nobis
suspicio, veteresque superni numinis irae
nota nimis sunt, et nimium memorare necesse est.
ille suo versat nunc candida sidera nutu:
ille polo regnat. nos hostes, atque rebelles   75
ducimur. ille idem pura pro luce diei,
pro sole aureo, pro stellantis circulo axis,
carcere nos taetro, caecoque inclusit Averno
ne quisquam nostrum ad summos aspiret honores.
ille dehinc (heu quam durum, indignumque relatu est: 80
hoc est, hoc, nostrum foede quod vulnus acerbat)
ille dehinc hominem coelestum sede locavit,
de vili argilla, atque informi pulvere fictum.
nec satis. ipsum etiam natum crudelibus umbris
mactandum, superis genitor demisit ab astris,   85
nostra in damna furens. venit Deus, atraque fregit
limina Tartareasque impulso cardine portas.
ausus et in nostris vestigia ponere regnis,
tot mihi sorte datas animas, tot debita fato
lumina detraxit, spoliisque Acherontis onustus,   90
contemptum in nostrum victor caelestibus oris
signa triumphati pandit pallentia Ditis.
sed quid ego antiquos fando renovare dolores

insequor, et notas demens iterare querelas?
aut quibus haec ille in terris, quo tempore cessat, 95
moliri? sat iam, sat coeli iniuria nobis
explorata vetus. praesenti appellere mentes
nunc deceat. nec enim (credo) nescitis, ut omnes
ille sui ad cultum gentes revocare laboret.
nobis pigra dies, et inertis vita trahetur, 100
nullaque in amissum stimulis accendet amaris
cura decus. semperne novas acquirere vires
Hesperias domito turmas Oriente sinemus?
imperioque suo Solymam subiungere gentem?
ille suos late terris diffundat honores? 105
atque alias hominum linguas? alia aera? novumque
impleat egregio concisum nomine marmor?
nostra autem contra pedibus disiecta prophanis
provolui simulachra solo patiemur, et uni
thure calere omnes, caesisque bidentibus, aras? 110
uni aurum, myrrhamque dari? suspensaque sacro
stare tholo? et memori signari carmine vota?
atque ubi iam nobis per terras cuncta patebant
atria templorum, et luci, nunc artibus ille,
et nostris impune dolis obsepiat omnes 115
ille vias? vacuasque domos et inania Pluton
regna colam, census animarum, et sanguinis expers?
non ita: namque etsi segnis torpensque resedit,
non tamen in vobis extinctus tabuit ardor,
ille prior, cum iam ferro flammisque sub auras 120
accincti superas contra pugnavimus arces.
congresssu (fateor) victi discessimus illo.
at non nostra altis tum virtus defuit ausis,
invictisque animis stetimus, quae gloria nobis
uno parta die, nullo delebitur aevo. 125
vincere quicquid ei dederit, casusve solusve.
verum agite unanimes Erebo nunc ite. (quid ultra
conqueror, et vestras nequicquam demoror iras?)
ite, mei socii, mea fida potentia, sontes

opprimite, atque Asiae crescentem extinguite
flammam.   130
ante Palaestina, ante omnis quam flagret Idume,
Iesseaeque ruant arces. nunc fraudibus usus,
nunc opus est animis. supero vos reddite coelo,
et mediis miscete vires. hic castra relinquat
exul, et ignotis Arabum vagus erret arenis.   135
ille cadat: Veneris curis hic mollibus undans,
effigie ut sacra divum, mortalis ab ore
pendeat, alloquio risuve elusus amico.
fatum esto, quodcunque volo. tela, horrida tela
ductorem in patrium dextrae conversa rebelles   140
divisaeque ferant acies. pugnentque cadantque
omnes. nulla huius superent vestigia motus."
vix ea fatus erat, cum illi nil verba morati
ultima, prosiluere, Chaos noctemque profundam
linquentes, coelique auras atque astra petentes   145
speluncis veluti patriis cum forte procella
turbine ventorum vario, fremituque sonoro
acta ruit, terras, pelagique natantia regna
verrit, agens imbrem, subtexitque aethera nimbis.
haud aliter curva hi noctis regione feruntur,   150
et geminas tollunt pennis stridentibus alas.
dispersique Asia in magna nova condere furta
incipiunt, variosque dolos, et mille nocendi
secum quisque artes foecundo in pectore versant.

Bibliography

Printed works

Alabaster, William, *"The Elisaeis" of William Alabaster* (ed. Michael O'Connor, *Studies in Philology* monograph 76, 1979).

Anon., *A Discourse on the maner of the discouery of this late Intended Treason*: printed with James I, King of England, *His majesties speach in this last sesssion of Parliament etc.* (printed by R. Barker, London, 1605).

— *A true and perfect relation of the proceedings at the severall arraignments of the late most barbarous Traitors* (printed at London by R. Barker, 1606).

— *A True and Plaine Declaration of the Horrible Treasons Practiced by William Parry* (printed by C. B., London, undated).

Aubin, R. A., *Topographical Poetry in Eighteenth Century England* (New York, 1936).

Baldwin, W. T., *William Shakspere's Small Latine & Lesse Greeke* (Urbana, 1944).

Bentham, James, *History and Antiquity of the Cathedral Church of Ely* (Cambridge, 1771).

Binns, J. W., *Intellectual Culture in Elizabethan and Jacobean England: The Latin Writing of the Age* (Leeds, 1990).

Black, J. B., *The Reign of Elizabeth, 1558 - 1603* (Oxford, 1936).

Boas, Frederick S., *University Drama in the Tudor Age* (Oxford, 1914, reprinted New York, 1966).

Boggs, Edmund, *Old Kingdom Emet: York and the Ainsty District* (London, 1902).

Bonney, Margaret, *Lordship and the Urban Community* (Cambridge, U. K., 1990).

Bowen, Emmanuel and Thomas Kitchen, *The Royal English Atlas* (London, 1760, reprinted Newton Abbot, Devonshire, 1970).

Boyd, William K. (ed.), *Calendar of the State Papers Relating to Scotland and Mary Queen of Scots* (Edinburgh, 1910).

Bradner, Leicester, *Musae Anglicanae: A History of Anglo-Latin Poetry 1500 - 1925* (New York, 1940, reprinted New York, 1966).

Brooke, C. F. Tucker, "The Life and Times of William Gager (1555 - 1622)," *Proceedings of the American Philosophical Society* 95 (1951) 401 - 31.

Burton, Elizabeth, *The Elizabethans at Home* (London, 1958).

Camden, William, *Britannia*, first edition printed by Ralph Newbery, London, 1586; second and considerably expanded edition printed by George Bishop and John Norton, London, 1607 (reprinted Hildesheim, 1970).

Campion, Thomas, *Campion's Works* (ed. Percival Vivian, Oxford, 1909, reprinted Oxford, 1966).

— *Thomas Campion: de Pulverea Coniuratione* (ed. David Lindley with the help of Robin Sowerby, Leeds Texts and Monographs n.s. 10, Leeds, 1987).

Carleton, Bishop George, *The life of Bernard Gilpin, a man most holy and renowned among the northerne English* (London, 1629).

Carter, Harry, *A History of the Oxford University Press* (Oxford, 1975).

Chambers, E. K., *Sir Henry Lee* (Oxford, 1936).

— *William Shakespeare* (Oxford, 1930).

Cheek, Macon, "Milton's 'In Quintum Novembris': An Epic Foreshadowing," *Studies in Philology* 54 (1957) 172 - 84.

Child, Francis James, *The English and Scottish Popular Ballads* (Boston - New York, 1888 - 90).

Clark, The Rev. Andrew, *Register of the University of Oxford* (Oxford, 1887).

Corbett, Richard, *The Poems of Richard Corbett* (edd. J. A. W. Bennett and H. R. Trever-Roper, Oxford, 1955).

Cross, Claire, *The Puritan Earl* (London, 1966).

— *The Royal Supremacy in the Elizabethan Church* (London - New York, 1969).

Davis, Walter R., *The Works of Thomas Campion* (New York, 1967).

Defoe, Daniel, *A Tour Thro' the Whole Island of Great Britain* (London, 1727, reprinted London, undated).

Donne, John, *Donne's Ignatius his Conclave* (ed. T. S. Healy S. J., Oxford, 1969).

Eccles, Mark, "Barnabe Barnes" in C. J. Sisson (ed.) *Thomas Lodge and Other Elizabethans* (Cambridge, Mass., 1933, repr. New York, 1966) 165 - 242.

Eedes, Richard, *Six learned and godly sermons* (printed by A. Islip for E. Bishop, London, 1604).

— *Three sermons now published by R. Horn* (printed by C. Meredith for P. Stevens, London, 1627).

Fletcher, Phineas, *The Poems of Phineas Fletcher B. D., Rector of Hilgay, Norfolk* (ed. the Rev. Alexander H. Grosart, privately printed, 1869).

— *The Poetical Works of Giles Fletcher and Phineas Fletcher* (ed. Frederick S. Boas, Cambridge, U. K., 1909).

Forsett, Edward, *Pedantius* (printed by Robert Mylbourn, London, 1631, photographic reproduction published as as *Edward Forsett, Pedantius, Prepared with an Introduction by E. F. J. Tucker*, Hildesheim, 1989). This play has been edited and annotated (but not translated) by G. C. Moore Smith, *Pedantius: A Latin Comedy Formerly Acted in Trinity College, Cambridge* (Materialien zur Kunde des älteren Englischdramas VIII, Louvain, 1905).

Foster, Joseph, *Alumni Oxonienses* (London, 1891 - 92, reprinted Nendeln, Luxembourg, 1968).

— *The Visitation of Yorkshire made in the Years 1584/5 by Robert Glover, Somerset Herald* (London, 1875).

Freer, W. H., *The English Church in the Reigns of Elizabeth and James I (1558 - 1625)* (London, 1905, reprinted New York, undated).

Fuller, Thomas, *The History of the Worthies of England* (ed. P. Austin Nutall, London, 1840, reprinted New York, 1965).

Gager, William, *Complete Works* (ed. D. F. Sutton, New York, 1994).

— (ed.) *Exequiae Illustrissimi Equitis D. Philippi Sidnaei, Gratissimae Memoriae ac Nomini Impensae* (printed at Oxford by Joseph Barnes, 1587).

Gentili, Scipio, *Plutonis Concilium* (printed at London by John Wolfe, 1584).

Gerard, John, *The Herball or Generall Historie of Plants* (London, 1633, repr. New York, 1973).

Graves, Robert, *The Greek Myths* (New York , 1955).

Greene, Mary Anne Everett (ed.), *Calendar of State Papers (Domestic)* (London, 1872, reprinted Nendeln, Luxembourg, 1967) vol. XII.

Harington, Sir John, *A Briefe View of the State of the Church of England as it Stood in Q. Elizabeths and King James his Reigne, to the Yeere 1608,* edited by his descendant John Harington under the title *Nugae Antiquae* (London, 1779, reprinted Hildesheim, 1968).

Herring, Francis, *Pontifica Pietas* (printed for Richard Boyle, London, 1606); edited by Estelle Haan, "Milton's *In Quintum Novembris* and the Anglo-Latin Gunpowder Epic," *Humanistica Lovaniensia* 41 (1992) 221 - 95.

— The same, *ab authore recognita* (printed at London for Joseph Windet, 1609). This volume also contains a continuation under the separate title *Venatio Catholica.*

Hibbert, Christopher and Edward, *The Encyclopaedia of Oxford* (London, 1988).

Holinshed, Raphael, *Chronicles of England, Scotland, and Ireland* (1587); I have consulted the London edition of 1807 - 8 (reprinted New York, 1965).

Horne, David H., *The Life and Minor Works of George Peele* (New Haven, 1952).

Kelley, J. N. D. *The Oxford Dictionary of Popes* (Oxford, 1986).

Leland, John, *Itinerary* (ed. Lucy Toulmin Smith, Oxford, 1907 - 10, reprinted Carbondale, Ill., 1964).

Lilliat, John, *Liber Lillliati* (ed. Edward Doughtie, Newark, N. J., 1985).

Melville, Sir James, *Memoirs of His Own Life* (Edinburgh, 1827).

Metcalfe, Walter C., *The Visitations of Northamptonshire made in 1564 and 1618-19* (London, 1887).

Milton, John, *The Poems of John Milton* (edited by John Carey and Alistair Fowler, London - New York, 1968).

— *Poems upon Several Occasions, English, Italian, and Latin, with Translations, by John Milton* (ed. Thomas Warton, 2nd ed., London, 1791).

Molen, Gesina H. van der, *Alberico Gentili and the Development of International Law, his Life, Work, and Times* (2nd ed., Leiden, 1968).

Mussett, P., *Lists of Deans and Major Canons of Durham 1541 - 1900* (Durham, 1974).

Nicholas, Sir Harris, *Memoirs of the Life and Times of Sir Christopher Hatton, K. G.* (London, 1847).

Page, William (ed.), *The Victoria History of the County of Durham* (London, 1968).

— *The Victoria History of the Country of Northamptonshire* (London, 1970).

— *The Victoria History of the Counties of England: Yorkshire* (London, 1974).

Panizza, D., *Alberico Gentili, Giurista Ideologo nell' Inghilterra Elisabettiana* (Padova, 1981).

Peele, George, *Pareus* (printed anonymously at Oxford by Joseph Barnes, 1586); transcription printed by C. F. Tucker Brooke, "A Latin Poem by George Peele (?)," *Huntington Library Quarterly* 3 (1939 - 40) 47 - 67.

Poole, Mrs. Reginald Lane, *Catalogue of Portraits in the Possession of the University, Colleges, City and County of Oxford* (Oxford, 1927).

Read, Conyers, *Mr. Secretary Walsingham* (Oxford, 1925).

Reid, R. R., *The King's Council in the North* (London - New York, 1921).

Ringler, William A., Jr., *The Poems of Sir Philip Sidney* (Oxford, 1962).

Rollins, Hyder Edward (ed.), *The Phoenix Nest* (Cambridge, Mass., 1931).

Rosenberg, Eleanor, *Leicester, Patron of Letters* (New York, 1955).

Ryder, Peter. F., *Medieval Buildings of Yorkshire* (Ashbourne, Derbyshire, 1982).

Seccombe, Thomas and H. Spencer Scott (edd.), *In Praise of Oxford: An Anthology in Prose and Verse* (London, 1910).

Smart, John Semple, *Shakespeare Truth and Tradition* (London, 1928).

Strype, John, *Annals of the Reformation and Establishment of Religion and Various Other Occurrences in the Church of England during Queen Elizabeth's Happy Reign* (Oxford, 1824, reprinted New York, undated).

Surtees, Robert, *The History and Antiquities of the County Palatine of Durham* (London, 1816 - 40, reprinted East Arsley, Wakefield, Yorkshire, 1972).

Swift, Jonathan, and others, *Miscellaneous Poems, Original and Translated by several hands, viz., Dean Swift, Mr. Parnel, Dr. Delany, Mr. Brown, Mr. Ward, Mr. Sterling. Mr. Concawen and others. Published by Mr. Concawen* (London, 1724).

Tasso, Torquato, *Gerusalemme Liberata,* translated into English under the title *Godfrey of Bulloigne, or the Recouerie of Ierusalem* by Edward Fairfax (1600). This is available in a critical edition by Kathleen M. Lea and T. M. Gang (Oxford, 1981).

Tilmot, P. M. (ed.), *A History of Yorkshire: The City of York* (printed at London for the Oxford University Press, 1961).

Venn, John and J. A., *Alumni Cantabrigienses* (Cambridge, U. K., 1922 - 24).

Wallace (Valesius), Michael, *In Serenissimi Regis Jacobi...Liberationem Foelicissimam Carmen* Ἐπιχάρτικον (printed by John Field, London, 1606). Edited by Estelle Haan, "Milton's *In Quintum Novembris* and the Anglo-Latin Gunpowder Epic, Part II," *Humanistica Lovaniensia* 42 (1993), 368 - 401.

Watson, Thomas, *Amintae Gaudia* (printed at London by William Ponsonby, 1592).

— *The* Ἑκατομπαθία, *or, Passionate centurie of loue* (printed at London by G. Canwood, 1582). Most recently edited by Cesare G. Cecioni, vol. 20 of the series Pubblicazioni della Facolta di lettere e filosofia (Catania, 1964).

Wood, Anthony à, *Athenae Oxonienses, Fasti Oxonienses,* and *Life of Anthony à Wood* (edited by Philip Bliss, London, 1813 - 22, reprinted Hildesheim, 1969).

— *Survey of the Antiquities of the City of Oxford Composed in 1661 - 6* (ed. the Reverend Andrew Clark, Oxford, 1899).

Yates, Frances A., *John Florio* (Cambridge U. K., 1934).

Manuscripts (by provenance)

London: British Library Additional ms. 22583, containing dramatic, poetic, and prose works by William Gager including *Musa Australis.*

London: British Library Additional ms. 30352, containing Richard Eedes' *Iter Boreale* under the title *Musae Boreales sive Iter Boreale, 1584.*

London: British Library ms. Harleian 6910, containing "Luigi Groto his New Philosophie Englished by Doct. Eedes."

London: Inner Temple ms. Petyt 538.43, containing a dialogue on love attributed to Richard Eedes in this manuscript (but to other writers elsewhere).

Oxford, Bodleian Library ms. D'Orville, containing Alberico Gentili's *de Papatu Romano Antichristo Assertiones ex Verbo Dei et SS. Patribus.*

Oxford: Bodleian Library ms. Rawlinson B 223, containing Richard Eedes' *Iter Boreale* and related material.

Oxford: Bodleian Library ms. Rawlinson Poet. 148, containing English poetry by Richard Eedes.

Oxford: Bodleian Library ms. Rawlinson Poet. 172, containing English poetry by Richard Eedes.

Oxford: Bodleian Library ms. Wood 8853, containing Richard Eedes' *Iter Boreale.*

Oxford: Corpus Christi College ms. 309, containing Richard Eedes' *Iter Boreale.*

FINIS

For Product Safety Concerns and Information please contact our EU
representative GPSR@taylorandfrancis.com
Taylor & Francis Verlag GmbH, Kaufingerstraße 24, 80331 München, Germany